Noël Coward

COLLECTED PLAYS: SIX

SEMI-MONDE, POINT VALAINE,
SOUTH SEA BUBBLE, NUDE WITH VIOLIN

"Reading Noël Coward's plays encourages the belief that there is a point where Literature and Show Business meet ... It [his style] is a matter, too, of his remarkable gifts of pace, discretion and construction, and the inspired creation of surprises ... Coward was the recorder, or inventor, of that quick-witted, snappy speech which has become the vinegar in which the myth of the privileged and disenchanting English 1920s is pickled." Douglas Dunn, *Encounter*

Semi-Monde: "Only in *Semi-Monde* does Coward find a successful metaphor for the sexual complications that lie behind his posturing. *Semi-Monde* is easily the most visually daring of his comedies, and the most intellectually startling ... *Semi-Monde* is made up of sexually mischievous *tableaux vivants* and gets much nearer the homosexual knuckle than Coward's public image allowed." *London Review of Books*

Point Valaine: "A picture of lust and rough manners in a tropical setting ... The simple story has the ring of truth, and its central character is portrayed full length, full depth." *The Times*, 1947
"Unmistakably the work of a master of the stage." *New York Times*

South Sea Bubble: "The main theme concerns the Governor's lady in the Isle of Samolo who plays with native fire, nearly gets her wings singed, bashes her native admirer with a bottle, and at one of those Coward next-morning-at-breakfast scenes slips her way out of the scrape with feline grace." *Manchester Guardian*, 1956

"*Nude With Violin* is a satirical light comedy which received almost unanimous abuse from the critics and ran to capacity for eighteen months ..." wrote Coward in 1962, "although it achieved its original purpose, which was to entertain the public and at the same time satirize certain aspects of 'Modern Art appreciation'."

Noël Coward

COLLECTED PLAYS

SIX

SEMI-MONDE

POINT VALAINE

SOUTH SEA BUBBLE

NUDE WITH VIOLIN

Introduced by Sheridan Morley

Methuen Drama

METHUEN WORLD CLASSICS

3 5 7 9 10 8 6 4 2

This collection first published in Great Britain in 1999
by Methuen Publishing Ltd
215 Vauxhall Bridge Road, London SW1V 1EJ

Semi-Monde was first published in 1999 in this edition
Point Valaine was first published in 1935 by
Heinemann and republished in 1962 in Play Parade Vol. 6
South Sea Bubble was first published in 1956 by
Heinemann and republished in 1962 in Play Parade Vol. 6
Nude With Violin was first published in 1956 by
Heinemann and republished in 1962 in Play Parade Vol. 6

Copyright in all the plays is by the Estate of the late Noël Coward
Introduction copyright © 1999 by Sheridan Morley
Chronology copyright © 1987, 1999 by Jacqui Russell

The right of the authors to be identified as the authors of this work has
been asserted by them in accordance with the Copyright, Designs and Patents
Act, 1988

ISBN 0 413 73410 2

Methuen Publishing Limited Reg. No. 3543167

A CIP catalogue record for this book
is available from the British Library

Typeset by Deltatype Ltd, Birkenhead, Merseyside
Printed and bound in Great Britain by
Cox & Wyman Ltd, Reading, Berkshire

CAUTION

These plays are fully protected by copyright throughout the world.
Application for performance, etc., should be made *by professionals* to Alan
Brodie Representation Ltd, 211 Piccadilly, London W1V 9LD and *by amateurs* to
Samuel French Ltd, 52 Fitzroy Street, London W1P 6JR. No performance may
be given unless a licence has been obtained.

CONTENTS

The four plays in this sixth volume of Coward's collected plays form an intriguing cross-section of his dramatic writing over thirty years. One, *Semi-Monde*, is here published for the first time; another, *Point Valaine*, is a dark 1930s drama of love and lust in a tropical setting; while the other two are more familiar early-1950s comedies which ran here and in New York, but have been infrequently revived since – *South Sea Bubble*, a comedy inspired by Noël's late-life love for Jamaica, and *Nude With Violin* which, some forty years before Yasmina Reza's global triumph with *Art*, was a satire on the nature and perception of modern paintings.

Semi-Monde has always been high on the "lost" Coward playlist; written in 1926 and originally entitled *Ritz Bar*, it had to wait all of fifty years for a first full staging, directed and designed by Philip Prowse for his Glasgow Citizens Company. Noël himself describes it best in his first autobiography, *Present Indicative*:

> The whole action took place in the public rooms of the Ritz Hotel in Paris over a period of three years. It was well-constructed and, on the whole, well-written; its production in London or New York seemed however unlikely, as some of the characters (owing to lightly suggested abnormalities) would certainly be deleted by the censor. Max Reinhardt was however enthusiastic about it, and it was translated into German and taken in due course to Berlin where for years it escaped production by a hair's breadth, until Vicky Baum wrote *Grand Hotel* and *Semi-Monde*, being too closely similar in theme, faded gently into oblivion.

What Noël glossed over, in the interests of not startling the 1937 readers of his first memoirs, was that of course the "abnormalities" concerned several gay and lesbian characters, not to mention a couple of wife-swappers. In its epic cast of thirty, true to the pattern of many hotel and ship dramas, Noël had lightly sketched in a whole cross-section of smart society, and there was a world-weariness about them which appealed, at the 1977 Glasgow stage premiere, to Michael Billington of the *Guardian*:

> As so often with Coward, it is not so much the people themselves that grip you as his own equivocal attitude towards them. He was, by instinct, a puritan dandy with a Martini in one hand and a moral sampler in the other. And in *Semi-Monde* you can see clearly that while Coward envies the rich their style, he also has the true lower-middle-class boy's belief that a life without work cannot be pure. Even his attitude to homosexuality is not exactly encouraging; he seems to suggest that it should be practised but not preached ... Significantly, the one homosexual who earns Coward's approval here is a student-singer who is encouraged to devote himself to his career. This fits in with Coward's own code of constant work and sexual discretion ... the whole point of Coward in the mid-twenties was that he was uneasy about being prophetic.

Philip Hoare, in an admirable 1995 biography of Noël which some of Coward's older allies found nevertheless to be somewhat over-obsessed with his homosexuality, describes *Semi-Monde* as his "most daring play to date. In a chic Parisian hotel, a series of sexual pairings take place through rendezvous, arguments, infidelities and reconciliations; sexual deviance is undisguised, and it appears to have been written for a very sophisticated audience. Promiscuity is pursued by visitors from England and the United States in this unreal world, isolated by geography and happenstance. Set in the bisexual 1920s, the play could easily be populated by characters of Coward's society: dandy aesthetes Harold Acton, Brian Howard, Cecil Beaton, Stephen Tennant; and their female counterparts, Nancy Cunard, Diana Cooper, Iris Tree and Tallulah Bankhead. None was averse to sexual experimentation, as their exploits bore witness: Vita Sackville-West's elopement to France with her girlfriend, Violet Trefusis, pursued by their respective husbands (one of whom, Harold Nicolson, was homosexual), could have inspired a sub-plot of

Semi-Monde, amorous adventures conducted in foreign hotels to escape British censure and law, by sleek-haired men and boyish women."

Well, yes, it could have been, but in fact it wasn't; Noël was really not here writing a *roman à clef* or even a *drame à clef*. He was too astute a dramatist, too eager for his plays to live long, to let them be limited to any one contemporary group of real-life people, even assuming he didn't fear they would have sued if he made them too immediately recognisable.

For the *New Yorker* critic John Lahr, writing his 1982 *Coward the Playwright* (Methuen), *Semi-Monde* was "easily the most visually daring of his comedies, and the most intellectually startling . . . it gets much nearer the homosexual knuckle than Coward's public image allowed."

By 1957 however, with *Semi-Monde* still unproduced, Noël himself was taking a rather more jaded view of it and its period, in a preface to Beverley Nichols's memoir *Sweet and Twenties* (*Ritz Bar* was a working title):

> Were we really happy in the twenties? On the whole I think most of us were, but we tried to hide it by appearing to be as blasé, world-weary and "jagged with sophistication" as we possibly could. Naturally we had a lot of fun in the process. I remember I had a lovely time writing a play called *Ritz Bar*, as jagged with sophistication as all get-out: the characters were either demi-mondaine or just plain mondaine, shared their apartments and their lives with members of the opposite, or the same, sex, and no wife dreamed for one instant of doing anything so banal as living with her husband. The play was typical of the phase we all went through and, taken by and large, quite harmless; to call it good clean fun would perhaps be going too far, but at least it wasn't about the Death Wish and, compared with Existentialism, it becomes *Rebecca of Sunnybrook Farm*.

So much for *Semi-Monde*. Eight years later Noël wrote *Point Valaine*, another "lost" drama, this one seen in New York in 1935, but not in London until two years after World War Two, when critics already found it out of time and place; there has been only one major British revival since, on the Minerva stage in Chichester early in the 1990s when its hothouse quality was intelligently recaptured and reinterpreted, and the play richly deserves its place in this collection as an example of Coward's range as a dramatist.

Point Valaine was written by Noël for his beloved Alfred Lunt and Lynn Fontanne when, in the summer of 1934, he happened to be at home in Kent recuperating from an operation to remove his appendix. With their triangular triumph in *Design for Living* only two years before, Noël decided that this time he would direct for the Lunts on Broadway but not take any other part, though he did as usual find work for some other old friends in the company, notably his old child-actor colleague Philip Tonge and Philip's mother Lilian. Before rehearsals started, Noël went for a weekend to stay with his old friend the *New Yorker* humourist and critic Alexander Woollcott, who had first named him "Destiny's Tot".

Noël announced after dinner one night that he would read *Point Valaine* to Woollcott's assembled guests. "Where?" asked Woollcott icily, and taking the hint, Noël never did read his play aloud. It was in any case always going to be problematic, as Noël himself later noted, "neither big enough for tragedy, nor light enough for comedy".

It is perhaps more than coincidental that *Point Valaine* is dedicated to Somerset Maugham, one of Noël's earliest mentors and the one he was eventually to characterise with wicked accuracy in his last play, *A Song At Twilight*, in 1967. For in its plot and characters, *Point Valaine* is unlike any other play of Coward's; indeed some of the characters here seem to have drifted in from a road company of *Rain*.

For Noël however, this was a valiant attempt to break entirely new ground; he was experimenting with new moods and feelings, above all trying to find ways to convey a sense of impending horror on the stage without, until the bitter end, being forced to give any actual reason for it. As a short story it might have worked better, but neither the mood nor the plot really sustain this drama, and the characters are for the most part a vaguely defined and deeply unattractive lot who seem to deserve all that they ultimately get.

The opening night in Boston was a gloomy way to spend Christmas 1934, and it is not altogether surprising that this production marked the low-water mark in Coward's near-lifelong friendship with the Lunts. They became as depressed about the play's chances as Noël himself, and the result was a mutual irritability that lasted all through rehearsals and into Boston, where a rain machine flooded the stage by accident and all the sets were found not to fit.

The Broadway opening a couple of weeks later was equally unhappy; audiences who had come expecting another chic Coward comedy were quickly reduced to stony indifference, and the reviews were quick to point out that this was not the best of Coward. Brooks Atkinson for the *New York Times* pinpointed the main reason for this disappointment: "Coward's gifts are so multitudinous, his range so bewildering and his success so dazzling, that we are all inclined to expect too much of him. When we come to one of his new plays, we are feverishly prepared as for a sign from God."

This time the sign was not good. *Point Valaine* limped along for eight weeks on Broadway, and when it finally made it to Britain in 1947 it was only to Liverpool and the Embassy in Swiss Cottage where it collected more bad reviews, including an especially savage one from Graham Greene. Noël refused to authorise a West End transfer, noting simply "I have never really considered it quite good enough".

The *Observer* took a similar line: "Once the decorations, racial and climatic, have been stripped, we are left with a harsh melodrama of one woman and two men ... only the novelist shows gleams of a wittier, other Coward as he peeps and botanises with a grim pleasure which has begun to fray into boredom."

Point Valaine remains memorably the only Coward play in which a man literally throws himself to the sharks, but George Jean Nathan still described it as "zymotic bilge", and reckoned it was the kind of script Maugham might just have written for

Hollywood if he was getting a hundred thousand dollars and suffering from prolonged jetlag and influenza at the time.

In sharp contrast, the last two plays in this volume achieved comparative success in the 1950s. *South Sea Bubble* was first written in 1949 under the title *Home and Colonial*, and first staged in 1951 in America as *Island Fling*, before reaching its last title with the London opening in 1956. Noël himself explains:

> I wrote this originally for Gertrude Lawrence [his lifelong friend and partner from 1912 until she settled and married in America in 1940] and if her tragic death in 1952 had not intervened, she would probably have played it after the end of the run of *The King and I*. While I am prepared to admit that it does not rank among my best comedies, it still has, to my prejudiced eye, a great deal to recommend it. I find Sandra an enchanting character, so much so that I introduced her in my later novel *Pomp and Circumstance* along with some of the play's minor characters. To be honest I now find the first act rather verbose and lacking in action, but from then on the play gathers momentum and I have found it highly entertaining both to write and to read.

The play is set on the mythical isle of Samolo, in reality of course Jamaica, where Noël spent many of his last years and is in fact buried; the character of the Governor, in both play and novel, owes a lot to the then Jamaican governor Sir Hugh Foot, while the socialist Norman Manley, later to become prime minister, is also recognisable. In the play and novel, Coward was (as often, ahead of his time) keen to satirise the kind of racial barriers that still then existed between the white planters and the native blacks, with whom Princess Margaret was, even on state visits, not allowed to dance. By the time (as *Island Fling*) the play had its first performance in Westport, Connecticut, on 22 July 1951, Coward addicts were already familiar with the setting, since the mythical Samolo had first been used by him in the 1936 *We Were Dancing*, and again in a disastrous post-war musical, *Pacific 1860*, where Noël had even gone to the trouble of providing audiences with a "map".

With Gertie unavailable, the leading role went first to

Claudette Colbert in a production by Jack Wilson, Coward's long-time lover and manager, that was apparently bad enough to damage a friendship which soon collapsed entirely under financial and other disputes. Noël never saw this staging, which ran only briefly for a week at each of two summer-stock theatres, Westport and then the Cape Playhouse, but accounts were not encouraging and it wasn't until five years later that Coward redrafted the script as a vehicle for his beloved Vivien Leigh, then in one of her more unstable periods because her husband Laurence Olivier was off filming with the supposedly dangerous Marilyn Monroe.

This first London production in 1956 also got off to a rocky start, because Noël had just announced his decision to take up residence abroad for tax reasons, a decision common enough in later years but at this time greeted with a savage press, notably Beaverbrook's then-powerful *Daily Express* which had never forgotten or forgiven Coward's opening shot in the wartime film *In Which We Serve*, which has a battleship steaming down the Clyde ready for action while in the water we see an old newspaper bearing the infamous 1939 *Express* headline "THERE WILL BE NO WAR". Even so the reviews, as distinct from press commentaries, were a great deal warmer than Coward had been accustomed to since the war, notably Harold Hobson, writing in the *Sunday Times*:

> Mr Noël Coward, at over fifty, still retains that power to surprise, scandalise and amuse which made him the adored, as well as the abused, *enfant terrible* of the 1920s. You never know whether he will be stormy petrel, petard, pianist, puritan or even, very occasionally puerile; though you can be certain he will never be peasant, poet, pedant or Pecksniff . . . but it is, of course, precisely in this provocative unexpectedness of his attitude, and the calculated but apparently casual wit with which he expresses it, that Mr Coward's entertainment lies.

Tynan in the *Observer* was somewhat less impressed: "Through the characters one sees the father-figure of Mr Coward, guardian of empire, promoter of the tedious fiction that all coloured people are happy, smiling, backward Tories while all British administrators are seedy and frustrated socialists ... if the message sticks in one's throat, one positively chokes over the dialogue through which he transmits it."

After its first American try-out with Claudette Colbert, *South Sea Bubble* was in fact turned down by such stars of the time as Diana Wynyard and Kay Hammond, and when Vivien Leigh finally took it on for London she was already in a precarious mental state; after a few months she abruptly left the cast, having suddenly announced that she was pregnant by Olivier. Sadly, the day after she left the cast she miscarried, and the play staggered on for a few more months with Elizabeth Sellars. Noël, living out the start of his tax exile in Bermuda, felt somewhat betrayed.

A few months later, he was however able to go to Dublin for the premiere of another new comedy. This one, *Nude With Violin*, had been on and off his typewriter for a couple of years and was offered to a vast range of stars from Rex Harrison to Yvonne Arnaud before Noël eventually settled on Sir John Gielgud as director and star. This was the first time the two men had been together since, thirty years earlier, Gielgud had replaced Coward in both *The Vortex* and *The Constant Nymph*, but it too ran into the storm of publicity over the author's decision to live abroad; indeed an early edition of ITV's *This Week* turned itself over to a ponderous tele-discussion over whether or not Coward had the right to live where he chose.

"I arrived in Dublin," he wrote in his diaries, "to find that John had directed it with such loving care for my play that he had forgotten his own performance, so I helped a little with that."

Reviews in Dublin and on the pre-London tour were rather better than those Noël was now getting for his personal life, but in the West End the notices were good only for Gielgud, making only his second stage appearance in modern dress since the beginning of the war. "Billed as a comedy," said Milton Shulman for the *Evening Standard*, "*Nude With Violin* emerged as a farce and ended as a corpse."

Nevertheless, the play ran to good business on Shaftesbury Avenue for all of eighteen months, during which time Gielgud was replaced first by Michael Wilding ("He brought to the play large audiences," wrote Noël, "immense personal charm and quite startling inaudibility"), and then by Robert Helpmann. Noël himself, soon to direct and play the lead on Broadway, reckoned that "although the play achieved its original purpose, which was to entertain the public and at the same time satirise certain aspects of the 'Modern Art Appreciation' movement, it did not completely succeed because the situation of the play as established at the end of the first act becomes a trifle threadbare by the end of the last. I was acutely aware of this structural defect when I played the part of Sebastien myself, much more so than when I wrote it. The critics pounced on this failing with ill-concealed satisfaction, and of course they were quite right to do so. They were not quite right, however, to dismiss the whole play with withering contempt; it has in it some excellent character drawing and some fine comedy scenes."

A few months later, Noël himself with Eva Gabor opened the play on Broadway to generally tepid reviews; this was the year of John Osborne's *Look Back in Anger*, and rapidly changing theatrical fashions were apt to make Coward look somewhat dated and stranded. The Broadway run was brief, not helped by Noël having an equally brief homosexual affair with a bit-part actor, Bill Traylor, who subsequently tried (luckily unsuccessfully) to take his own life in what was generally believed to be a spasm of Catholic guilt.

The American press was as uncharitable as the West End reviews had been some months earlier: "Great to have Noël Coward back," wrote Walter Kerr in the *New York Times*, "but it would have been even better to have had him back in a play." Noël remained resilient ("thanks to all the vilification poured on my head in recent months I am now as famous as Debbie Reynolds, which is most gratifying"). In some desperation, as the box-office fell steeply, Noël decided to move the same cast into his old *Present Laughter*, and then have the plays alternate nightly, first in New York and then on tour, where they did rather better. All in all however, Coward was keen to pack his bags and head back to the place in the sun he had now found in Bermuda. On the way he had another of his lucky escapes – Mike Todd asked him to fly on his private plane to New York for a Liz Taylor (Mrs

Todd) celebration. Noël declined, and the Todd plane crashed a few hours later, killing all its passengers.

Neither *Nude With Violin* nor *South Sea Bubble* has ever had a major London or New York revival, though both plays were seen on television soon after their British stage runs.

Sheridan Morley
1998

CHRONOLOGY

1899   16 December, Noël Pierce Coward born in Teddington, Middlesex, eldest surviving son of Arthur Coward, piano salesman and Violet (née Veitch). A "brazen, odious little prodigy", his early circumstances were of refined suburban poverty.

1907   First public appearances in school and community concerts.

1908   Family moved to Battersea and took in lodgers.

1911   First professional appearance as Prince Mussel in *The Goldfish*, produced by Lila Field at the Little Theatre, and revived in same year at Crystal Palace and Royal Court Theatre. Cannard, the page-boy, in *The Great Name* at the Prince of Wales Theatre, and William in *Where the Rainbow Ends* with Charles Hawtrey's Company at the Savoy Theatre.

1912   Directed *The Daisy Chain* and stage-managed *The Prince's Bride* at Savoy in series of matinees featuring the work of the children of the *Rainbow* cast. Mushroom in *An Autumn Idyll*, ballet, Savoy.

1913   An angel (Gertrude Lawrence was another) in Basil Dean's production of *Hannele*. Slightly in *Peter Pan*, Duke of York's.

1914   Toured in *Peter Pan*. Collaborated with fellow performer Esmé Wynne on songs, sketches, and short stories – "beastly little whimsies".

1915   Admitted to sanatorium for tuberculosis.

1916   Five-month tour as Charley in *Charley's Aunt*. Walk-on in *The Best of Luck*, Drury Lane. Wrote first full-length song, "Forbidden Fruit". Basil Pycroft in *The Light Blues*, produced by Robert Courtneidge, with daughter Cicely also in cast, Shaftesbury. Short spell as dancer at Elysée Restaurant (subsequently the Café de Paris). Jack Morrison in *The Happy Family*, Prince of Wales.

1917   "Boy pushing barrow" in D.W. Griffith's film *Hearts of the World*. Co-author with Esmé Wynne of one-acter *Ida Collaborates*, Theatre Royal, Aldershot. Ripley Guildford in *The Saving Grace*, with Charles Hawtrey, "who . . . taught me many points of comedy acting", Garrick. Family moved to Pimlico and re-opened boarding house.

1918 Called-up for army. Medical discharge after nine months. Wrote unpublished novels *Cats and Dogs* (loosely based on Shaw's *You Never Can Tell*) and the unfinished *Cherry Pan* ("dealing in a whimsical vein with the adventures of a daughter of Pan"), and lyrics for Darewski and Joel, including "When You Come Home on Leave" and "Peter Pan". Also composed "Tamarisk Town". Sold short stories to magazines. Wrote plays *The Rat Trap*, *The Last Trick* (unproduced) and *The Impossible Wife* (unproduced). Courtenay Borner in *Scandal*, Strand.
Woman and Whiskey (co-author Esmé Wynne) produced at Wimbledon Theatre.

1919 Ralph in *The Knight of the Burning Pestle*, Birmingham Repertory, played with "a stubborn Mayfair distinction" demonstrating a "total lack of understanding of the play". Collaborated on *Crissa*, an opera, with Esmé Wynne and Max Darewski (unproduced). Wrote *I'll Leave It to You*.

1920 Bobbie Dermott in *I'll Leave It to You*, New Theatre. Wrote play *Barriers Down* (unproduced). *I'll Leave It to You* published, London.

1921 On holiday in Alassio, met Gladys Calthrop for the first time. Clay Collins in American farce *Polly with a Past*: during the run "songs, sketches, and plays were bursting out of me". Wrote *The Young Idea*, *Sirocco*, and *The Better Half*. First visit to New York, and sold parts of *A Withered Nosegay* to *Vanity Fair* and short-story adaptation of *I'll Leave It to You* to *Metropolitan*. House-guest of Laurette Taylor and Hartley Manners, whose family rows inspired the Bliss household in *Hay Fever*.

1922 *Bottles and Bones* (sketch) produced in benefit for Newspaper Press Fund, Drury Lane. *The Better Half* produced in "grand guignol" season, Little Theatre. Started work on songs and sketches for *London Calling!* Adapted Louise Verneuil's *Pour avoir Adrienne* (unproduced). Wrote *The Queen Was in the Parlour* and *Mild Oats*.

1923 Sholto Brent in *The Young Idea*, Savoy. Juvenile lead in *London Calling!* Wrote *Weatherwise*, *Fallen Angels*, and *The Vortex*.

1924 Wrote *Hay Fever* (which Marie Tempest at first refused to do, feeling it was "too light and plotless and generally lacking in action") and *Easy Virtue*. Nicky Lancaster in *The Vortex*, produced at Everyman by Norman MacDermott.

1925 Established as a social and theatrical celebrity. Wrote *On With the Dance*, with London opening in spring followed by *Fallen Angels* and *Hay Fever*. *Hay Fever* and *Easy Virtue* produced, New York. Wrote silent screen titles for Gainsborough Films.

1926   Toured USA in *The Vortex*. Wrote *This Was a Man*, refused a licence by Lord Chamberlain but produced in New York (1926), Berlin (1927), and Paris (1928). *Easy Virtue, The Queen Was in the Parlour*, and *The Rat Trap* produced, London. Played Lewis Dodd in *The Constant Nymph*, directed by Basil Dean. Wrote *Semi-Monde* and *The Marquise*. Bought Goldenhurst Farm, Kent, as country home. Sailed for Hong Kong on holiday but trip broken in Honolulu by nervous breakdown.

1927   *The Marquise* opened in London while Coward was still in Hawaii, and *The Marquise* and *Fallen Angels* produced, New York. Finished writing *Home Chat*. *Sirocco* revised after discussions with Basil Dean and produced, London.

1928   Clark Storey in Behrman's *The Second Man*, directed by Dean. Gainsborough Films productions of *The Queen Was in the Parlour, The Vortex* (starring Ivor Novello), and *Easy Virtue* (directed by Alfred Hitchcock) released – but only the latter, freely adapted, a success. *This Year of Grace!* produced, London, and, with Coward directing and in cast, New York. Made first recording, featuring numbers from this show. Wrote *Concerto* for Gainsborough Films, intended for Ivor Novello, but never produced. Started writing *Bitter-Sweet*.

1929   Played in *This Year of Grace!* (USA) until spring. Directed *Bitter-Sweet*, London and New York. Set off on travelling holiday in Far East.

1930   On travels wrote *Private Lives* (1929) and song "Mad Dogs and Englishmen", the latter on the road from Hanoi to Saigon. In Singapore joined the Quaints, company of strolling English players, as Stanhope for three performances of *Journey's End*. On voyage home wrote *Post-Mortem*, which was "similar to my performance as Stanhope: confused, under-rehearsed and hysterical". Directed and played Elyot Chase in *Private Lives*, London, and Fred in *Some Other Private Lives*. Started writing *Cavalcade* and unfinished novel *Julian Kane*.

1931   Elyot Chase in New York production of *Private Lives*. Directed *Cavalcade*, London. Film of *Private Lives* produced by MGM. Set off on trip to South America.

1932   On travels wrote *Design for Living* (hearing that Alfred Lunt and Lynn Fontanne finally free to work with him) and material for new revue including songs "Mad about the Boy", "Children of the Ritz" and "The Party's Over Now". Produced in London as *Words and Music*, with book, music, and lyrics exclusively by Coward and directed by him. The short-lived Noël Coward Company, independent company which enjoyed his support, toured UK with *Private Lives*, *Hay Fever*, *Fallen Angels*, and *The Vortex*.

1933   Directed *Design for Living*, New York, and played Leo. Films of *Cavalcade*, *To-Night Is Ours* (remake of *The Queen Was in the Parlour*), and *Bitter-Sweet* released. Directed London revival of *Hay Fever*. Wrote *Conversation Piece* as vehicle for Yvonne Printemps, and hit song "Mrs. Worthington".

1934   Directed *Conversation Piece* in London and played Paul. Cut links with C. B. Cochran and formed own management in partnership with John C. Wilson. Appointed President of the Actors' Orphanage, in which he invested great personal commitment until resignation in 1956. Directed Kaufman and Ferber's *Theatre Royal*, Lyric, and Behrman's *Biography*, Globe. Film of *Design for Living* released, London. *Conversation Piece* opened, New York. Started writing autobiography, *Present Indicative*. Wrote *Point Valaine*.

1935   Directed *Point Valaine*, New York. Played lead in film *The Scoundrel* (Astoria Studios, New York). Wrote *To-Night at 8.30*.

1936   Directed and played in *To-Night at 8.30*, London and New York. Directed *Mademoiselle* by Jacques Deval, Wyndham's.

1937   Played in *To-Night at 8.30*, New York, until second breakdown in health in March. Directed (and subsequently disowned) Gerald Savory's *George and Margaret*, New York. Wrote *Operette*, with hit song "The Stately Homes of England". *Present Indicative* published, London and New York.

1938   Directed *Operette*, London. *Words and Music* revised for American production as *Set to Music*. Appointed adviser to newly-formed Royal Naval Film Corporation.

1939   Directed New York production of *Set to Music*. Visited Soviet Union and Scandinavia. Wrote *Present Laughter* and *This Happy Breed*: rehearsals stopped by declaration of war. Wrote for revue *All Clear*, London. Appointed to head Bureau of Propaganda in Paris to liaise with French Ministry of Information, headed by Jean Giraudoux and André Maurois. This posting prompted speculative attacks in the press, prevented by wartime secrecy from getting a clear statement of the exact nature of his work (in fact unexceptional and routine). Troop concert in Arras with

Maurice Chevalier. *To Step Aside* (short story collection) published.

1940   Increasingly "oppressed and irritated by the Paris routine". Visits USA to report on American isolationism and attitudes to war in Europe. Return to Paris prevented by German invasion. Returned to USA to do propaganda work for Ministry of Information. Propaganda tour of Australia and New Zealand, and fund-raising for war charities. Wrote play *Time Remembered* (unproduced).

1941   Mounting press attacks in England because of time spent allegedly avoiding danger and discomfort of Home Front. Wrote *Blithe Spirit*, produced in London (with Coward directing) and New York. MGM film of *Bitter-Sweet* (which Coward found "vulgar" and "lacking in taste") released, London. Wrote screenplay for *In Which We Serve*, based on the sinking of HMS Kelly. Wrote songs including "London Pride", "Could You Please Oblige Us with a Bren Gun?", and "Imagine the Duchess's Feelings".

1942   Produced and co-directed (with David Lean) *In Which We Serve*, and appeared as Captain Kinross (Coward considered the film "an accurate and sincere tribute to the Royal Navy"). Played in countrywide tour of *Blithe Spirit*, *Present Laughter*, and *This Happy Breed*, and gave hospital and factory concerts. MGM film of *We Were Dancing* released.

1943   Played Garry Essendine in London production of *Present Laughter* and Frank Gibbons in *This Happy Breed*. Produced *This Happy Breed* for Two Cities Films. Wrote "Don't Let's Be Beastly to the Germans", first sung on BBC Radio (then banned on grounds of lines "that Goebbels might twist"). Four-month tour of Middle East to entertain troops.

1944   February–September, toured South Africa, Burma, India, and Ceylon. Troop concerts in France and "Stage Door Canteen Concert" in London. Screenplay of *Still Life*, as *Brief Encounter*. *Middle East Diary*, an account of his 1943 tour, published, London and New York – where a reference to "mournful little boys from Brooklyn" inspired formation of a lobby for the "Prevention of Noël Coward Re-entering America".

1945   *Sigh No More*, with hit song "Matelot", completed and produced, London. Started work on *Pacific 1860*. Film of *Brief Encounter* released.

1946   Started writing "Peace in Our Time". Directed *Pacific 1860*, London.

1947   Gary Essendine in London revival of *Present Laughter*. Super-vised production of *"Peace in Our Time"*. *Point Valaine* produced, London. Directed American revival of *To-Night at 8.30*. Wrote *Long Island Sound* (unproduced).

1948   Replaced Graham Payn briefly in American tour of *To-Night at 8.30*, his last stage appearance with Gertrude Lawrence. Wrote screenplay for Gainsborough film of *The Astonished Heart*. Max Aramont in *Joyeux Chagrins* (French production of *Present Laughter*). Built house at Blue Harbour, Jamaica.

1949   Christian Faber in film of *The Astonished Heart*, Wrote *Ace of Clubs* and *Home and Colonial* (produced as *Island Fling* in USA and *South Sea Bubble* in UK).

1950   Directed *Ace of Clubs*, London. Wrote *Star Quality* (short stories) and *Relative Values*.

1951   Deaths of Ivor Novello and C. B. Cochran. Paintings included in charity exhibition in London. Wrote *Quadrille*. One-night concert at Theatre Royal, Brighton, followed by season at Café de Paris, London, and beginning of new career as leading cabaret entertainer. Directed *Relative Values*, London, which restored his reputation as a playwright after run of post-war flops. *Island Fling* produced, USA.

1952   Charity cabaret with Mary Martin at Café de Paris for Actors' Orphanage. June cabaret season at Café de Paris. Directed *Quadrille*, London. *"Red Peppers"*, *Fumed Oak*, and *Ways and Means* (from *To-Night at 8.30*) filmed as *Meet Me To-Night*. September, death of Gertrude Lawrence: "no one I have ever known, however brilliant . . . has contributed quite what she contributed to my work".

1953   Completed second volume of autobiography, *Future Indefinite*. King Magnus in Shaw's *The Apple Cart*. Cabaret at Café de Paris, again "a triumphant success". Wrote *After the Ball*.

1954   *After the Ball* produced, UK. July, mother died. September, cabaret season at Café de Paris. November, Royal Command Performance, London Palladium. Wrote *Nude With Violin*.

1955   June, opened in cabaret for season at Desert Inn, Las Vegas, and enjoyed "one of the most sensational successes of my career". Played Hesketh-Baggott in film of *Around the World in Eighty Days*, for which he wrote own dialogue. October, directed and appeared with Mary Martin in TV spectacular *Together with Music* for CBS, New York. Revised *South Sea Bubble*.

1956   Charles Condomine in television production of *Blithe Spirit*, for

CBS, Hollywood. For tax reasons took up Bermuda residency. Resigned from presidency of the Actors' Orphanage. *South Sea Bubble* produced, London. Directed and played part of Frank Gibbons in television production of *This Happy Breed* for CBS, New York. Co-directed *Nude With Violin* with John Gielgud (Eire and UK), opening to press attacks on Coward's decision to live abroad. Wrote play *Volcano* (unproduced).

1957 Directed and played Sebastien in *Nude With Violin*, New York. *Nude With Violin* published, London.

1958 Played Gary Essendine in *Present Laughter* alternating with *Nude With Violin* on US West Coast tour. Wrote ballet *London Morning* for London Festival Ballet. Wrote *Look After Lulu!*

1959 *Look After Lulu!* produced, New York, and by English Stage Company at Royal Court, London. Film roles of Hawthorne in *Our Man in Havana* and ex-King of Anatolia in *Surprise Package*. *London Morning* produced by London Festival Ballet. Sold home in Bermuda and took up Swiss residency. Wrote *Waiting in the Wings*.

1960 *Waiting in the Wings* produced, Eire and UK. *Pomp and Circumstance* (novel) published, London and New York.

1961 Alec Harvey in television production of *Brief Encounter* for NBC, USA. Directed American production of *Sail Away*. *Waiting in the Wings* published, New York.

1962 Wrote music and lyrics for *The Girl Who Came to Supper* (adaptation of Rattigan's *The Sleeping Prince*, previously filmed as *The Prince and the Showgirl*). *Sail Away* produced, UK.

1963 *The Girl Who Came to Supper* produced, USA. Revival of *Private Lives* at Hampstead signals renewal of interest in his work.

1964 "Supervised" production of *High Spirits*, musical adaptation of *Blithe Spirit*, Savoy. Introduced Granada TV's "A Choice of Coward" series, which included *Present Laughter*, *Blithe Spirit*, *The Vortex*, and *Design for Living*. Directed *Hay Fever* for National Theatre, first living playwright to direct his own work there. *Pretty Polly Barlow* (short story collection) published.

1965 Played the landlord in film, *Bunny Lake is Missing*. Wrote *Suite in Three Keys*. Badly weakened by attack of amoebic dysentry contracted in Seychelles.

1966 Played in *Suite in Three Keys*, London, which taxed his health further. Started adapting his short story *Star Quality* for the stage.

1967 Caesar in TV musical version of *Androcles and the Lion* (score by

Richard Rodgers), New York. Witch of Capri in film *Boom*, adaptation of Tennessee Williams's play *The Milk Train Doesn't Stop Here Any More*. Lorn Loraine, Coward's manager, and friend for many years, died, London. Worked on new volume of autobiography, *Past Conditional*. *Bon Voyage* (short story collection) published.

1968 Played Mr. Bridger, the criminal mastermind, in *The Italian Job*.

1970 Awarded knighthood in New Year's Honours List.

1971 Tony Award, USA, for Distinguished Achievement in the Theatre.

1973 26 March, died peacefully at his home in Blue Harbour, Jamaica. Buried on Firefly Hill.

SEMI-MONDE

Characters

TANIS MARSHALL

DAY PORTER

YOUNG GIRL

YOUNG MAN

DOROTHY PRICE

SUZANNE FELLINI

MIKE CRAVEN

MR. FLETCHER

MRS. FLETCHER

BERYL FLETCHER

BEVERLEY FORD

CYRIL HARDACRE

ALBERT HENNICK

OWEN MARSHALL

INEZ ZULIETA

CYNTHIA GABLE

MARION FAWCETT

JEROME KENNEDY

NORMA KENNEDY

JULIUS LEVENOVITCH

ELISE TRENT

HARRY LEFTWICH

GEORGE HUDD

MAÎTRE D'HÔTEL

TWO BARMEN

LUKE BELLOWS

JOSHUA DRAKE

BENNY TYRELL

FREDDY PALMER

VIOLET EMERY

MR. JEVON

MRS. JEVON

MR. HANCOX

MRS. HANCOX

PHYLLIS HANCOX

EDGAR DARRELL

WAITERS, LIFT-BOYS, HOTEL GUESTS, *etc.*

The action of the play passes in a hotel in Paris.

ACT I—1924

Scene I.   *The Lounge (Place du Cœur). January. Late afternoon.*

Scene II. *Communicating passage between Place du Cœur and Rue Gilon sides. A few days later—before lunch.*

Scene III. *The Bar—lunch time—March.*

ACT II—1925

Scene I.   *The Lounge (Rue Gilon side). January. After lunch.*

Scene II. *The Bar again. February. Before lunch.*

Scene III. *Corner of the terrace outside the Grill Room. June—lunch time.*

ACT III—1926

Scene I.   *The Men's Bar—before dinner—January.*

Scene II. *The Lounge (Rue Gilon side). The same night. 3 a.m.*

Scene III. *The Lounge (Place du Cœur). June. Late afternoon.*

NOTE

Whoever produces this play must use his own discretion as to the breaking up of scenes by various necessary interruptions, such as the entrances and exits of non-speaking parts, at places in which he considers such interruptions least harmful to the action. I have purposely minimised my stage directions realising that grouping and movement in a production of this sort can only satisfactorily be decided in actual rehearsal.

ACT I: Scene I

TIME: *January 1924. Late afternoon.*

SCENE: *The Reading and Waiting Room of a hotel in Paris. The Bureau, lifts and doors opening onto Place du Cœur are in the background. The foreground is occupied by a small writing desk and a few chairs, also a table strewn with periodicals.*

When the curtain rises, TANIS MARSHALL *is seated at writing desk writing postcards. A* YOUNG GIRL *is seated near by looking through an illustrated weekly. She occasionally looks up as though expecting someone. The swing doors admit two people, a man and woman, who pass across the back on their way to tea. Music can be heard from the tea lounge. At last the* YOUNG MAN *she is expecting comes in. She half rises and then goes on reading the paper as though she hadn't seen him; he approaches her.*

YOUNG MAN: I'm terribly sorry.

YOUNG GIRL: I've been here for ages.

YOUNG MAN: Please forgive me. I couldn't get away.

YOUNG GIRL: It doesn't matter.

YOUNG MAN: Where shall we go?

YOUNG GIRL: Anywhere.

YOUNG MAN: The same as last time?

YOUNG GIRL: If you like.

YOUNG MAN: You're not really angry, are you?

YOUNG GIRL: I do hate waiting about.

YOUNG MAN: It can't be helped, you know, really—every now and then I have to be so damned careful.

YOUNG GIRL: So have I.

YOUNG MAN: Sweetheart!

YOUNG GIRL (*taking his arm, half smiling*): Shhh!

> *They go out.*

TANIS *beckons to the* DAY PORTER, *who is standing just by the swing doors. He comes over to her.*

TANIS: Mr. Marshall hasn't come in yet, has he?

DAY PORTER: No, madam.

TANIS: When he does, tell him I'm in here, in case he doesn't see me.

DAY PORTER: Yes, madam.

He goes back and takes up his stand by the doors.

DOROTHY PRICE *and* SUZANNE FELLINI *come out from the direction of the lifts and stand talking.* DOROTHY PRICE *is chic, beautifully dressed, on the flashy side.* SUZANNE *is also well dressed but less ostentatious.*

DOROTHY: He makes me tired—he really does.

SUZANNE: Why argue with him?

DOROTHY: He's so damned pig-headed.

SUZANNE: Wait until we get to Zoë's and he's had a cocktail or two, then all will be well.

DOROTHY: He's more trouble than he's worth.

SUZANNE (*laughing*): Don't be silly, dear!

DOROTHY (*almost laughing too*): I don't know what I should do without you, Suzanne. Honestly I don't; you must come to Cannes with us.

SUZANNE: He'd hate the sight of me in a week.

DOROTHY: That doesn't matter—I can manage him.

SUZANNE: There are other reasons too why I can't come.

DOROTHY: I can arrange all that.

SUZANNE: You mean you can make him arrange it.

DOROTHY: Well, it doesn't matter, does it, as long as you're there? You must come. I shall go mad, if you don't.

SUZANNE: Here he is—for God's sake be a little nicer to him.

MIKE CRAVEN *comes from the lift, small but rather pugnacious looking.*

DOROTHY: Did you find it?

MIKE: Yes, here it is. (*He gives her a small cigarette box.*) I had to search the room out for it.

DOROTHY (*sweetly*): I'm so sorry, Mike dear.

The FLETCHERS *arrive. The* PORTER *brings in their hand luggage.* MRS. FLETCHER *is stout and rich middle-class American.* MR.

6

FLETCHER is spare and appears depressed. BERYL is young, rather over-smart and extremely lovely. She stares at DOROTHY with great interest.

MIKE: We'd better be moving along, hadn't we—we can't stand about here all day.

DOROTHY: I should hate to, darling. (*She winks at SUZANNE.*)

As they go out of the swing doors——

MR. FLETCHER (*in uneasy French*): Il ya un autre valise encore.

DAY PORTER (*in perfect English*): Very well, sir. I will get it. (*He motions him towards the Bureau.*)

BERYL: Did you see her bangles, Mother?

MRS. FLETCHER: Whose bangles?

BERYL: The woman that just went out.

MRS. LETCHER: I do hope they've made the reservations all right.

BERYL: They were heavenly—and that little cigarette case was darling.

MRS. FLETCHER: I know what European hotels are like . . .

They disappear in the direction of the Bureau, where MR. FLETCHER is talking to the ASSISTANT MANAGER.

BEVERLEY FORD and CYRIL HARDACRE come through the swing doors, carrying small bags and followed by the DAY PORTER, carrying their larger ones. BEVERLEY is about forty, extremely well dressed.

CYRIL is in his twenties—good-looking and slim.

BEVERLEY (*to the DAY PORTER*): Pay the taxi, will you? I haven't any change.

DAY PORTER (*putting down the bags*): Yes, sir.

CYRIL: I have.

BEVERLEY: No—he'll do it.

The DAY PORTER goes out.

Well, my dear—here we are at last. Paris is a virgin for you, unsullied by memories. Are you happy?

CYRIL (*with faint impatience*): Of course I am.

BEVERLEY (*with a giggle*): You blush so beautifully when I make affected remarks.

CYRIL: Oh shut up, Beverley.

BEVERLEY: That's why I make them.

ALBERT HENNICK *enters from the direction of the Lounge. He is a dapper little man of about twenty-eight. His voice is rather shrill.*

ALBERT: Beverley—by God, it *is* you. I was having tea with Violet; she saw you first. This is divine—how are you?

BEVERLEY: Completely shattered at the moment. We had a filthy crossing. Do you know Cyril Hardacre? Albert Hennick.

ALBERT: How are you?

The DAY PORTER *has returned by this time and gives* BEVERLEY *his change.* BEVERLEY *tips him.*

BEVERLEY: Leave the bags while I go and see about our rooms. Talk to Cyril for a moment, Albert.

He goes to the Bureau.

ALBERT: I've seen you before somewhere, haven't I?

CYRIL: In London, perhaps.

ALBERT: How long are you staying?

CYRIL: Not long. Beverley wants to go down to Cannes.

ALBERT: Are you going with him?

CYRIL (*frowning slightly*): Yes.

ALBERT: My dear, how marvellous! You must both come to a party a friend of mine is giving on Thursday—Nicco Benelli—d'you know him?

CYRIL: No. I'm afraid I don't.

ALBERT: He's completely mad—you'll love him. Italian you know—dark and flashy eyes and plays the piano like an angel. Eric Burnett always says—D'you know Eric?

CYRIL: No.

ALBERT (*giggling*): Well, you will soon – he's terribly funny.

BEVERLEY *rejoins them.*

BEVERLEY: We're on the Rue Gilon side.

ALBERT: You must talk to Violet on the way through. She's dying to see you.

BEVERLEY: All right. (*To the* DAY PORTER.) Have the bags sent over as soon as possible.

DAY PORTER: Yes, sir.

BEVERLEY: Come along.

CYRIL *walks off a few paces in front.*

ALBERT (*to* BEVERLEY *as they go off*): My dear—where did you find that? It's divine!

> *Three people—two women and a man walk in from the lounge and—*
> *—out through the swing doors talking as they go.*
> *As they go out,* OWEN MARSHALL *comes in. He is a good-looking man of about thirty. The* DAY PORTER *intercepts him.*

DAY PORTER: Madame is in there, sir—writing letters.

OWEN: Oh, is she? Thanks. (*He comes forward and sees* TANIS.)

TANIS: Hallo, dear. You've been ages!

OWEN (*glancing at his watch*): Three-quarters of an hour.

TANIS: It seemed ages.

OWEN: I was engaged upon a very noble mission.

TANIS: What?

OWEN: Buying you a present.

TANIS: Oh, darling, you shouldn't have. What is it?

OWEN: Here. (*He flings down on the desk a small package.*) I'm giving it to you carelessly as though it meant nothing.

TANIS (*playing up*): It's such a bore receiving presents—can't you wait until I'm less busy.

OWEN: Open it for God's sake. (*He gives a cautious look around and kisses the back of her neck.*)

> *She proceeds to open the package. During the whole of the ensuing scene various people arrive with luggage, etc., or pass out through the swing doors. One fails to catch their conversation, being so completely engrossed in* TANIS *and* OWEN.

TANIS (*disclosing small box*): "Cartier"! Oh, darling!

OWEN: I felt the moment had come for a "*beau geste*".

> TANIS *opens the box and takes out an exquisite little cigarette case.*

TANIS: Owen!

OWEN: Do you like it?

TANIS: Like it? It's heavenly; it's perfect——

OWEN: I saw it in the window—leering at me.

TANIS: I can't begin to tell you how I love it—and you.

> *She gives a swift glance round, then draws his head down and kisses him.*

OWEN: I suppose I should have waited until we were in our room to give it to you.

TANIS (*smiling*): Yes—you should have, really.

OWEN: I couldn't.

TANIS: It's going to stay here out of its box right by me—while I finish these postcards.

OWEN: It's frightful of you to write postcards on a honeymoon.

TANIS: You'd better send some too.

OWEN: Heaven forbid.

TANIS: Do—there's a darling—send one to George from us both—and Freda. They're on my mind.

OWEN: Oh, all right. (*He sits down opposite her.*)

TANIS: You only need say, "Here we are in Paris."

OWEN: They know that already.

TANIS: Never mind—they'll love to be sure of it.

> *While they are both concentrating on their writing* INEZ ZULIETA *and* CYNTHIA GABLE *come through the swing doors.* INEZ *is slightly older than* CYNTHIA. *They are both dressed with rather affected simplicity.*

INEZ (*coming forward and sitting by the table*): I'll wait here.

CYNTHIA: Don't be so silly.

INEZ: I'll be quite happy. You needn't worry about me. (*She assumes a martyred expression.*)

CYNTHIA: I do wish you wouldn't be so difficult.

TANIS (*looking up at* OWEN): The Bath Club will find Philip, won't it?

OWEN: Yes. They'll forward it on, anyhow.

INEZ: I'm not being in the least difficult.

CYNTHIA: There are moments when you're infuriating.

INEZ: Thank you.

CYNTHIA (*lowering her voice*): What is there to be jealous about?

INEZ: Everything—you don't know her like I do.

CYNTHIA (*sharply*): That's true enough.

INEZ: Why say things like that?

CYNTHIA: Well, you told me yourself.

INEZ: That was all over years ago.

CYNTHIA: I didn't say it wasn't.

INEZ: You're damnably cruel sometimes.

CYNTHIA: Why don't you trust me?

INEZ: Trust you——

CYNTHIA: Yes; I feel as though I were in a cage.

INEZ: Cynthia darling——

CYNTHIA: What?

INEZ: I do trust you—really—but don't go and see her now.

CYNTHIA: Why not?

INEZ: You know perfectly well.

CYNTHIA: Just because you've worked yourself up into a ridiculous state . . .

INEZ: I haven't done anything of the sort.

CYNTHIA: You have.

INEZ: I wish you'd give me back my pride.

CYNTHIA: Don't be melodramatic.

INEZ: And with it the courage never to see you again.

> *She gets up abruptly and goes out.*

CYNTHIA (*following her*): Inez—Inez——

> *She goes out after her.*

OWEN (*blotting a postcard and sitting back*): I've got seats for the Guitrys.

TANIS: Grand! I love them.

OWEN: You're really awfully nice to go on a honeymoon with—so appreciative.

TANIS: I'm intensely happy.

OWEN: Are you—honestly?

TANIS: Can't you see?

OWEN: Yes, I suppose so. I never thought I should be able to get away with it.

TANIS: What?

OWEN: Making you happy.

TANIS: Neither did I—at first.

OWEN (*almost hurt*): Tanis!

TANIS (*gently*): I love you now, you know—that makes all the difference.

OWEN: And you didn't before?

TANIS (*looking down*): No. I felt awfully ashamed—marrying you.

OWEN (*definitely hurt—leaning towards her*): I don't understand.

TANIS: I liked you.

OWEN (*with faint sarcasm*): I'm very glad, I'm sure.

TANIS: Don't be cross, darling. It really is all right now.

OWEN: Is it?

TANIS: It's frightfully difficult to love people right away, you know.

OWEN: I never found it difficult with you.

TANIS: I was very grateful to you for that.

OWEN: Dear—what are you talking about?

TANIS: Nothing particular. I feel amazingly free and content and I just wanted to explain why.

OWEN: Explain away then.

TANIS: No—not now—this is neither the time or the place.

OWEN: Is there anything on your mind?

TANIS: No, darling, and even the things that were are rapidly sliding off.

OWEN: Oh, darling!

TANIS: Well?

OWEN: I'm afraid you're being a little tiresome.

TANIS: I know—maddening. Please forgive me.

OWEN (*rising*): I suppose we'd better go up and dress.

TANIS: And linger over it.

OWEN: You always do.

TANIS: Darling. (*She pinches his arm.*)

OWEN (*picking up a postcard*): You've forgotten a beautiful bird's-eye view of Versailles. (*He turns it over.*) I didn't know you knew Benny Jowett.

TANIS: That's the last postcard I shall ever send him.

OWEN: Why?

TANIS (*sighing*): Oh dear!

OWEN: What on earth is the matter with you to-day?

TANIS: I'm going to be awfully true to you. I've got a tremendous ideal about it.

OWEN: I can't begin to imagine not being true to you.

TANIS (*with utter sincerity*): I love you so very deeply.

OWEN: Sweetheart! (*He kisses her.*)

TANIS (*taking his arm*): Darling—I'm sure that woman saw us!

> They go out, pausing at the entrance to the lounge to allow a group of people to pass on their way out.

CURTAIN SLOWLY FALLS

Scene II

TIME: *A few days after Scene I. Just before lunch.*

SCENE: *The communicating passage-way between the Place du Cœur and the Rue Gilon side. There are several show-cases exhibiting clothes, jewellery, perfume, etc., standing at equal distances from one another.*

Apart from the individual characters in the play, other people pass back and forth. There is a kiosk of magazines and papers a little to the R., a GIRL *in black is in charge of it, seated on a stool by the side.*

When the curtain rises, the stage is empty with the exception of the GIRL. *A man, dapperly dressed, walks rapidly across from R. to L. He is obviously in a hurry and might almost be French.*

MARION FAWCETT *enters from L. She is somewhere between thirty and forty and dressed smartly. She has almost reached the kiosk when* INEZ *and* CYNTHIA *enter from R.*

MARION: Hallo, Inez. How are you?

INEZ: Exhausted, dear. You know Cynthia, don't you?

MARION: Of course. (*She shakes hands with* CYNTHIA.) You haven't seen a dark little American girl with a sort of wood-violet face loitering about, have you?

INEZ: Yes, hundreds.

MARION: Gloria Craig gave her a letter of introduction to me. I must find her and give her lunch.

CYNTHIA: Well, if you don't succeed, come and lunch with us.

INEZ: I'm not lunching.

CYNTHIA (*warningly*): Inez!

INEZ: I have to go to Chanel's.

CYNTHIA (*to* MARION): Well, lunch with *me* then. I'll be in the Restaurant.

MARION: Thanks, my dear. See you later, Inez.

She goes off.

INEZ (*as they walk across*): I suppose it's too much to expect that you should ever wish to lunch with me alone.

CYNTHIA: Don't be ridiculous.

INEZ: I'm not ridiculous. You know I loathe Marion Fawcett.

CYNTHIA: I don't know anything of the sort.

INEZ (*angrily*): Go and lunch with her then—lunch and dine and sup with all the people I hate most—and discuss me with them and break up everything.

CYNTHIA (*quickly*): I will—if you're not careful!

> *As they are about to go off*—CYRIL *walks on L.*

CYRIL: Oh, how do you do?

INEZ (*shaking hands*): I'd no idea you were in Paris.

CYRIL: I'm over here with Beverley.

INEZ: My dear boy, how unoriginal.

CYRIL: Is it?

INEZ: How's Francis?

CYRIL: Oh, all right, I think.

INEZ: Give him my love when you see him.

CYRIL: Certainly I will. Good-bye. (*He bows and walks on.*)

> *They go off.*
>
> JEROME KENNEDY *and* NORMA *enter from R.* JEROME *is about forty, slightly grey-haired and distinctly attractive.* NORMA *is about eighteen—fair and slim and self-assured.*

CYRIL: Did you say Restaurant or Grill?

JEROME: Restaurant.

NORMA: I thought you'd muddle it.

CYRIL: I say—I'm most awfully sorry.

JEROME: Have you been waiting long?

CYRIL: About twenty minutes.

JEROME: We'll go to the Grill, the Restaurant's teeming with angry women.

NORMA: Oh no, Father.

JEROME: Well, we'll see what it looks like anyhow.

> *They stroll across towards L.*
>
> ALBERT *and* BEVERLEY *enter from L.*

BEVERLEY (*to* CYRIL): Hallo.

CYRIL (*irritably*): Oh, hallo.

> ALBERT *and* BEVERLEY *pass on.*
> *The* KENNEDYS *and* CYRIL *stroll off.*

ALBERT (*just as they are nearly off*): Have you been having a row?

BEVERLEY: Good-looking people are always difficult to manage.

ALBERT (*giggling*): You're right. We are.

BEVERLEY (*to* GIRL *at kiosk*): Have you got *Vanity Fair*?

  GIRL: Oui, monsieur. (*She hands it to him.*)

BEVERLEY (*paying her for it*): Here.

GIRL: Merci, monsieur.

ALBERT: Do get *La Vie Parisienne*, it's so defiantly normal!

BEVERLEY: Be quiet, Albert.

> *They go off.*
> *The stage is empty for a moment.* DOROTHY *and* JULIUS *stroll on from R., pausing in front of show-cases.* JULIUS LEVENOVITCH *is a tall, good-looking slightly over-dressed Russian.*

DOROTHY: And didn't they give you any food?

JULIUS: Just black bread every day or so. One did not feel like eating much.

DOROTHY: I understand.

JULIUS: I know you do.

DOROTHY: It seems so unfair that people should have to suffer so much.

JULIUS: Perhaps I deserved it. Who knows.

DOROTHY: You must teach me Russian.

JULIUS: I would love to.

DOROTHY: I know just a few words already.

JULIUS: What are they?

DOROTHY (*smiling*): I can't tell you now.

JULIUS: Why not?

DOROTHY: I don't know you well enough. (*At show-case.*) Do look at that frock. Isn't it frightful?

JULIUS: Are you staying here long?

DOROTHY: Only a few days. We're going to Cannes.

JULIUS: We?

DOROTHY: Suzanne and me—and Mike.

JULIUS: That short man you were dining with last night?

DOROTHY: Yes, Mike Craven. You must meet him.

JULIUS: Must I?

DOROTHY (*laughing*): You really are terrible.

> *They go off.*

CYNTHIA *walks on from* L. ELISE TRENT *enters at the same moment from* R. *They exchange a long look and* ELISE *passes on.* MARION *enters from* R. *with* BERYL. *They are talking gaily.*

CYNTHIA: You found her all right then?

MARION: Yes. Beryl Fletcher—Cynthia Gable.

CYNTHIA: How d'you do.

BERYL: I'm so pleased to meet you. I know you by sight.

CYNTHIA: How nice of you.

MARION: Where's Inez?

CYNTHIA: She stamped out into the Rue Gilon.

MARION (*laughing*): You are divine, Cynthia.

CYNTHIA: I'm very cross.

MARION: Come and lunch with us in the Grill.

CYNTHIA: I asked you to lunch with me if you didn't find Miss Fletcher.

MARION: Well, let's all lunch with each other.

CYNTHIA: All right.

BERYL (*as they go off*): I'm coming over by myself in the Fall to learn French properly.

They all three go off L.
OWEN *and* TANIS *come in from* R. TANIS *stops at kiosk.*

TANIS: Let's stop and load up with magazines for the train.

OWEN: All right.

The KENNEDYS *enter from* L. *with* CYRIL.

JEROME: Why don't you come South with us?

CYRIL: God, I should love it, but——

NORMA: Anyhow, we shall see you somewhere about, shan't we?

CYRIL: Yes—oh yes.

Just as they are passing the kiosk TANIS *turns to* JEROME, *thinking it is* OWEN.

TANIS (*brandishing the sketch*): Darling, do look at this awful photograph of Sylvia. (*Realising her mistake.*) Oh, I beg your pardon.

JEROME (*smiling*): Not at all.

He and NORMA *and* CYRIL *exit.* NORMA *laughs.*

TANIS: Owen, I'm covered in shame. I've called a perfectly strange man "Darling"!

CURTAIN

Scene III

TIME: *March. Before lunch.*

SCENE: *The Bar on the Rue Gilon side. It is a small compact room with entrance back C., facing the entrance to the Men's Bar. There are small tables round the walls and dishes of olives and crisp potato flakes on each table.*

There is a group of three people sitting at a table L. upstage. They are drinking cocktails and talking in undertones. Their conversation is inaudible, being immaterial to the action of the play.

CYRIL HARDACRE enters, looks round and sits at table R. A WAITER comes in with fresh cocktails for the people L. After he has delivered them CYRIL calls him.

CYRIL: Garçon.

WAITER: Monsieur?

CYRIL: Two Martinis with a dash.

WAITER: Bien, monsieur.

CYRIL: Make one of them double.

WAITER: Oui, monsieur.

> *The WAITER departs.*
> *CYRIL looks at his wrist watch and lights a cigarette. DOROTHY PRICE and SUZANNE FELLINI enter and seat themselves at table down L.*

SUZANNE: I think you're an awful fool to do this.

DOROTHY: Oh, shut up, Suzanne.

SUZANNE: Well, I do.

DOROTHY: There's no harm in lunch, is there?

SUZANNE: A good deal, I should imagine.

DOROTHY: That's your dirty mind, dear.

SUZANNE: Thanks.

DOROTHY: I don't intend to be a slave to anyone ever.

SUZANNE: Slaves don't get as much out of life as you do.

DOROTHY: Mike doesn't arrive until this evening anyhow.

SUZANNE: He might fly over.

DOROTHY: Not he—he'd be too frightened of getting into an air pocket.

SUZANNE: Your passion for intrigue will wreck you one day.

DOROTHY: Don't croak.

SUZANNE: It wrecked me.

DOROTHY: That was different—you weren't discreet.

SUZANNE: I thought I was.

DOROTHY: My dear, Mike is far too conceited to imagine anyone could be unfaithful to him.

SUZANNE: Are you sure?

DOROTHY: Anyhow I haven't been—yet.

SUZANNE: He's no fool really, you know.

DOROTHY: He is over me.

SUZANNE: You're so sure of yourself.

DOROTHY (*exasperated*): Now look here, Suzanne—I'm merely lunching here with you and Julius.

SUZANNE: No, dear—you're merely lunching here with Julius.

DOROTHY: How's Mike to know that?

SUZANNE: Here's the waiter.

The WAITER *has returned with* CYRIL'S *cocktails which he places on the table.* CYRIL *pays him.*
The three people upstage L. get up and go out.

DOROTHY: Garçon.

WAITER: Oui, madame.

DOROTHY: One Bronx—what do you want, Suzanne?

SUZANNE: Porto Flip.

DOROTHY: How disgusting! (*To* WAITER.) And one Porto Flip.

SUZANNE: And bring some more of these potatoes, will you.

WAITER: Bien, madame.

He takes empty potato dish and goes off.

SUZANNE: Do you honestly think Julius is worth all this trouble?

DOROTHY: There hasn't been any trouble.

SUZANNE: There will be.

DOROTHY (*with sarcasm*): You're being *such* a comfort, dear.

SUZANNE: I've known Mike longer than you have.

DOROTHY: Yes, but not so intimately.

SUZANNE: Exactly—one can see better when one's not too close.

DOROTHY: You've got a hangover this morning. That's what it is.

SUZANNE: Why not wait until Mike goes away?

DOROTHY: I'll be an old woman before he does that—he keeps putting it off—putting it off——

SUZANNE: Has it ever struck you that he's pretty deeply in love with you?

DOROTHY: Don't, dear, you're breaking my heart.

SUZANNE: And I think making a fool of him after all you got from him is not only dangerous but rather second-rate.

DOROTHY: Now look here, Suzanne.

SUZANNE: I mean it.

DOROTHY: To hear you talk anyone would think I was never out of bed with Julius.

SUZANNE: He's nothing but a cheap little Russian pimp, anyhow!

DOROTHY (*furious*): How dare you say that!

SUZANNE: The nearest he ever got to the old nobility was seeing their pictures in the *Daily Mirror*.

DOROTHY: You're jealous—anyone could see that.

SUZANNE: Jealous! That's funny!

DOROTHY: I think it's pathetic.

SUZANNE (*rising*): You self-satisfied little fool—you can manage your own filthy intrigues—I'm not going to be mixed up in them.

DOROTHY (*acidly*): Aren't you going to wait for your Porto Flip, darling?

SUZANNE (*irately*): You know what you can do with that, don't you?

DOROTHY: Oh, go to hell!

> SUZANNE *stalks out—nearly banging into——*
> NORMA *who is coming in.* CYRIL *rises.*

NORMA: Am I terribly late?

CYRIL: No, not a bit—I was early.

NORMA: I've been shopping.

CYRIL: Here's a cocktail for you.

NORMA (*sitting down and loosening her furs*): Thank God.

CYRIL: When are you going back to London?

NORMA: To-morrow—or the day after.

CYRIL (*despondently*): Oh!

NORMA: Don't look so gloomy.

CYRIL: I can't help it.

NORMA: Cyril dear—you mustn't be silly, you know.

CYRIL: I'm not silly.

NORMA: You are—a little.

CYRIL: You were much nicer to me in Cannes.

NORMA: Was I?

CYRIL: You know you were.

NORMA: How's your singing going?

CYRIL: Damn my singing!

NORMA: Are you working hard?

CYRIL: Yes—far too hard.

NORMA: How's Beverley Ford?

CYRIL: I don't know—I haven't seen him since Cannes.

NORMA: I'm glad of that.

CYRIL: Why?

NORMA: I'm not a fool, Cyril.

CYRIL: I don't know what you mean.

NORMA: Yes, you do—perfectly well.

CYRIL: I wish you wouldn't insinuate things.

NORMA (*lightly*): You forget, dear, that apart from being an extremely bright modern young girl, I happen to be the daughter of a novelist—life holds out no surprises for me. I'm occasionally pained but never shocked.

CYRIL: Oh God!

NORMA: What's the matter?

CYRIL: You frighten me.

NORMA: Don't be ingenuous, Cyril, or you'll arouse the maternal in me.

CYRIL: I love you.

NORMA (*gently*): Shut up.

CYRIL: Why should I?

NORMA: Because as I've told you before—it's no use.

CYRIL: I suppose you were only sweet to me in Cannes, because you felt I needed reforming.

NORMA: I certainly felt that you were on the wrong track.

CYRIL: And you didn't care for me at all?

NORMA: Of course I did—I do now—I think you're a dear.

CYRIL: I see.

NORMA: I'm afraid you don't.

CYRIL: Are you in love with anyone else?

NORMA: No.

CYRIL: Honestly!

NORMA (*with faint hesitation*): I don't think so.

CYRIL: I suppose you don't want to lunch with me.

NORMA: Yes, I do—very much.

CYRIL: I'm not going to be very gay or amusing.

NORMA: I don't want you to be.

CYRIL: I'm utterly miserable.

NORMA: Look here, Cyril—don't be weak and self-pitying. I'm not going to be false and play up to you. I respect you too much.

CYRIL (*contemptuously*): Respect!

NORMA: Yes—and you're wrong about me trying to reform you—I wouldn't try to reform anybody—I realised in Cannes that you were in quite the wrong métier and not particularly happy in it. It's awfully difficult to find one's level these days—nothing matters really except being sure of what you want—and you weren't.

CYRIL: I am now—and I'm more wretched than I've ever been in my life.

NORMA: You'll get over that—and anyhow you do *know* about yourself.

The WAITER *comes in with a cocktail and Porto Flip for* DOROTHY.

DOROTHY: I don't want the Porto Flip after all—will you take it back?

WAITER: Oui, madam.

DOROTHY (*paying him*): Here.

WAITER: Merci, madame.

CYRIL: Do you want another cocktail?

NORMA: No, thanks.

CYRIL: I think I do.

NORMA: You've already had a double one.

CYRIL: Oh, all right—let's go and have lunch.

They get up to go and meet JEROME *coming in. Two people come in after him and sit at a table up stage R.*

NORMA: Hallo, Father!

JEROME: Hallo. (*He shakes hands with* CYRIL.) Are you two lunching here?

CYRIL: Yes.

JEROME: It's all right. Don't look scared, Cyril. I don't intend to join you. I'm lunching with the Marshalls.

NORMA: The Marshalls?

JEROME: Yes, you remember that woman in Cannes who played tennis with us—and her husband?

NORMA: Oh yes—I remember.

JEROME: We're dining at 7.30, remember—so don't be late.

NORMA: Don't fuss, dear—I'll be there.

JEROME (*to* CYRIL): Good-bye, young man.

CYRIL: Good-bye.

JEROME: Look us up if you come over to London.

CYRIL: Thanks awfully—I will.

Goes out with NORMA.

JEROME *goes and sits at the table they've just left. He rings the bell for the* WAITER *and lights a cigarette.* CYNTHIA *and* ELISE *enter and sit at a table just below* DOROTHY.

ELISE: They did the whole thing with masks.

CYNTHIA: Marvellous!

ELISE: I really feel that they're getting somewhere, you know.

CYNTHIA: Inez doesn't—she resents anything progressive in opera.

ELISE: Naturally—she still clings to the old school.

The WAITER *enters and goes over to* JEROME—*his ensuing dialogue with the* WAITER *and* CYNTHIA *and* ELISE *should be spoken simultaneously.*

JEROME: Garçon.

WAITER: Monsieur?

JEROME: Bring me a double Manhattan.

WAITER: Oui, monsieur.

JEROME: And some Turkish cigarettes.

WAITER: Abdullah, monsieur?

JEROME: Yes, they'll do—bring them quickly.

WAITER: Tout de suite, monsieur.

ELISE: What do you want, dear?

CYNTHIA: I don't care.

ELISE: Stingers are delicious.

CYNTHIA: Stingers?

ELISE: Yes, very potent—crème de menthe and brandy.

CYNTHIA: We shall be under the table.

ELISE: Never mind; we ought to celebrate really.

CYNTHIA: Darling. (*She squeezes* ELISE'*s hand under the table.*)

ELISE: Garçon.

WAITER: Madame?

ELISE: Two Stingers.

WAITER: Bien, madame.

> *He goes off.*
> DOROTHY *rises from her table with slight irritability and goes and stands just outside the door waiting.*

ELISE: Does Inez know—d'you think?

CYNTHIA: I can't help it if she does.

ELISE: But does she?

CYNTHIA: She suspects.

ELISE: I shouldn't think that was anything new.

CYNTHIA: You're right—it isn't.

ELISE: I can't imagine how you've stood it for so long.

CYNTHIA: Neither can I—now.

ELISE: Will she make a scene?

CYNTHIA: I expect so.

ELISE: You don't seem to mind much.

CYNTHIA: I'm used to them.

ELISE: Poor Inez.

CYNTHIA: It serves her right really—she's always so untrusting.

ELISE (*laughing*): Darling—that's funny!

CYNTHIA (*laughing too*): Yes, I suppose it is rather.

ELISE: I feel a bit guilty.

CYNTHIA: Why?

ELISE: It was my fault in the first place.

CYNTHIA: No, it wasn't. I saw you before you ever saw me.

ELISE: Where?

CYNTHIA: Philippe's about two years ago—dining with a red-haired woman.

ELISE: Nadia Balaishieff.

CYNTHIA: Where is she now?

ELISE: New York, I think. I really don't know.

CYNTHIA: Tell me, Elise—are you as utterly ruthless as you pretend to be?

ELISE: I don't pretend ever.

CYNTHIA: I'm glad.

ELISE: It's funny you remembering me all that time—life's made up of circles, isn't it?

CYNTHIA: Perhaps.

ELISE: Are you going to tell Inez?

CYNTHIA: Yes, I suppose so.

ELISE: When?

CYNTHIA: I don't know.

ELISE: Soon?

CYNTHIA: She's bound to know—very soon indeed.

ELISE: Why don't you get it over at once?

CYNTHIA: The opportunity will occur of its own accord.

ELISE: That's rather cowardly of you.

CYNTHIA: She's got to go to Dresden next month anyhow.

ELISE: Will you come to me then?

CYNTHIA: Yes.

ELISE: Next month—it's a long way ahead.

> *The* WAITER *appears with their cocktails,* ELISE *pays him.*

WAITER: Merci, madame.

> *The* WAITER *delivers* JEROME'S *cocktail and cigarettes.*

CYNTHIA (*sipping her drink*): This is delicious.

ELISE: They're awfully easy to make.

> INEZ *enters wrapped in furs and looking extremely sullen—she sees them and approaches the table.*

(*Affably.*) Good morning, Inez.

INEZ (*ignoring her—to* CYNTHIA): I want to speak to you.

ELISE (*half rising*): Shall I go?

CYNTHIA: Certainly not—stay where you are.

INEZ: I should like you to go, please.

CYNTHIA: Don't be a fool, Inez.

ELISE: This is very embarrassing.

INEZ: I'm surprised that you find it so—it's a situation you must be well accustomed to.

ELISE: I shouldn't raise your voice quite so much if I were you—it's rather silly.

INEZ: Mind your own business.

CYNTHIA: Inez!

INEZ: You've lied to me.

CYNTHIA: You're behaving fantastically.

INEZ: Will you go back to the flat sometime during the afternoon and pack your things.

CYNTHIA (*rising, furiously*): How dare you!

ELISE (*pulling her down*): Ssh, Cynthia.

INEZ (*softly*): I hate you—I hate you—I hate you!

> *She walks out.*

CYNTHIA (*after a pause—shuddering*): How horrible!

ELISE: Are you going after her?

CYNTHIA: No.

ELISE: Good! (*She finishes her drink.*)

CYNTHIA: How dare she talk to me like that—how dare she! (*She breaks into tears.*)

ELISE: Cynthia—for heaven's sake—don't be an idiot. (*She presses her arm.*)

CYNTHIA: Don't touch me.

ELISE: Darling, pull yourself together.

CYNTHIA: Let's go quickly—quickly——

ELISE: Very well—come along.

> *They go out as——*
> TANIS MARSHALL *comes in.* DOROTHY PRICE *also re-enters and returns to her table.* TANIS *sees* JEROME.

TANIS: I've been waiting for Owen over at the other side but I left a message with the porter.

JEROME: Good. D'you want a cocktail?

TANIS (*sitting down*): No, thanks—you'd better order for Owen.

> JEROME *rings bell for* WAITER.

JEROME: It's awfully nice seeing you again.

TANIS: I'm feeling awfully homesick for the South—all that lovely sunshine and everything.

JEROME: It was divine, wasn't it?

TANIS: When do you go back to London?

JEROME: The day after to-morrow, I think.

TANIS: So are we—we shall meet on the train.

The WAITER *appears.*

JEROME: What do you think your husband would like?

TANIS: Oh, anything—a Martini, I should think.

JEROME: Bring a Martini, will you?

WAITER: Oui, monsieur.

JEROME: Cigarette?

TANIS (*taking one*): Thanks. Are you working on a new book?

JEROME: I shall start directly I get back.

TANIS: You do lead a grand life, don't you?

JEROME: I enjoy myself, I think—on the whole.

TANIS: How's Norma?

JEROME: Frightfully well and extremely energetic as usual.

TANIS: She's awfully amusing.

JEROME: They all are—this younger generation.

TANIS: You talk as though you were seventy!

JEROME: It's having a grown-up daughter—I feel seventy sometimes.

TANIS: Your tennis seems still to retain a certain amount of youthful vigour.

JEROME (*laughing*): Thanks.

TANIS (*looking across at* DOROTHY): There's that woman we saw in the Ambassadeur that night.

JEROME: Oh yes—so it is. Wasn't she the one who had a fearful scene with the little red-faced man?

TANIS: Yes—look at her pearls.

JEROME: God bless the little red-faced man!

TANIS: People are amusing, aren't they, to watch?

JEROME: In this atmosphere they rather lack variety.

The WAITER *brings the cocktail.* JEROME *pays for it.*

TANIS: It's really very tiresome of Owen to be so late.

JEROME: I'm perfectly happy.

TANIS: I should like to have all the money in the world and rush
   up and down the Rue de la Paix with a barrow.

JEROME: I know that feeling.

    OWEN enters and approaches them.

TANIS: Here he is at last.

OWEN: I'm terribly sorry——(*He shakes hands with* JEROME.)

JEROME: It doesn't matter a bit—here's a Martini for you.

OWEN: Thanks—I'll swallow it down in one gulp. (*He does so.*)

TANIS: Where *have* you been?

OWEN: At the bank, dear—hedged in by enthusiastic tourists.

JEROME: Shall we go and lunch?

TANIS (*crushing out her cigarette*): Yes, let's.

JEROME: Come along, then.

TANIS (*as they go out*): Isn't it fun, Owen—Mr. Kennedy is going
   over to London on Thursday with us.

    They go out.
    A group of people enter and sit down. DOROTHY, *by this time*
    extremely impatient, gathers herself together preparatory to leaving.
    Finally JULIUS *enters hurriedly.*

JULIUS: Dorothy!

DOROTHY: I was just going.

JULIUS: Forgive me, please.

DOROTHY: I've been here for hours.

JULIUS: Don't be angry.

DOROTHY: I'm not angry—only bored.

JULIUS: Please smile.

DOROTHY: Why are you so late?

JULIUS: Just one smile.

DOROTHY: You haven't answered me.

JULIUS: There is only one way I could answer you.

DOROTHY: Well, why don't you?

JULIUS: It's too public.

DOROTHY: Now then.

JULIUS: Do you want to lunch here?

DOROTHY: I don't care.

JULIUS: Don't you?

DOROTHY: Not a bit.

JULIUS: You look wonderful.

DOROTHY: Thanks.

JULIUS: I'm glad I was late.

DOROTHY: Why?

JULIUS: Because I've never seen you angry before—I want to know you in every mood.

DOROTHY: I'd begun to think you weren't coming at all.

JULIUS: Where is Suzanne?

DOROTHY: Suzanne's a bloody fool.

JULIUS: I didn't say what is she—I said where is she?

DOROTHY: I don't know and I don't care.

JULIUS: I'm glad you got rid of her.

DOROTHY: Do you want a cocktail?

JULIUS: No thank you. Do you?

DOROTHY: I've had one.

JULIUS: Another?

DOROTHY: No.

JULIUS: Come, then.

DOROTHY: We haven't decided where to go yet.

JULIUS: We'll decide in the taxi.

DOROTHY: I'd rather walk.

JULIUS: Don't be cruel.

DOROTHY: Well, I would—I know about you in taxis.

JULIUS: You haven't smiled yet.

DOROTHY: There——(*She grimaces at him.*)

JULIUS: Beautiful!

DOROTHY: Where are we lunching?

JULIUS: The other side of the river.

DOROTHY: Oh no, we're not.

JULIUS: Yes—please.

DOROTHY: Some awful little café?

JULIUS: No.

DOROTHY: Where then?

JULIUS: No café at all.

DOROTHY: Do you mean——?

JULIUS: Yes, please.

DOROTHY: Well, really—you have got a nerve.

JULIUS: Lunch is all ready—delicious—that's why I was late.

DOROTHY: Suppose I don't come?

JULIUS: I shall throw it all out of the window.

DOROTHY: You are absurd! (*She smiles.*)

JULIUS: The smile—at last——

DOROTHY (*as they go out*): Alone in Paris with an amorous
Russian—so help me God!

CURTAIN

ACT II: Scene I

TIME: *January 1925. Just after lunch.*

SCENE: *The lounge—Rue Gilon side. On the right is the exit to the Rue Gilon and entrances to the Bars off stage. To the left down stage, entrance to the Grill Room. French windows up left opening onto terrace. There is a big sofa across middle of stage behind which is entrance to communicating passage far up left and far up right the lifts.*

When the curtain rises four people come out of the Grill Room. The women depart for the Ladies' room and the men to get their hats and coats R. CYRIL enters from communicating passage. He comes down and looks into Grill Room, then goes over to sofa and sits down. The two men return to view, hatted and coated, and wait for the women who presently rejoin them and they all go out together. INEZ enters from R.

INEZ: My dear boy, how can you manage to look so hearty and well after that *fearful* party?

CYRIL (*having risen*): I feel marvellous really—considering.

INEZ: You sang quite beautifully—why did I never know you had a voice like that?

CYRIL (*pleased*): Well, you see, I——

INEZ: Are you studying?

CYRIL: Yes—with Farelli.

INEZ: My dear, you must leave him at once.

CYRIL: Oh—why?

INEZ: He shuts up people's throats like mouse-traps—Look at poor Griselda Menken—the most constipated Carmen I've ever heard.

CYRIL: I thought she was rather good.

INEZ: Why don't you come and have tea with me sometime?

CYRIL: Thanks, most awfully—I'd love to.

INEZ: Do you live in this hotel?

CYRIL: No.

INEZ: Well, you shouldn't loiter about here so much—you'll make people think you do.

CYRIL: Do you think that would be bad for my reputation?

INEZ: I know a good deal more about your reputation than you imagine. I'm afraid you're rather a naughty boy, aren't you?

CYRIL (*laughing*): In what way?

INEZ: The usual ways.

CYRIL: You know you're quite different from when I met you first—last year.

INEZ: Am I?

CYRIL: Yes—I used to be terrified of you.

INEZ: I was passing through a tiresome phase.

CYRIL: I would like to hear you sing sometime.

INEZ: I'm rehearsing this afternoon for my concert—you can come if you promise to sit quietly and not say a word.

CYRIL: I'd love to—where shall I come?

INEZ: Soixante-sept rue des Saint Pères—five o'clock.

CYRIL: It's awfully sweet of you to let me.

> BEVERLEY FORD *enters from the Grill Room.*

BEVERLEY: Cyril?

CYRIL: Hallo, Beverley.

BEVERLEY: Inez, my dear—you're looking marvellous.

INEZ (*to* CYRIL): Beverley's so insincere—I adore him.

BEVERLEY: Lady Gailby's in the Grill Room wearing a hat like a Directoire wedding cake.

INEZ (*laughing*): Isn't he ridiculous.

BEVERLEY: I couldn't take my eyes off it—Would you like to dine with me tonight, Cyril?

CYRIL: I'm afraid I can't tonight.

INEZ: Lest old acquaintance be forgot!

BEVERLEY: Really, Inez, you're divine—tongue like a scorpion. (*To* CYRIL.) Beware of her, Cyril—she's the most dangerous woman in Paris—prima donnas always know far too much anyhow.

INEZ: None of the ones I've met know anything. I must go now,

my dears. I promised to meet Helen Saville in the Restaurant
at two o'clock sharp—it's now at least four.

CYRIL (*glancing at his wrist watch*): Twenty-past two to be exact.

INEZ (*patting his arm*): You'll never be a good singer if you're
exact in your private life—don't forget, five o'clock. Soixante-
sept rue des Saint Pères—Good-bye, Beverley. Do come to my
concert.

BEVERLEY: *Nothing* could keep me away.

> INEZ *waves gratefully and goes off in the direction of the*
> *communicating passage.*

Inez is so much more amusing when she's not in love.

CYRIL: So is everybody else.

BEVERLEY: I think Cynthia behaved pretty badly all the same.

CYRIL: Oh, do shut up, Beverley!

BEVERLEY: You're becoming far too hearty these days, Cyril. You
were awfully rude to Albert the other day—he'll never forgive
you.

CYRIL: I don't want him to.

BEVERLEY: Even if you are reverting to the commonplace, surely
there's no necessity to be so truculent about it. (*He walks over*
to get his hat and coat.)

> NORMA *enters hurriedly from the Grill Room.*

CYRIL: Norma.

NORMA: Cyril—I haven't seen you for ages.

CYRIL: I know you haven't.

NORMA: How are you?

CYRIL: All right, thanks.

NORMA: Studying hard?

CYRIL: Yes—I told you I was in my letters.

NORMA: Of course you did.

CYRIL: Which you never answered.

NORMA: I'm always terrible about answering letters.

> *There is a slight pause.*

CYRIL: I suppose you're not going to be in Paris for long, are
you?

NORMA: No—we go to St. Moritz to-morrow.

CYRIL: Oh, I see.

There is another pause.

NORMA (*conversationally*): I wish we were staying longer really—
I'd rather be in Paris than anywhere.

CYRIL: I wish you were, too.

NORMA: Have you still got your studio?

CYRIL: Yes.

NORMA: I'd love to come and see it when we come back.

CYRIL: You wouldn't really, you know—you're just being polite.

NORMA: Don't be so silly, Cyril.

CYRIL: Why don't you say outright that I bore you stiff?—it
would be more honest.

NORMA: What on earth is the matter with you?

CYRIL: Do you think it was quite fair of you to be as nice to me
as you were last year and then leave me utterly flat?

NORMA: I haven't done anything of the sort.

CYRIL: You had such tremendous plans about improving my life.

NORMA: Perhaps you don't feel that my tremendous plans were
necessary?

CYRIL: I did then.

NORMA: And you don't now? Is that it?

CYRIL: I certainly haven't got much out of it.

NORMA: I'm sorry. I thought you had more intelligence.

CYRIL: Thank you.

NORMA: I must go now—I'm frightfully late.

CYRIL (*turning away*): All right—good-bye.

NORMA (*relenting a little*): Cyril—please don't be horrid.

CYRIL (*with bitterness*): Horrid?

NORMA: Yes—I'm sorry I didn't answer your letters or anything—I am honestly.

CYRIL: Rot—you don't give a damn.

NORMA (*angry*): Cyril!

CYRIL: It's perfectly true and you know it—you don't care if I
live or die.

NORMA: If you feel like that about it, there's nothing more to be
said.

CYRIL: There's this to be said—next time you feel the urge to
reform someone—don't muddle it up with your own desire to
be made love to.

NORMA: How dare you say that!

CYRIL: I suppose you found it amusing to see how far you could make me give myself away to you—Well, you succeeded beautifully.

NORMA: Shut up or I'll never speak to you again.

CYRIL: I should be far happier if you didn't!

> *He walks off quickly in the direction of the communicating passage.* NORMA *stands looking after him for a moment, then with a slight shrug of her shoulders—goes out R.*
>
> BERYL FLETCHER *and* MARION FAWCETT *enter from Grill Room.* BERYL *has changed perceptibly since her first arrival in Act I. She is smarter and more assured.*

BERYL: I do think you might come too, Marion.

MARION: Certainly not. I don't approve.

BERYL (*laughing*): Harry adores you—he said so the other night.

MARION: It's very sweet of him, I'm sure.

BERYL: We might do a little shopping on the way.

MARION (*patiently*): Will you take one word of advice from me, dear— go easy on the shopping. Harry's never been renowned for his generosity.

BERYL: He's a perfect darling—I won't hear a word against him.

MARION: You won't be able to help it in some quarters.

BERYL: If I hadn't been staying with you I shouldn't have met him anyhow.

MARION: Oh yes, you would—Harry's always on the track of the fresh and ingenuous.

BERYL (*irately*): I'm *not* fresh and ingenuous.

MARION: Not now, dear.

BERYL (*with slightly forced indignation*): Marion, how can you?

MARION: If I had any sense, I'd pack you off home.

BERYL: I wouldn't go. I'm having far too grand a time.

MARION: You're quite incorrigible. What time are you meeting him?

BERYL: He just said—after lunch.

MARION: He would . . . I must go now. I'll be in about six.

BERYL: I doubt if I shall.

MARION: You must—we're dining early.

BERYL (*laughing*): All right, dear. I'll try.

MARION *goes off up L.*

BERYL *sits down on the sofa and lights a cigarette.* DOROTHY PRICE *and* MIKE CRAVEN *come out of the Grill Room quarrelling and go up back R. to the lifts.*

DOROTHY: Oh, for God's sake shut up about it.

MIKE: The next time I hear anything like that there's going to be trouble.

DOROTHY: I don't care.

MIKE: You will.

DOROTHY: Who do you think you are anyway—Pontius Pilate?

They pass out of earshot and eventually disappear into the lift.
HARRY LEFTWICH *enters from direction of street. He is excellently dressed and about forty-five—nice-looking in a fulsome way.*

HARRY: Beryl!

BERYL: Hallo!

HARRY: You're smoking again—that's awfully naughty.

BERYL: I had to do something while I was waiting for you.

HARRY: Have you been waiting long?

BERYL: About half an hour.

HARRY: Where's Marion?

BERYL: I don't know. I haven't seen her since this morning.

HARRY: I thought you were lunching with her.

BERYL: Oh no, I was lunching with someone else.

HARRY: Who?

BERYL: Let's go now—shall we?

HARRY: Who were you lunching with?

BERYL: Don't be so inquisitive.

HARRY: Why should you try to hide it from me?

BERYL: I'm not trying to hide anything—if you must know, it was a boy I met coming over on the boat last year.

HARRY: Have I ever seen him?

BERYL: I don't know—he's tall and fair and rather athletic-looking.

HARRY: What's his name?

BERYL: Why should you want to know?

HARRY: I don't particularly—come along, my child.

BERYL: I'm not your child.

HARRY: Aren't you?

BERYL: His name's Leo Williams.

HARRY: You've got too much lip rouge on.

BERYL (*pursing up her lips at him*): I think it looks rather nice.

HARRY: It's unnecessary.

BERYL (*sweetly*): Are you mad at me?

HARRY: You're spoiling yourself.

BERYL: That's funny coming from you.

HARRY: What do you mean?

BERYL: You know quite well what I mean.

HARRY (*handing her his handkerchief*): Wipe it off.

BERYL (*smiling*): You *do* frighten me, Harry. (*She wipes her lips.*) Is that better? (*She holds her face towards him.*)

HARRY: Much—darling. (*He is about to kiss her when——*)

> A group of people come out of the Grill Room and——
> Walk off R. talking.

BERYL: Here's your handkerchief. (*She gives it to him.*)

HARRY (*pressing it to his lips*): That's for you.

BERYL (*enraptured*): Oh, Harry!

HARRY: Come along now.

BERYL: Where are we going?

HARRY: We'll decide in the car—it's outside.

BERYL: Let's stop for a moment at Coty's.

HARRY: Why?

BERYL: I must get some perfume.

HARRY: You don't want to use scent at your age.

BERYL: Yes, I do.

HARRY: Oh, very well.

BERYL: I think Marion suspects about us.

HARRY (*sharply*): What!

BERYL: Don't look so scared—what does it matter?

> *Enter* GEORGE HUDD *from back L. He is a thick-set stocky man.*

GEORGE: Hallo, Harry.

HARRY (*irritably*): Hallo, George.

GEORGE: I've just got in from Holland.

HARRY: Really?

GEORGE: I pulled off a pretty big deal. (*He looks at* BERYL, *obviously anxious to be introduced.*)

HARRY: That's splendid. (*Grudgingly.*) Miss Fletcher—Mr. Hudd.

GEORGE (*shaking hands*): How do you do?

BERYL (*with great charm*): I'm so pleased to meet you.

GEORGE: Didn't I see you at Ciro's one night last week?

BERYL: Perhaps you did—I often go there.

GEORGE: I'm going to be here for a few days, Harry—can't we get up a nice little party?

HARRY: I'm rather off parties, George.

GEORGE: You're getting old—that's what it is—eh, Miss Fletcher? (*He laughs.*)

> DOROTHY *comes out of the lift and advances towards them followed by* MIKE. *They are both apparently in better tempers.*

DOROTHY: George! Fancy seeing you. I thought you were in America?

GEORGE (*shaking hands*): No. I've put off going until May. Hallo, Mike. (*They shake hands.*) Do you know Miss Fletcher?

MIKE (*shaking hands with* BERYL): How are you?

BERYL: I'm awfully pleased to meet you.

DOROTHY: I've got a message for you, Harry, from Hazel Clark.

HARRY: Oh, really? I haven't seen her for ages.

DOROTHY: Yes—that was the message—she's furious with you.

GEORGE: Miss Fletcher—Miss Price.

DOROTHY: How do you do—I know you very well by sight.

BERYL: I know you too.

GEORGE: I've been trying to make Harry get up a little party with me.

DOROTHY: Oh yes—when?

GEORGE: What about Thursday?

DOROTHY: That'll be lovely, won't it, Mike? We can have it in our suite.

MIKE: I shan't be here on Thursday.

DOROTHY: Stay over till Friday.

MIKE: I can't.

GEORGE: Make it Wednesday then.

MIKE: Oh, all right.

GEORGE: Does that suit you, Miss Fletcher?

BERYL: I didn't know I was asked.

DOROTHY: Of course you are.

BERYL: How gorgeous—Harry will bring me—won't you, Harry?

HARRY (*without enthusiasm*): Yes, if you like.

GEORGE: Well, that's settled. About 11.30.

DOROTHY: Number 517.

HARRY: All right. Come along, Beryl, we must go.

BERYL (*with a ravishing smile at everybody*): Thanks ever so much.

HARRY: Good-bye, Dorothy.

> *He and* BERYL *go off.*

GEORGE: Who is that girl?

DOROTHY: I don't know—apart from being Harry's latest.

MIKE: He does like 'em young.

DOROTHY: She's pretty in a funny sort of way.

> JULIUS *enters, bows politely to* DOROTHY *and sits down in an armchair left.*

MIKE (*as he and* GEORGE *and* DOROTHY *walk off*): Who's that man?

dorothy: A friend of Suzanne's. Russian I think.

GEORGE: Can I drop you anywhere?

> *They go off talking R.*
> TANIS *and* JEROME *enter from Grill Room.*

TANIS: Jerry dear, I *have* enjoyed my nice lunch.

JEROME: So have I.

TANIS: Don't trouble to wait with me—Owen will be here soon.

JEROME: I shall certainly wait.

TANIS: I'll just go and collect my rich fur coat.

JEROME: All right.

> *She goes off to cloakroom.*
> JEROME *walks over to windows left and stands looking out.*
> DOROTHY *re-enters hurriedly,* JULIUS *rises.*

dorothy (*furtively*): I can't manage this afternoon.

JULIUS: You promised.

DOROTHY: I know—but I can't—I'll call you up this evening.

JULIUS: I must see you—I told you why.

DOROTHY: Haven't you heard from them yet?

JULIUS: No—it's awful.

DOROTHY: Poor old darling—I'll see what I can do this afternoon.

JULIUS: I do hate bothering you, dear.

DOROTHY: Don't be silly—Mike may have to dine out to-night.

JULIUS: You will call me up?

DOROTHY: Yes, about six.

JULIUS: Promise?

DOROTHY: Promise—I must fly now—I said I'd left my bag.

JULIUS: You are an angel.

DOROTHY (*putting her finger to her lips*): Shhh!

> *She goes out again quickly.*
>
> TANIS *comes out of the cloakroom.* JEROME *comes down from the windows and meets her.* JULIUS *bites his lip in obvious annoyance and goes out up stage L.* JEROME *and* TANIS *sit on sofa.*

JEROME: Would you like a cigarette?

TANIS: No, thanks. I smoked far too many at lunch.

JEROME: I wish you were coming to Switzerland instead of Italy.

TANIS: So do I.

JEROME: Winter sports are divine.

TANIS: We're rather making conversation, you know.

JEROME: Yes—we are, I'm afraid.

TANIS: Why?

JEROME: I still feel a little dazzled.

TANIS: Dazzled?

JEROME: Yes—lunch was wonderfully illuminating.

TANIS: You mean I've talked too much.

JEROME: Perhaps—in a way.

TANIS: Oh, Jerry—why did you let me?

JEROME: I was fascinated.

TANIS: Life is awfully complicated, isn't it, at moments?

JEROME: Only at moments.

TANIS: No—all the time, really.

JEROME: I feel terribly guilty.

TANIS: Why should you?

JEROME: It's my fault.

TANIS: No—no it isn't.

JEROME: But I don't think I could have helped myself.

TANIS: People change so strangely as one gets to know them better. When we first met I saw you only as a sort of celebrity—nice and rather glamorous.

JEROME: And now the glamour has departed?

TANIS: Yes—that side of it.

JEROME: When did it go?

TANIS: London, I think—when you and Norma came and dined that night. I suddenly found you were a real person.

JEROME: Were you glad?

TANIS: Yes—but rather scared.

JEROME: My dear.

TANIS: Lunch has been illuminating for me, too.

JEROME: Has it really?

TANIS (*looking down*): Yes.

JEROME: I was trying terribly hard not to make love to you.

TANIS: I know.

JEROME: I'm afraid I didn't succeed very well.

TANIS (*half smiling*): I'm afraid you didn't.

JEROME: You're not angry, are you—anywhere deep down inside you? I couldn't bear that.

TANIS: No, I'm not angry.

JEROME: It would serve me right if you were.

TANIS: Why?

JEROME: I'm such an anti-romanticist—on paper.

TANIS: That doesn't count.

JEROME: If you were scared in London—I'm scared now.

TANIS (*pressing his arm lightly*): Don't be frightened, Jerry.

JEROME: We've got to behave decently—that's what's so damnable.

TANIS: Yes.

JEROME: To hell with society and all its rotten little codes.

TANIS: It isn't that either, really.

JEROME: No—I suppose it isn't.

TANIS: I'll write to you—now and again.

JEROME: Yes, please.

TANIS: Oh, don't look like that.

JEROME: Wait—I'll put up a smoke screen. (*He lights a cigarette.*)

TANIS: Good-bye, Jerry dear.

JEROME: Good-bye, Tanis dear. (*There is a pause.*) They say the new farce at the Capucines is very good.

TANIS: Yes, I heard it was.

JEROME: I went last night.

TANIS: What was it like?

JEROME: Awful!

TANIS: Yes, I heard it was. Have you seen the new Folies Bergère Revue?

JEROME: Yes, last year.

TANIS: So did I.

> OWEN *enters from the street.*

OWEN: There you are, dear.

TANIS: Yes, here I am.

OWEN: Hallo, Jerry.

JEROME: You seem to have a triumphant air—as though you'd achieved something great.

OWEN: I have—I've been to Cook's.

TANIS: Thank God, at last—He's been putting it off every day.

OWEN: We leave on Thursday.

TANIS (*without enthusiasm*): Splendid!

OWEN: What do you want to go to Switzerland for, Jerry? Nasty cold place.

JEROME: The call of the snow.

OWEN: You'd much better come to Rapallo with us.

JEROME: I hate Rapallo, Owen—it's filled with double-breasted American matrons. Good-bye Tanis—we'll meet again eventually, I suppose.

TANIS: Of course we shall.

JEROME: Thank you for having lunch with me.

TANIS: I loved it.

JEROME: Good-bye, Owen.

OWEN: Good-bye. Don't climb about too much—it's bad for the liver.

JEROME: I'll remember.

> *He looks once at* TANIS *and goes off up L. quickly.*

OWEN: What do you want to do?

TANIS: I don't care.

OWEN: It's quite nice out.

TANIS: I know—I've been out.

OWEN: Well, don't snap at me—I thought we might drive round a bit.

TANIS: I must buy some stockings.

OWEN: Oh, God!

TANIS: Why not?

OWEN: You're always buying stockings.

TANIS: That's not true.

OWEN: You bought heaps the day after we arrived.

TANIS: Well, I want to buy heaps more.

OWEN: Oh, all right—come on.

TANIS: For heaven's sake, don't be so disagreeable.

OWEN: I'm not disagreeable—I merely find it a little dull standing
at a crowded stocking counter surrounded by angry women.

TANIS: You can wait outside.

OWEN: Do you want to go to a play to-night?

TANIS: Yes, if you like.

OWEN (*as they go off*): We'll go to that thing at the Capucines.

CURTAIN

Scene II

TIME: *February. Before lunch.*

SCENE: *The Bar (same as Act I, Scene III).*

*When the curtain rises the Bar is crowded. Apart from the
characters already familiar to the audience there are several other
groups of people smoking and talking. At a table down L. are
DOROTHY and BERYL. CYNTHIA and ELISE are sitting against
the wall up R. MARION FAWCETT, SUZANNE FELLINI and
GEORGE HUDD are seated together just below ELISE and
CYNTHIA. JEROME is seated just above DOROTHY and BERYL,
reading a paper and sipping a cocktail. ALBERT HENNICK is
devoting himself assiduously to a rich old lady who is slightly deaf
but determined to be vivacious. The ensuing scene must be played
simultaneously by everybody. The dialogue being immaterial to the*

play but the general effect of noise essential. INEZ *and* CYRIL *are sitting silently in a corner.*

CYNTHIA:	I waited for twenty-five minutes.
ELISE:	How infuriating!
CYNTHIA:	And when she arrived with that dreadful Merrivale woman.
ELISE:	Why didn't you go?
CYNTHIA:	How could I—it would have been too pointed.
DOROTHY:	My dear, you needn't worry about that.
BERYL:	I haven't got your perfectly wonderful poise.
DOROTHY:	Nonsense!
BERYL:	It's true—I get embarrassed terribly easily.
DOROTHY:	I wish you'd telephoned me.
ALBERT:	It's really worth seeing.
OLD LADY:	What?
ALBERT:	I say it's really worth seeing—she's entrancing.
OLD LADY:	I didn't know it was a musical play.
ALBERT:	It isn't.
OLD LADY:	You said she was dancing——
MARION:	Never again as long as I live.
GEORGE:	It was damn funny though.
MARION:	It may have been to you—I was furious.
SUZANNE:	She always gets bad-tempered when she's drunk.
GEORGE:	I couldn't help laughing——
ELISE:	I can't understand what she sees in her.
CYNTHIA:	Neither can anyone else.
ELISE:	It's that sort of mind that prevents her being a good artiste.
CYNTHIA:	She's never real for a moment.
ELISE:	She deceives a lot of people though—Freddie Carrol was raving about her——

BERYL:	I will another time.
DOROTHY:	You see I've known him for years.
BERYL:	Yes, he said heavenly things about you.
DOROTHY:	That's damn nice of him.
BERYL:	But he did—honestly.
ALBERT:	No—entrancing—marvellous.
OLD LADY:	I love anything a little risqué.
ALBERT:	Well, it's certainly that.
OLD LADY:	What?
ALBERT:	I say it's certainly that.
OLD LADY:	What a pity—she used to be so lovely.
SUZANNE:	I must say I see Marion's point.
GEORGE:	Who was the little fair girl who sang?
MARION:	I don't know—she made me feel uncomfortable.
SUZANNE:	Marie something or other—she used to be at the Casino de Paris.
GEORGE:	Damned attractive-looking!
ALBERT:	Shall we go and have lunch now?
OLD LADY:	What?
ALBERT:	Lunch?
OLD LADY:	Oh yes—I'm dieting, you know—I shan't eat much.
ALBERT (*rising*):	I'm not particularly hungry.
OLD LADY:	We might walk through to the Restaurant.

ALBERT *pilots her out.*

SUZANNE:	Thanks for the cocktail, George—I wish you were eating with us.
GEORGE:	I shall wait ten minutes more.
MARION (*rising*):	Come on, Suzanne.
SUZANNE:	Give us a call when you get back.
GEORGE:	We'll have a party.

MARION: Lovely. Good-bye.

GEORGE: I shall probably be at the Crillon—I'm sick of this place.

SUZANNE: So am I—but it's a sort of habit one can't shake off.

SUZANNE *and* MARION *go out—leaving* GEORGE *at the table. Several other people have left by this time, so the atmosphere has become less congested and the individual dialogue easier to distinguish.* GEORGE *catches* BERYL'S *eye—she nods to him and smiles.* DOROTHY *looks over and waves.*

BERYL: He's nice, isn't he?

DOROTHY: Who—George?

BERYL: Yes.

DOROTHY: Not bad.

BERYL: He was sweet to me at that party.

DOROTHY: I think you made a hit.

BERYL: Do you—really?

DOROTHY: Not that you had much chance with Harry hanging round you all the time.

BERYL: Harry's getting on my nerves—he's so possessive.

DOROTHY: Never mind, dear.

BERYL: I should never have rowed with Marion if it hadn't been for him.

DOROTHY: I didn't know you had.

BERYL: We're not speaking now—Didn't you see her sweep out just then without looking at me?

DOROTHY: She's no loss to anyone—are you doing anything to-night—late?

BERYL: I'm supposed to be supping with Harry—why?

DOROTHY: I wondered if you'd do me a great favour.

BERYL: Of course. What is it?

DOROTHY: Come out with Julius and me—I daren't be seen with him alone when Mike's in Paris.

BERYL: I'll have to put off Harry.

DOROTHY: Does it matter?

BERYL: Not much—I'll telephone him.

DOROTHY: You're a dear.

BERYL: You've been perfectly darling to me.

DOROTHY: I like you.

> GEORGE *rises and comes over to their table.*

GEORGE: Hallo, Dorothy.

DOROTHY: Oh, hallo.

GEORGE: Good morning, Miss Fletcher—may I join you for a moment?

DOROTHY: Of course.

> *He sits down.*

GEORGE: Will you both have a cocktail with me?

BERYL: No, thank you.

DOROTHY: I've already had two—I'm waiting for Mike.

GEORGE (*to* BERYL): Are you lunching anywhere?

BERYL: Yes—I'm afraid I am.

GEORGE: I'm sorry—I thought you might have lunched with me.

BERYL: It's terribly sweet of you—I should have loved to—
but . . .

GEORGE: I'm leaving Paris on Friday.

BERYL (*disappointed*): Oh—what a shame.

DOROTHY: What time did you say you'd meet Harry?

BERYL: One o'clock.

DOROTHY (*glancing at her watch*): It's nearly half-past.

BERYL: Harry's always late.

GEORGE: Rotten bad manners.

BERYL: Yes, I suppose it is.

DOROTHY: I'm sorry you're leaving so soon, George.

GEORGE (*looking at* BERYL): So am I—damned sorry.

DOROTHY: Listen—I've got an appointment at two o'clock
anyhow. Why don't we three lunch together—it'll teach Mike
and Harry a lesson.

BERYL: Oh, Dorothy!

GEORGE: I wish you would.

DOROTHY: Come on—we'll go somewhere quiet.

BERYL: I ought to wait really.

DOROTHY: Don't be a fool, dear—do what you want to do.

BERYL: He'll be furious.

DOROTHY: So will Mike—serve them right.

GEORGE: I've got to buy a birthday present for my sister this
afternoon—you might help me to choose it.

BERYL: Can't I leave a message or anything?

DOROTHY: Tell the doorman to say you couldn't wait any
longer.

BERYL: All right—let's go quickly.

> *They go out.*
> GEORGE *squeezes* DOROTHY'S *arm gratefully.* TANIS *comes in as
> they go out. She goes over to* JEROME.

JEROME (*rising*): My dear.

TANIS: Well, Jerry?

JEROME: I wondered if you'd come.

TANIS: That was silly of you.

JEROME: You have a tremendously stern conscience at moments. I felt a bit apprehensive.

TANIS: I think my conscience must have died.

JEROME: When?

TANIS: You know when.

JEROME: You're exultant and defiant to-day—I do love you for it.

TANIS: I'm extraordinarily happy—you see, it hasn't been entirely our fault—we put up a good fight at first. There was no reason for me ever to have known you were here if Fate hadn't led us both to the opera on Monday.

JEROME: It's cowardly to blame Fate—and yet I'm inclined to agree with you.

TANIS: Dear Jerry.

JEROME: Don't use that voice to me when there are other people about—it isn't fair.

TANIS: I told Owen I was lunching with you.

JEROME: Did you?

TANIS: Yes, here.

JEROME: If he tries to find us—he'll search in vain.

TANIS: I'm afraid he will.

> *They go out.*
> MIKE *enters hurriedly—looks round and sits at table down L.* ELISE *and* CYNTHIA *rise and walk out.*

ELISE (*as they go*): What's the use of arguing?

CYNTHIA: No use at all—obviously.

ELISE: Why do it then?

CYNTHIA: You're impossible.

ELISE: I'm honest—anyhow.

CYNTHIA: I wonder!

> *They go out.*

MIKE (*calling* WAITER): Garçon!

WAITER: Monsieur?

MIKE: You know Miss Price, don't you?

WAITER: Yes, monsieur.

MIKE: Has she been here this morning?

WAITER (*thinking*): Yes, monsieur—she went out a few minutes ago.

MIKE: Was she alone.

WAITER: No, monsieur—there was a lady and gentleman.

MIKE: A dark gentleman?

WAITER: I don't remember, monsieur.

MIKE: She left no message.

WAITER: Non, monsieur.

MIKE: All right.

> *The* WAITER *departs.*
> MIKE *rises angrily and is about to go out when* HARRY *enters.*

HARRY: Hallo!

MIKE: Hallo!

HARRY: What's the matter?

MIKE: Nothing.

HARRY: Come and have a drink.

MIKE: No, thanks.

> *He goes out and leaves* HARRY *looking after him in some surprise.*
> HARRY *looks round Bar for* BERYL, *then with an exclamation of annoyance, goes out.* INEZ *and* CYRIL *rise and go towards the door back.*

INEZ: I believe that in some people a sullen silence is considered rather attractive. Cyril darling, in your case I find it a little irritating.

CYRIL (*impatiently*): Oh, I'm sorry.

INEZ: So am I—and very hurt.

CYRIL: Now look here, Inez.

INEZ: I'm beginning to realise that you've cheated with me.

> *As they reach the door,* NORMA *enters hurriedly.*

CYRIL (*his voice changing*): Norma!

NORMA (*glancing at him and then at* INEZ): Oh, hallo——(*She walks down and seats herself at a table.*)

> CYRIL *hesitates, looking at her.*

INEZ (*at door*): Cyril——

CYRIL (*hopelessly*): All right—I'm coming.

> *They go out.*
> NORMA *pulls off her gloves and summons a* WAITER.

NORMA: Garçon.

WAITER: Madame?

NORMA: Bring me a Bronx, please.

WAITER: One, madame?

NORMA (*as an afterthought*): You'd better bring two.

WAITER: Bien, madame.

> *He whips up two used glasses from her table and departs.* NORMA *lights a cigarette and waits.* OWEN *enters.*

NORMA: Beautifully timed.

OWEN: Have you only just arrived?

NORMA: A minute ago—I ordered you a Bronx.

OWEN: Splendid!

NORMA: I'm dead—I've been rushing about all the morning.

OWEN: So am I—we'll both relax completely.

NORMA: Thank God, there's no one here—I get so sick of people all over the place.

OWEN: It's a tiring spot Paris—do you mind if I have one of your cigarettes?—I've run out.

NORMA: Of course not—here.

> *She pushes her case along the table to him—he looks at her and smiles.*

CURTAIN

Scene III

TIME: *June.*

SCENE: *The scene is a corner of the terrace outside the Grill Room. There are only three tables visible—the one down R. is in the sun and is protected by a large umbrella. The one down L. is occupied by* SUZANNE FELLINI *and* DOROTHY. *The one above it is empty, as is also the one down R.*

DOROTHY: I don't know what to do.

SUZANNE: Well, I gave you advice before and you were furious
  with me.

DOROTHY: That was different.

SUZANNE: No, it wasn't.

DOROTHY: What shall I do now? I think I'm going crazy.

SUZANNE: Leave Paris.

DOROTHY: You know I can't.

SUZANNE: Why not?

DOROTHY: I should never see him again.

SUZANNE: Exactly.

DOROTHY: It's all very fine for you to sit there and say "exactly".
  You don't know how I feel.

SUZANNE: Yes, I do—but you must pull yourself together.

DOROTHY (*almost crying*): I can't—I can't.

SUZANNE: Listen, dear—you're no fool—you know perfectly
  well he's using you.

DOROTHY: I don't care—I love him.

SUZANNE: Mike's as crazy about you as ever he was—why can't
  you be satisfied with that?

DOROTHY: Mike drives me mad.

SUZANNE: Only because you give way to it—if Julius weren't
  about, you'd be all right.

DOROTHY: Oh, Suzanne—I'm so damned miserable——

SUZANNE: You wouldn't be for long if you made a real effort and
  got away.

DOROTHY: You think Julius doesn't love me a bit.

SUZANNE: That's not the point.

DOROTHY: It *is* the point—do you think that?

SUZANNE: I don't know him well enough to judge—but I do
  know that if you let Mike go on his account, you're mad.

DOROTHY: Mike need never know.

SUZANNE: He suspects now.

DOROTHY: How do you know?

SUZANNE: Of course he does—and there'll be trouble soon, bad
  trouble.

DOROTHY: I'm not afraid of him.

SUZANNE: I am.

DOROTHY: What could he do anyhow?

SUZANNE: That depends how drunk he is when he finds out.

DOROTHY: Here comes that little fool Beryl Fletcher with George.

SUZANNE: I must go—Come round to the flat at tea time.

DOROTHY: All right.

SUZANNE: And for God's sake think over what I've said.

> GEORGE *and* BERYL *come up to the table.* BERYL *is wearing pearls and some expensive bangles.*

BERYL: We had to come over and say hallo.

SUZANNE (*shaking hands with* GEORGE): How are you, George?

GEORGE: Fine! We're going down to Le Touquet this afternoon.

BERYL: George gambles terribly.

GEORGE: Pretty successfully though, just lately. How's everything, Dorothy?

DOROTHY: Rotten, thanks.

SUZANNE: Dorothy's got a hangover today.

DOROTHY (*with some malice*): I saw Harry yesterday.

BERYL (*sweetly*): Did you? How was he?

DOROTHY: He seemed very bright.

BERYL: Poor old Harry.

DOROTHY: Come on Suzanne—we must be going.

BERYL (*as they all four go out*): We're going to be in Deauville all July. George has taken the cutest little villa you've ever seen— you must come and stay—mustn't they, George?

GEORGE: Oh yes, rather.

> *They go off.*
> *During the latter part of their scene* OWEN *and* NORMA *have entered and sat at the table down R.* OWEN *is ordering lunch—with the* MAÎTRE D'HÔTEL.

OWEN: Two canteloup ...

MAÎTRE (*writing it down*): Bien, monsieur.

OWEN: What then, Norma?

NORMA: Something frightfully light and cool. I'm not a bit hungry.

OWEN: Cold soup?

NORMA: No—no soup—just one thing and a salad.

MAÎTRE: A little cold duckling.

NORMA: Yes, that'll do.

OWEN: Very well—duckling for two.

NORMA: And ordinary cœur de laitue with French dressing.

MAÎTRE: Entremets?

OWEN: We'll decide afterwards.

MAÎTRE: Very well, monsieur.

He goes away.

OWEN: I do loathe ordering things.

NORMA: So do I.

OWEN: I feel awfully gay this morning.

NORMA: Do you, Owen?

OWEN: Yes. I've been arguing for days with fat German business men and now out of a clear sky, I find myself lunching with you.

NORMA (*smiling*): How lovely for you.

OWEN: It is—really.

NORMA: You're a strange man.

OWEN: Why strange?

NORMA: I didn't like you much at first.

OWEN: Do you now?

NORMA: Of course—you were awfully sweet when we were all here in February.

OWEN: Friendships take a long time to build up—I was frightened of you.

NORMA: Frightened?

OWEN: Yes—you seemed so sure and determined—I watched that poor young Cyril Hardacre battering his head against your supreme detachment.

NORMA: That sounds frightfully attractive, I'm afraid he didn't batter much, though.

OWEN: You were rather unkind to him, weren't you?

NORMA: No.

OWEN: A little heartless?

NORMA: I don't believe in pretending things I don't feel.

OWEN: There comes a time when one has to.

A WAITER arrives with the melon.

NORMA: It does look delicious, doesn't it?

OWEN: Beautiful.

NORMA: Cyril's terribly weak anyhow—I hate weak people.

OWEN: You make me feel fearfully old at moments.

NORMA: Sorry.

OWEN: When do you leave for Biarritz?

NORMA: To-morrow—then Father and I are coming back through Spain.

OWEN: Is he working on a new book there?

NORMA: Supposed to be—but he's awfully lazy. How's Tanis?

OWEN: All right—I had a card from her two days ago in Berlin.

NORMA: Is she in London?

OWEN: Yes.

NORMA: Give her my love.

OWEN: Of course I will.

NORMA: I don't think she likes me much.

OWEN: Nonsense—why shouldn't she?

NORMA: I have a feeling about it.

OWEN: I'm sure you're wrong.

NORMA: I wish I knew you better—there are so many things I should like to say to you.

OWEN: You can say anything you want to.

NORMA: No, I can't—not yet.

OWEN: Why not?

NORMA: We've met so often casually in crowds—I feel tongue-tied when we're alone.

OWEN: You needn't a bit.

NORMA: I'm so desperately curious about you.

OWEN: Curious?

NORMA: Yes, it's cheap of me, I know—but I'm longing to know about you really—private, personal things.

OWEN: What, for instance?

NORMA: Well—are you in love with Tanis?

OWEN: Norma!

NORMA: I'm sorry—I was afraid you'd be embarrassed.

OWEN: I'm not embarrassed—only rather surprised.

NORMA: You're quite right—I deserve to be snubbed—please forgive me and let's talk about something else.

OWEN: Why did you ask that?

NORMA: Sheer cheap curiosity.

OWEN: Of course I'm in love with Tanis.

NORMA: That's all right then, isn't it?

OWEN: How do you mean?

NORMA: Here comes the duckling.

> The WAITER *serves duckling and salad and takes away remains of*
> *melon.*

OWEN: Is your salad all right?

NORMA: Grand, thanks.

OWEN: I thought you were probably going to marry Cyril.

NORMA: You were wrong.

OWEN: He's a nice boy.

NORMA: Yes—but I don't love him.

OWEN: That might come afterwards.

NORMA: I doubt it.

OWEN: Why?

NORMA: Things don't pan out as easily as that.

OWEN: He's got a nice private income, hasn't he?

NORMA: Don't be horrid.

OWEN: Are you in love with someone else?

NORMA: Yes.

OWEN: Oh, I see.

NORMA: No, you don't.

OWEN: I'm being curious now.

NORMA: I know.

OWEN: Fairly itching with it.

NORMA: Owen, we'd really better talk about something quite
different.

OWEN: It's more interesting talking about ourselves.

NORMA: You headed me off just now when I wanted to.

OWEN: No, I didn't.

NORMA: Yes, you did—you told me a smart little lie.

OWEN: You mean about Tanis?

NORMA: Yes.

OWEN: What does it matter anyway?

NORMA: A good deal.

OWEN: I'm sorry.

NORMA: Has the drifting apart been mutual?

OWEN: Yes, I think so.

NORMA: Poor Owen.

OWEN: You're behaving awfully badly, Norma.

NORMA: Yes, I suppose I am.

OWEN: Why are you?

NORMA: Don't you know?

OWEN: I half guess—but I'm not sure.

NORMA: I love you.

OWEN (*smiling at her*): My dear—how ridiculous of you.

NORMA: I expect it is—but it can't be helped.

OWEN: I don't know what to do now.

NORMA: It is rather awkward, isn't it?

OWEN: Damnably.

NORMA: I suppose the whole lunch is going to be a failure now owing to my lack of restraint.

OWEN: We'll try not to let it be.

NORMA: I had to tell you, you know—it's been going on inside me for months.

OWEN: That's an awfully nice hat.

NORMA: I'm glad you like it—I bought it yesterday morning.

OWEN (*suddenly resting his hand on hers*): Do you want anything more to eat—darling?

NORMA (*emotionally*): Owen! (*She buries her head in her arms.*)

OWEN: Don't, dear—don't be silly——

CURTAIN

ACT III: Scene I

TIME: *January 1926.*

SCENE: *The scene is the Men's Bar—Rue Gilon side. It is before dinner. On the left of the stage is a bar with two men in white coats serving drinks. The entrance is on the right. There are tables along the back wall.*

When the curtain rises, HARRY LEFTWICH *and* GEORGE HUDD *are drinking at the bar down left. At a table up right are a fair young man and a dark young man, engrossed in conversation.* JULIUS LEVENOVITCH *finishes a drink, glances at his wrist watch and goes out.* GEORGE *and* HARRY *turn to look after him.*

GEORGE: What women can see in that beats me.

HARRY: He's just one of those mournful Russians—they're always successful.

GEORGE: Shifty-looking swine.

HARRY: Is Dorothy Price still playing around with him?

GEORGE: Yes, I think so.

HARRY: He's probably getting a good bit out of her.

GEORGE: Well, good luck to him if she's such a fool.

HARRY: Have another?

GEORGE: All right.

HARRY: Two more Martinis with a dash.

GEORGE: No dash for me.

BARMAN: Very good, sir.

    BEVERLEY *and* ALBERT *enter and cross to the bar.*

ALBERT: And we'd just got half way down the street when I realised what the game was.

BEVERLEY: My God!

ALBERT: I was terrified.

BEVERLEY: What did you do?

ALBERT: I turned and ran, my dear.

BEVERLEY: You should have been more careful.

ALBERT: Well, how was I to know? It was all Eric's fault anyhow.

BEVERLEY: What do you want?

ALBERT: A Manhattan, please. I love the little cherry at the bottom.

BEVERLEY: One Manhattan, one Bronx.

BARMAN: Very good, sir.

BEVERLEY: Jimmy's got a party to-night.

ALBERT: I *know* he'll be turned out of that flat.

> CYRIL *enters and crosses to bar.*

BEVERLEY: Hallo, Cyril—want a cocktail?

CYRIL: Yes, thanks.

BEVERLEY: Manhattan?

CYRIL: Yes, that'll do.

BEVERLEY: Another Manhattan.

BARMAN: Yes, sir.

> *The other* BARMAN *serves drinks to* GEORGE *and* HARRY.

HARRY: Here you are.

GEORGE: Thanks.

HARRY: Here's how.

GEORGE: Cheerio.

ALBERT: How's Inez, Cyril?

CYRIL: I don't know—I haven't seen her for ages.

BEVERLEY: Your little friend Norma What's-her-name is in Paris.

CYRIL (*looking up sharply*): Is she?

ALBERT: Startled fawn very difficult.

BEVERLEY: Don't tease Cyril, Albert—we must all try to be broadminded.

CYRIL: Is she staying here?

BEVERLEY: How do I know?

CYRIL: You generally know everything about everybody.

BEVERLEY: Only the people I'm interested in.

> *The* BARMAN *brings them their cocktails*—BEVERLEY *pays for them.*
> GEORGE *and* HARRY *stroll out.*
>
> LUKE BELLOWS *enters with* JOSHUA DRAKE. LUKE *is a good-looking young man of about twenty-eight; his clothes are sack-like. He possesses a rugged, boyish charm enhanced by a Middle Western accent.* JOSHUA DRAKE *is small and fair and untidy.*

ALBERT: Why, Luke! This is marvellous!

LUKE: Hallo, Albert.

ALBERT: When did you arrive?

LUKE: Yesterday on the *Leviathan*.

JOSHUA: I found him wandering along the Rue Castiligone.

ALBERT: Do you know Beverley Ford—Luke Bellows.

LUKE: Glad to meet you, Mr. Ford.

> *They shake hands.*

BEVERLEY: I've heard of you, of course—hundreds of times.

LUKE: That's terribly nice of you.

ALBERT: When are you playing again?

LUKE: Not until the Fall—I'm going over to London. They want me to do *Chummy* there.

ALBERT: They'd love you. He's marvellous in *Chummy*, Beverley.

LUKE: Do you think they would like me—honestly?

ALBERT: Of course.

LUKE: I guess I'm not elegant enough for London.

JOSHUA: Don't take any notice of him—he always goes on like that—it's a stunt.

LUKE (*winsomely*): Isn't Paris wonderful?

JOSHUA: Let's all go and sit down, for God's sake.

> *They all go over to table up left and order drinks.*
> *Enter* BENNY TYRELL *and* FREDDY PALMER. BENNY *is about thirty;* FREDDY *about twenty-two. They cross straight over to the bar.*

BENNY: What d'you want?

FREDDY: Champagne cocktail.

BENNY: Two champagne cocktails.

BARMAN: Yes, sir.

BENNY (*looking across at* LUKE): Now I know why you wanted to come here.

FREDDY: Don't start a scene.

BENNY: I suppose you're going to pretend.

FREDDY: I'm not pretending anything.

LUKE (*rising*): Excuse me a moment. (*He comes over.*) Hallo, Freddy.

FREDDY: Hallo.

LUKE: How do you feel after the boat, Benny?

BENNY: Splendid, thanks—You look much better.

LUKE: Why don't you both come and lunch with me to-morrow—I'm just a boy from the West alone in Paris.

BENNY: I can't.

LUKE: What about you, Freddy?

FREDDY: All right.

BENNY: I can't wait any longer for the cocktails; I must go.

He goes.

LUKE: Sorry if I was butting in.

FREDDY: Benny's in a bad temper to-day, anyhow.

LUKE: Did you get the photographs?

FREDDY: Yes.

LUKE: Did you like them?

FREDDY: Here are the cocktails—you'd better take Benny's.

LUKE: Thanks—I wish you weren't so tied up.

FREDDY: I'm not really, but——

LUKE: You're so determined not to be friends.

FREDDY: I explained on the boat.

LUKE: Well, I can wait, Freddy old kid. (*He raises glass.*) Les Printemps.

FREDDY: Le Printemps.

LUKE: All right—I know your French is better than mine.

ALBERT (*calling*): Luke—do come and sit down.

LUKE: Come over and join us.

FREDDY: No, thanks—I must go and find Benny.

LUKE *rejoins his friends.* FREDDY *pays for the cocktails and departs.* OWEN *and* JEROME *enter and cross over to the bar.*

OWEN: You're right about this place—I'm sick to death of it.

JEROME: We're far more comfortable at the Crillon than we ever were here.

OWEN: I know—Norma told me.

JEROME: What shall we drink?

OWEN: Something innocuous.

JEROME: Martinis are safe and conventional.

OWEN: All right.

JEROME: Two Martinis.

BARMAN: Yes, sir.

JEROME: Why are you so depressed?

OWEN: Am I?

JEROME: Yes, I think so.

OWEN: I find life rather too hectic.

JEROME: You've never struck me as being a particularly hectic type.

OWEN: That's the trouble—I'm not.

JEROME: People like me who write and are supposed to have temperament always resent nerves in anyone else.

OWEN: I'm sorry, Jerry.

JEROME: Don't apologise.

OWEN: As a matter of fact, Paris doesn't seem to be stimulating you quite as much as usual this time.

JEROME: I'm beginning to hate it—I'm only waiting for something definite to happen.

OWEN: What sort of something?

JEROME: Some crisis—then I shall go away—thousands of miles—no more soft carpets and shaded lights and civilised conversation——

OWEN: The great open spaces?

JEROME: Yes, where men are men.

OWEN (*laughing*): You mustn't let this bar dishearten you.

JEROME: Oh, these don't matter—they're not even real of their kind—here's your drink. (*He pays the* BARMAN.)

BARMAN: Thank you, sir.

JEROME: I find it so difficult not to cheat when everyone else is cheating all round me.

OWEN: How do you mean?

JEROME: I expect you'll know some day.

OWEN: I'm more used to you when you're intellectually superior and sure of yourself.

JEROME: I suppose I am letting down a bit.

OWEN: Anyhow I don't know you at all, really.

JEROME: Neither do I.

OWEN: Strange bird.

JEROME: Thanks.

OWEN: Did you take that as a compliment?

JEROME: No—merely as a contribution to the conversation. I was duly grateful.

OWEN: You've always found me dull, haven't you?

JEROME: Not dull exactly—rather difficult.

OWEN: That's putting it nicely.

JEROME: All right, dull then.

OWEN: You've irritated me a good deal from time to time.

JEROME (*smiling*): I expect I have.

OWEN: I suppose I was envious of your knowledge of things and people.

JEROME: You needn't have been—that sort of knowledge only complicates one's own problems doubly.

OWEN: Cheer up!

> JULIUS *re-enters hurriedly and crosses to bar; he looks very white and rather scared.*

JULIUS: Give me a brandy and soda, please.

BARMAN: Yes, sir.

JULIUS: Double.

BARMAN: Right, sir.

JEROME: I suppose we'd better go. Tanis will be waiting.

OWEN: I doubt it—but we'll see.

> *There is a scream of laughter from* LUKE *and* JOSHUA *and* ALBERT *at something* BEVERLEY *has said.*

BEVERLEY: I always said it was worse than madness to shave off his moustache.

ALBERT: Jimmy wouldn't speak to him for days.

> *There is more laughter.* JEROME *and* OWEN *have just reached the door when* MIKE CRAVEN *bursts in, followed by* GEORGE HUDD. MIKE *is obviously drunk; he bangs into* JEROME *without apologising.*

JEROME (*glancing at him*): Don't mention it.

> *He and* OWEN *go out.*

MIKE: Where is he?

GEORGE (*endeavouring to calm him*): Don't be a fool, Mike.

> MIKE *goes up to* JULIUS *and swings him round.*

MIKE: Here, you!

GEORGE: Mike—for God's sake.

JULIUS: Take your hands off me.

MIKE: Come outside then, you swine!

JULIUS (*trying to push past him*): Leave me alone.

MIKE: I'll knock your damned head off.

GEORGE: Shut up, Mike.

JULIUS: You're drunk!

> MIKE *takes up* JULIUS' *drink and flings it in his face.* BEVERLEY, JOSHUA *and* ALBERT *and* LUKE *rise hurriedly.*

MIKE: I'll teach you to muck about with my women!

ALBERT: My God, there's a row on.

LUKE: Let's get out—I don't want to be mixed up in anything.

JULIUS (*white with rage and terror*): You'll regret that.

MIKE: Pimp! Crawling bloody pimp!

> *He takes a revolver from his pocket and shoots* JULIUS. *There is a scream from* ALBERT *and a concerted rush for the door.* JULIUS *falls down. A* BARMAN *vaults over the bar and assisted by* GEORGE *wrenches the revolver from* MIKE'S *hand. The other* BARMAN *rushes out. The dark young man and the fair young man disappear behind their table.*

MIKE (*beside himself*): I'll show him—I'll show him——

GEORGE (*kneeling beside* JULIUS): Fetch a doctor, quick!

QUICK CURTAIN

Scene II

TIME: *The same night. It is about 3 a.m.*

SCENE: *The Lounge, Rue Gilon side, same as Act II, Scene I.*

*The stage is empty—*INEZ *and* VIOLET EMERY *enter from the communicating passage up left. They are both in evening dress.* VIOLET *is extremely chic and wearing excellent jewellery.*

VIOLET: It was divine of you to drop me.

INEZ: We ought to have told the taxi to come to this entrance really.

VIOLET: I know—I never thought of it.

INEZ: It's been charming—meeting you. I've heard so much about you from Mary.

VIOLET: Not too much, I hope; so many things are spoiled by people saying too much.

INEZ: Will you lunch or dine with me sometime?

VIOLET: I should love to.

INEZ: Very well—I'll telephone you.

VIOLET: Any time before eleven thirty.

INEZ: Well, good-bye.

VIOLET: I suppose you wouldn't come up and talk to me while I go to bed—I'm wide awake.

INEZ: The taxi's waiting.

VIOLET: You could ring down from my room and have him sent away—the night porter will pay him.

INEZ: Just for a few minutes, then.

VIOLET (*ringing for the lift*): You're an awfully sympathetic person.

INEZ (*smiling*): Am I?

VIOLET: I felt it the moment you came into the room to-night.

INEZ: With all those people chattering?

VIOLET: That didn't matter.

INEZ: I'm glad.

VIOLET: And of course when you sang...

INEZ: Here's the lift.

> *They enter the lift and disappear.*
>
> SUZANNE FELLINI *enters from right. She is in travelling clothes. She glances at her watch, then sits on the sofa. A group of people pass through talking and go off up left.* DOROTHY *comes out of the lift, also in travelling clothes. She carries a small jewel case.*

DOROTHY: I saw you arrive—I've been at the window for hours.

SUZANNE: Are there any more developments?

DOROTHY: No, I haven't heard a thing—the telephone rang several times but I didn't answer it.

SUZANNE: Has the manager been up to see you?

DOROTHY: No—I don't think my name can have been mentioned yet.

SUZANNE: You can come to my flat until the train goes.

DOROTHY: You've been wonderful to me, Suzanne—I'll never forget it.

SUZANNE: Lucky for you he didn't kill him.

> *They go off hurriedly right.*

JEROME *and* TANIS *enter. They are in evening dress.*

TANIS: Good-night, my dear—you were a darling to bring me back.

JEROME (*holding her hand*): Don't be silly.

TANIS: By the way, where have we been?

JEROME: Oh, anywhere.

TANIS: Zelli's?

JEROME: It was Zelli's last time.

TANIS: Let's invent somewhere; we can always forget how to find it if anyone wants us to take them.

JEROME: La Grotte Bleu?

TANIS: Too obvious.

JEROME: Le Parapluie Vert?

TANIS: Lovely—the colour helps.

JEROME: Gypsies sang to us.

TANIS: Of course they did—Darling, I do love you.

JEROME: Shhh!

TANIS: Telephone me in the morning.

> *She goes towards the lift and meets* OWEN *and* NORMA *coming out of it.* OWEN *gives a start of embarrassment.*

Owen—I thought you were in bed?

OWEN: I felt better so I got up again—you're very late.

NORMA (*with great sang froid*): Hallo, Father.

JEROME: Where have you been?

NORMA: Talking to Owen.

JEROME: How long have you been talking to him?

NORMA (*casually*): I don't know—I went home to the Crillon after I left Ethel's party and you weren't there, so I called up Owen.

TANIS: What an odd thing to do.

JEROME: When did you come to the Crillon?

NORMA: About half an hour ago.

JEROME (*quickly*): Is this true, Owen?

NORMA: Father! What on earth's the matter?

OWEN: Of course it's true.

JEROME: How long has Norma been with you?

NORMA (*faintly flurried*): Father, don't be so absurd.

OWEN: Only a little while—she just told you.

NORMA: I told you I went back to the hotel and you weren't there, and I wasn't a bit sleepy so . . .

JEROME: That's a lie—I was there.

TANIS: Jerry!

JEROME: I've been there for the last two hours.

OWEN: Where were you then, Tanis?

TANIS: This is all perfectly ridiculous—I'm going to bed.

OWEN: Where you at the Crillon, too?

TANIS: Certainly not. I . . .

JEROME: We'd all better stop lying now—Tanis was at the Crillon with me.

OWEN: Tanis!

TANIS: Don't look like that, Owen—you don't mind really.

OWEN (*aghast*): You mean——?

JEROME (*quickly*): I am your wife's lover, Owen.

OWEN: My God!

JEROME: That remark has no longer any dramatic significance— one says it when one can't find a taxi.

OWEN: Tanis, please go up to our room.

JEROME: You're so unconscious of irony—it's pathetic.

OWEN: Shut up, you cad!

JEROME: We've been lovers for months—oblivious to everything but one another—that's why we're all here in this vile situation. When did you seduce Norma, Owen?—Was it to-night or ages ago?—Let's be frank and outspoken . . .

NORMA (*clutching his arm*): Father!

JEROME (*pushing her aside*): Keep away from me—we must all be calm and just and honest with one another. I feel terribly wise and ashamed just for a moment—it won't last—nothing lasts ever—I shall creep back to the usual refuge of codes and pretences—utter futility. It's quite natural really. We're all silly animals, gratifying our own beastly desires, covering them with a veneer of decency and good behaviour. Lies—lies— complete rottenness . . .

TANIS: For God's sake, stop talking like that!

JEROME (*laughing*): Why—it's true, isn't it?—I'm your lover— Owen is Norma's lover. Owen's your husband—Norma's my

daughter—there's real life for you—love—romance—beauty—
happy ever after . . .

OWEN: How dare you talk like that—you've no proof.

JEROME: I don't need proof—I have a splendid knack of knowing
things by instinct—it earns me my daily bread.

OWEN (*stubbornly*): It's not true—I don't love Norma.

JEROME: If you lie any more, I shall strangle you.

NORMA: Stop, Owen—don't say a word.

TANIS (*sinking into the sofa burying her face in her hands*): Horrible—
horrible—horrible——

JEROME: There's nothing to be done, you know—nothing at all.
We might of course start our lives all over again—that would
be interesting—or we might rush into convents and monas-
teries and repent in religious seclusion—hasn't anyone a
suggestion to make—I don't wish to monopolise the conversation.

NORMA (*crying*): Stop, Father—please, please, stop——

OWEN: Come away, Tanis.

JEROME: That's right—take her away—please, please, take her
away.

OWEN *and* TANIS *go towards the lift*. NORMA *stands still, sobbing.*
MR. *and* MRS. JEVON *enter from right; they are a young married
couple.*

MRS. JEVON (*recognising* JEROME): Why, Mr. Kennedy—I'd no
idea you were in Paris.

JEROME: We're leaving to-morrow.

MRS. JEVON: Well, isn't that a pity now. I should have loved to
see something of you. This is my husband—I don't think
you've met.

MR. JEVON: How do you do.

They shake hands.

MRS. JEVON: Paris is terrible—one never gets any sleep.

MR. JEVON: The lift's just going up.

MRS. JEVON: All right—good-night, Mr. Kennedy—perhaps we
shall see something of you in London?

JEROME: Delightful! Good-night.

MR. JEVON: Good-night.

JEROME: Good-night.

> *They go to the lift and disappear with* TANIS *and* OWEN.
> NORMA *has been standing by the window with her back turned; she turns.* JEROME *clasps her in his arms.*

NORMA: Father!
JEROME: Oh, Christ!

CURTAIN

Scene III

TIME: *June. It is late afternoon.*
SCENE: *The Lounge (Place du Cœur side). The same as Act I, Scene I.*

NORMA *is writing at the bureau. A* YOUNG MAN *is seated down right, reading an illustrated paper. He occasionally glances up as though expecting someone. Music can be heard from the direction of the Tea Lounge. A group of people come in through the swing doors. Finally a* YOUNG GIRL *comes in. The* YOUNG MAN *rises.*

YOUNG MAN: I thought you were never coming.
YOUNG GIRL: I couldn't get away—Mother's gone home to rest.
YOUNG MAN: It's awfully late.
YOUNG GIRL: Don't be angry.
YOUNG MAN: I'm not, but . . .
YOUNG GIRL: You are—just a little.
YOUNG MAN: Come along.
YOUNG GIRL: I ought to telephone really—I'm supposed to be having tea with Mrs. Banks.
YOUNG MAN: Not now—please not now.
YOUNG GIRL: All right.

> *They go out through the swing doors.*
> LUKE BELLOWS *and* FREDDY PALMER *enter. The* DAY PORTER *brings their bags after them.*

LUKE: Have you got any change?

FREDDY: Yes.

LUKE: Tip him then, will you?

FREDDY: All right. (*He does so.*)

LUKE: Leave them here till we find the number of our room, then we'll send a bell boy.

PORTER: Yes, sir. Thank you, sir.

LUKE: Isn't Paris marvellous—one gets a thrill every time.

FREDDY: Yes.

LUKE: Are you happy?

FREDDY: Of course.

    ALBERT HENNICK *appears from direction of Lounge.*

ALBERT (*effusively*): Luke—my dear, this is divine. I thought it was you but I wasn't sure—Hallo, Freddy.

FREDDY: Hallo.

LUKE (*obviously*): We just arrived a minute ago.

ALBERT: That's grand—Jimmy's giving a party to-night—you must both come.

FREDDY: Jimmy who?

ALBERT: Jimmy Collett—you don't mean to say you don't know Jimmy?

LUKE: We've neither of us been here since January.

ALBERT: Of course you haven't. Jimmy came in March from Rome—he was going to be a priest and now he isn't—you'll adore him.

LUKE: We're only staying a few days.

ALBERT: He's living with Bob Trevor—you know Bob, don't you?

FREDDY: Yes, I do.

LUKE: I don't . . .

ALBERT: He's a scream—like a great Newfoundland puppy, melting eyes and a divine sense of humour—Is it true you're going to play *Ghosts* in New York with Myra Pelly?

LUKE: Yes, I think so—we're going to give alternate performances.

FREDDY: I can't see Myra Pelly as a boy.

ALBERT: Never mind. I'm sure *she* can.

LUKE: Come and help us find out about our room.

ALBERT (*as they go up back*): How's Benny?

68

FREDDY (*stiffly*): I don't know; I haven't seen him for ages.

ALBERT: Poor Benny. He was always so tiresome.

> *They go out of earshot and finally disappear into the lift after pausing at the desk.*
> *A* PORTER *fetches their bags.* INEZ ZULIETA *and* VIOLET EMERY *enter from Lounge.*

INEZ: I'm going straight home.

VIOLET: Don't be so unreasonable.

INEZ: Unreasonable! (*She laughs bitterly.*) You seem to take a delight in making me utterly miserable.

VIOLET: You will imagine things.

INEZ: I don't imagine—I know.

VIOLET: You're impossible.

INEZ: Thank you.

> *They go out through the swing doors.*
> *The* HANCOX *family arrives,* MR. *and* MRS., *typical wealthy middle-class, and their daughter,* PHYLLIS.

HANCOX: Stay here while they bring in the luggage. I'll go and see about the rooms.

MRS. HANCOX: We'll sit down—Come, Phyllis.

> *She and* PHYLLIS *come down stage and sit by the table. The* PORTER *is occupied with their luggage.* BERYL FLETCHER *appears from the direction of the lifts with* DOROTHY PRICE. DOROTHY *is less chic than she used to be.* BERYL *is radiant, wearing several expensive bangles and two or three strings of pearls.*

BERYL: My God, he isn't here. (*She looks around.*)

DOROTHY: Never mind, he will be in a minute.

BERYL: He knows I hate hanging about. Just wait, that's all. I'll teach him.

DOROTHY: Don't be silly, dear.

BERYL: Well, he's always doing things like this—annoying me.

DOROTHY: For heaven's sake don't have another scene with him—I can't bear it.

BERYL: He thinks he can do what he likes just because he's so damned rich.

DOROTHY: Here he is.

> EDGAR DARRELL *enters—thin and forty.*

BERYL (*disagreeably*): At last.

EDGAR: I'm sorry. I didn't know I was late.

BERYL: No, you never do know.

EDGAR: Hallo, Dorothy.

DOROTHY: Hallo.

EDGAR (*to* BERYL): Don't be unkind, little girl.

BERYL: Dorothy's coming to Deauville with us in July.

EDGAR (*despondently*): Oh, is she?

DOROTHY: Beryl said you wouldn't mind.

EDGAR: Of course I don't.

> *They go out through the swing doors.*
> MR. HANCOX *comes down from back.*

HANCOX: Come along.

PHYLLIS (*as they rise*): Mother.

MRS. HANCOX: What, dear?

PHYLLIS: Did you see her pearls?

MRS. HANCOX: Whose pearls?

PHYLLIS: That woman's—they were huge!

MRS. HANCOX: I suppose they'll send the trunks up later.

> *They all three go off upstage to the lifts.*
> CYRIL *enters through swing doors and comes over to* NORMA.

CYRIL: Pardon me, are you Mrs. Cyril Hardacre?

NORMA (*looking up*): Certainly not. How dare you address me!

CYRIL: Darling!

NORMA: You've been out far too long anyhow.

CYRIL: I've bought you a present.

NORMA: Cyril—that was awfully naughty of you.

CYRIL (*producing package from his pocket*): Here.

NORMA: No—wait until we go to our room.

CYRIL: I can't wait long—

NORMA: Baby.

CYRIL: Who are you writing to?

NORMA: Father.

CYRIL: Give him my love.

NORMA: Sit down—I shan't be a minute.

CYRIL: Very well. (*He sits down opposite to her and lights a cigarette.*)

NORMA: Light one for me.

CYRIL: All right. (*He does so.*) Here.

NORMA: Thanks, dear.

CYRIL: What have you said?

NORMA: Nothing much—just how happy I am.

CYRIL: Oh, is that all?

NORMA: There. (*She folds up the letter and addresses an envelope.*)

CYRIL: I've got the seats for to-night.

NORMA: Front row?

CYRIL: Yes.

NORMA: Lovely.

CYRIL: Are you really so happy?

NORMA (*seriously*): Yes.

CYRIL: Sure?

NORMA: Positive.

CYRIL: Oh, God!

NORMA: What's the matter?

CYRIL: It all seems too good to be true.

NORMA: I feel that, too—I didn't know I was going to love you quite so much.

CYRIL: Neither did I.

NORMA (*rising*): It's different from anything that's ever happened to me before. I'm going to be so careful to keep it always true and real like it is now.

CYRIL: We will both—darling.

NORMA: Come along up—I'm dying to see my present.

CYRIL: Pardon me, Mrs. Hardacre. (*He kisses her suddenly.*)

NORMA (*laughing*): Cyril! I'm sure that man saw us!

    They go off.

CURTAIN

POINT VALAINE

A play in three Acts

To

WILLIAM SOMERSET MAUGHAM

this play is affectionately dedicated

Characters

Point Valaine was first presented in the USA at the Colonial
Theatre, Boston, on 25 December 1934, with the following cast:

MRS. TILLETT	Grayce Hampton
MAJOR TILLETT	Fred Leslie
MRS. BIRLING	Lillian Tonge
ELISE BIRLING	Phyllis Connard
MORTIMER QUINN	Osgood Perkins
STEFAN	Alfred Lunt
LOLA	Ruth Boyd
MAY	Alberta Perkins
GEORGE FOX	Brod Crawford
TED BURCHELL	Philip Tonge
LINDA VALAINE	Lynn Fontanne
MRS. HALL-FENTON	Gladys Henson
GLADYS ⎫	Phyllis Harding
PHYLLIS ⎬ *her daughters*	Margaret Curtis
SYLVIA ⎭	Valerie Cossart
HILDA JAMES	Everley Gregg
MARTIN WELFORD	Louis Hayward

Produced by THE AUTHOR
Designed by G. E. CALTHROP

Point Valaine was first presented in the UK by the Old Vic Company at the Playhouse, Liverpool, on 18 October 1944. It was first presented in London by Envoy Productions at the Embassy Theatre, Swiss Cottage, on 2 September 1947. The cast was as follows:

MRS. TILLETT	Marjorie Hellier
MAJOR TILLETT	Charles Cameron
MRS. BIRLING	Doris Rogers
ELISE BIRLING	Audrey Fildes
MORTIMER QUINN	Anthony Ireland
STEFAN	Ben-Astar
LOLA	Pauline Henriques
MAY	Louise Toummavoh
GEORGE FOX	Basil Appleby
TED BURCHELL	Neville Mapp
LINDA VALAINE	Mary Ellis
MRS. HALL-FENTON	Isobel Ohmead
GLADYS ⎫	Pat Smythe
PHYLLIS ⎬ *her daughters*	Prudence Hyman
SYLVIA ⎭	Alexis Milne
HILDA JAMES	Ambrosine Phillpotts
MARTIN WELFORD	Allan Cuthbertson

Produced by PETER GLENVILLE
Designed by TANYA MOISEIWITSCH

ACT I

Scene I. *The verandah of the Point Valaine Hotel. Morning.*

Scene II. *Linda's sitting-room. Afternoon.*
Scene III. *The verandah. Late afternoon.*

ACT II

Scene I. *Linda's sitting-room. Afternoon. Four days later.*
Scene II. *The verandah. Evening. The next day. During this scene the*
curtain is lowered to denote lapse of a few hours.

ACT III

Scene I. *Linda's sitting-room. Night.*
Scene II. *The verandah. The next morning.*

TIME: The Present.

ACT I: Scene I

Point Valaine is a small island situated a mile or so south of one of the larger British West Indies. In the evening and the morning, when the light is clear, the coast of Venezuela can be seen, dim and mysterious, like a bank of clouds on the horizon.

The verandah of the Point Valaine Hotel is spacious and shabbily comfortable. There are several long chairs covered with faded chintz lined up against the balustrade in order that the guests of the hotel can sit back in comfort and admire the exceedingly beautiful view, with their feet up. A corrugated tin roof covers the verandah, and around the poles that support it circular tables have been built. One of these is used as a dumb waiter at meal times. Another has a portable gramophone on it, a lot of records, and a pile of old illustrated weeklies. There are two doors on the right-hand side of the stage, the lower one leading to the bedrooms and the rest of the hotel, and the upper one leading to the bar and the kitchen. On the left-hand side, down stage, is a door leading to LINDA VALAINE'S *private apartments. In the middle of the balustrade at the back there are steps leading down to the landing stage and the swimming pool.*

Profuse tropical foliage can be seen over the edge of the verandah at the back, and beyond it, on the right, the open sea. On the left, a mile away, is the main island, to and from which the hotel launch journeys twice daily. All round the verandah there are rather battered green shutters which are let down when it rains, imparting to everything an atmosphere of strange gloom, almost as though one were at the bottom of the sea. During the rainy season this faintly obvious simile is used several times a day by the majority of the guests.

When the curtain rises it is about 8.30 a.m. MAJOR *and* MRS. TILLETT, MRS. BIRLING, ELISE BIRLING, *and* MORTIMER QUINN *are finishing breakfast. The tables are set along the left side of the stage, close to the balustrade.* STEFAN, LOLA *and* MAY *are waiting on them. It is a steamy, oppressive morning in June. There*

*is no sun as yet, owing to the rainy season being in full swing, but
there is always the hope that in a little while it may burst through
the clouds for an hour or so.* MAJOR *and* MRS. TILLETT *are a
conventional elderly couple.* MRS. BIRLING *is vague with rather a
whining voice.* ELISE, *her daughter, is an anaemic girl in the
twenties.* MORTIMER QUINN *is an eminent writer of about forty-
five. There is a certain dry aloofness in his manner, but in spite of
his enviable detachment he is quite amiable and polite.* LOLA *and*
MAY *are coloured girls, products of the island.* STEFAN *is a
Russian. He might be any age between thirty and fifty. He speaks
briefly and seldom, with a strange Russian-American accent. He is
quiet and unobtrusive, even slightly servile at moments, but in his
movements there is always a suggestion of controlled force, again
detachment, but different from* MORTIMER QUINN'S *in that it is
animal rather than intellectual.*

MRS. TILLETT: Don't have any more coffee, Bertie, we don't
want to waste time, and it will only make you livery.

MAJOR TILLETT: There's only a drain left in the pot.

MRS. TILLETT: I mean don't order any more, you haven't packed
your suitcase yet.

MAJOR TILLETT: I mustn't leave without giving you back your
ointment, Miss Birling.

ELISE: Oh, you can keep it if you like, you might need it on the
voyage. I've got another tube, anyhow.

MRS. BIRLING: It's really wonderful stuff, isn't it?

MAJOR TILLETT: Extraordinary—absolutely extra-ordinary, the
little beggars won't come near it.

ELISE: I only got it as a sample to begin with. Mr. Harrison told
me about it, and so off I went to the chemist's—you know
that one just near the Royal—and they gave me a little tiny
tube no bigger than that——(*She measures in the air a minute tube
of mosquito ointment.*)

MRS. TILLETT: No smell, that's what I like about it—no smell at
all.

MRS. BIRLING: It will seem funny to be home again, won't it? I
mean, where you don't have to worry about insects or
anything.

MAJOR TILLETT: Oh, I don't know about that. We get pretty bad gnats in Horsham.

MRS. BIRLING: Yes, but gnats are different, I mean they're not dangerous.

MRS. TILLETT: A friend of ours once got blood-poisoning from a gnat, she couldn't put her leg to the ground for three weeks.

> GEORGE FOX *and* TED BURCHELL *come running up the verandah steps. They are wearing bathing trunks, and bath towels over their shoulders. They are both sugar planters, but* GEORGE *is American and* TED *is English.*

TED: Good morning, everybody.

GEORGE: Good morning.

> *Everybody replies with polite "good mornings".*

MRS. BIRLING: How is the water?

TED: A bit soupy.

GEORGE: I think Mrs. Valaine ought to have the net tightened, there was a whale of a jellyfish by the steps.

MRS. TILLETT: A whale of a jellyfish, doesn't that sound funny? (*She laughs immoderately.*)

TED: They slip in over the top at high tide.

ELISE: I hope it will have gone by eleven o'clock.

TED: It's gone now, I scooped it out with the canoe paddle.

MRS. TILLETT: I must go and finish packing—hurry up, Bertie.

MAJOR TILLETT: I'm ready.

MRS. TILLETT: The launch will be here in a minute.

GEORGE (*to* MORTIMER): Are you working this morning or do you want to come fishing with Ted and me?

MORTIMER: How far are you going?

GEORGE: Just off Mother Amos, the wind's wrong for going right round.

MORTIMER: I shall leave it to the weather. If it rains, I stay; if it doesn't rain, I go.

GEORGE: Good—come on, Ted.

TED: All right.

> *They go off upstairs to dress.*

MRS. TILLETT (*to the* BIRLINGS): Will you still be here when we come down?

MRS. BIRLING: Oh yes—I'm not going to let Elise bathe until eleven.

ELISE: I'm not sure I want to bathe anyhow.

MRS. BIRLING: We'll be on the landing stage to wave you good-bye.

MAJOR TILLETT: Splendid—splendid.

MRS. TILLETT: Come along, Bertie—hurry up.

MAJOR TILLETT: All right, all right——

> *They go off upstairs to finish their packing.*
> *The* BIRLINGS *get up from their table and move over to the balustrade right.* MRS. BIRLING *sits in a chair, and* ELISE *perches on the edge. She picks up the binoculars which are always lying about and gazes out to sea.* STEFAN, LOLA *and* MAY *clear away the vacant tables and fold them up.*

MORTIMER: Bring me some fresh coffee, will you, Stefan?

STEFAN: Yes, sir.

> *He goes right off.*

ELISE: There's a ship coming in.

MRS. BIRLING: A big one?

ELISE: One of the French Line, I think.

MRS. BIRLING (*taking the glass from her*): Let me see.

ELISE: I expect it's the *Colombie*—she's due to-day.

MRS. BIRLING (*putting down the glass*): Don't forget to take your iron jelloids.

ELISE: I took them just now, at breakfast.

> STEFAN *comes back with a pot of fresh coffee for* MORTIMER.

MORTIMER: Are you going over to the mainland to-day, Stefan?

STEFAN: I go to-morrow.

MORTIMER: Can you remember to get me some typewriter rubber?

STEFAN: Eraser?

MORTIMER: Yes, if you prefer it.

STEFAN: I will bring it.

MORTIMER: Thank you.

ELISE: Here it comes—here comes the rain——

> *There is a spatter of rain on the roof which rapidly swells into a downpour.* STEFAN, LOLA *and* MAY *let down the blinds all round the verandah.* STEFAN *goes off,* MAY *and* LOLA *tidy up a few things*

rather aimlessly, obviously waiting for MORTIMER *to finish his coffee
so that they can get the table out of the way.*

MRS. BIRLING: How tiresome.

ELISE: It won't last long.

MORTIMER (*with a glint in his eye*): It feels exactly as though one
were at the bottom of the sea, doesn't it?

MRS. BIRLING: That's what I always say.

MORTIMER: It's all right, Lola, you can snatch away the table
now if you want to—I'll finish my coffee in a chair.

LOLA (*giggling*): Yes, sir.

> MORTIMER *settles himself in a chair and takes a cigarette.* STEFAN
> *appears suddenly with a match and lights it for him and disappears
> again.* GEORGE *and* TED *re-enter dressed in old flannel trousers and
> sweaters.*

TED: This is cheerful, isn't it?

ELISE: It won't last long.

GEORGE (*calling*): Stefan—Stefan——

TED (*looking out to sea round one of the blinds*): The fish are jumping,
anyway.

> STEFAN *enters.*

GEORGE: Did you put any gas in the boat?

STEFAN: Two tins of gas.

GEORGE: Fine.

TED (*to* MORTIMER): Coming?

MORTIMER: God has sent rain so that I shall not be tempted to
go fishing and leave my work. God is very domineering.

ELISE (*laughing*): Oh, you are awful, Mr. Quinn! Isn't Mr. Quinn
awful, Mother?

MRS. BIRLING: It must be lovely to be a writer—I mean to be
able to work whenever you feel like it.

MORTIMER: It is lovely. Awful and lovely.

GEORGE: Oh, come on, we can be back in time for lunch.

MORTIMER: No, I shall go and sit on my balcony, very sadly,
with the blinds down, and meditate.

TED: You can meditate, in the boat.

MORTIMER: I've tried that, it's no good.

ELISE: The rain will stop soon—it never lasts long.

MORTIMER (*in a sinister whisper to* GEORGE): Has it ever struck you,

George, that when it is raining and the blinds are down it feels just as though one were at the bottom of the sea?

GEORGE (*cheerfully*): Not at all. It feels as though one were on the top of a mountain.

MORTIMER (*still whispering*): That's what I always say. (*He goes off upstairs.*)

The noise of a motor launch is heard, then two blasts of a Klaxon horn.

ELISE: There's the launch.

TED (*to* GEORGE): Shall we wait and say good-bye to the Tilletts, or slip away now?

GEORGE: Let's go now.

They are about to go when LINDA VALAINE *enters from the left. She is a handsome red-haired woman somewhere between thirty-five and forty-five. She wears heelless sand shoes, bare legs, a cheap faded cotton dress which is almost an overall, a short, vividly coloured Chinese jacket, and horn-rimmed glasses.*

LINDA (*brusquely*): Good morning.

TED: Good morning, Mrs. Valaine.

The BIRLINGS *and* GEORGE *also murmur "good mornings".*

LINDA (*to* GEORGE *and* TED): Are you taking the *Maria*?

GEORGE: Yes.

LINDA: Don't go round Mother Amos—it's not safe to-day: the wind's too strong.

TED: We won't go further than the point.

GEORGE: If the motor doesn't conk out before then.

ELISE: Mr. Fox says there was a jellyfish in the pool this morning.

LINDA: Tell Stefan to take it out.

GEORGE: I took it out myself.

LINDA: Good.

MRS. BIRLING: Don't you think the net ought to be tightened? I mean if a jellyfish could get in, a barracuda could get in, or even a shark—I mean—it's a little dangerous, isn't it?

LINDA: The net is examined carefully every few days. A moray might conceivably squeeze in through the wire—there's no preventing that; but there's no fear of either sharks or barracudas.

MRS. BIRLING: Jellyfish are bad enough: they can be very poisonous.

LINDA (*absently*): They are.

MRS. BIRLING: Well—I mean—I do think——

LINDA (*patiently*): The tides are always abnormally high at this time of the year, Mrs. Birling, and if jellyfish float in over the net, the best thing is not to bathe until they've floated out again.

GEORGE (*laughing*): That sounds reasonable.

LINDA (*calling*): Lola—May——

TED: We'll be getting along.

> LOLA *enters.*

LINDA (*at table*): Fetch the book, Lola, and refill this inkpot.

> *The* TILLETS *come bustling down the stairs followed by* MAY *and* STEFAN *with their luggage.*

MRS. TILLETT: Ah, there you are, Mrs. Valaine. We've enjoyed our time here so much.

MAJOR TILLETT: Best holiday I've ever had, far and away the best.

LINDA: I'm so glad. You'd better take down the luggage, Stefan.

MRS. TILLETT: Good-bye, Mr. Fox. Good-bye, Mr. Burchell.

GEORGE: Good-bye.

TED: Have a nice journey.

> *There are general good-byes, and handshakings all round.*

LINDA: Don't forget to write in the book.

MAJOR TILLETT: Of course—of course——

> MAY *comes running in with the visitors' book and an inkpot.*

LINDA: It's stopped raining. Pull up the blinds, May.

MAY: Yes, ma'am.

> MAY *goes round pulling up the blinds. The* TILLETTS *write in the visitors' book.* GEORGE *and* TED *go off down the steps.*

TED (*as they go*): Give my love to England—good-bye——

ELISE: Come on, Mother, let's go down to the landing stage.

MRS. BIRLING (*to* MAJOR TILLETT): What time does your boat sail?

MAJOR TILLETT: Four o'clock.

ELISE: It ought to pass here about half-past five—don't forget to wave.

> MRS. BIRLING *and* ELISE *go off down the steps.*

MRS. TILLETT: Well, good-bye, Mrs. Valaine.

LINDA (*shaking hands*): Good-bye.

MAJOR TILLETT: If ever we come out to the Islands again, we shall come straight here.

LINDA: I shall expect you.

MRS. TILLETT: And if those snapshots turn out well you will send them on to us, won't you?

LINDA: Of course. You left your permanent address?

MRS. TILLETT: It's in the book.

MAJOR TILLETT: Well, good-bye again. (*He shakes hands.*)

MRS. TILLETT: Come along, Bertie.

> *They go off down the steps.*
>
> LINDA *stands looking after them.* STEFAN *comes up the steps and on to the verandah. He passes* LINDA *and is about to go off.*

LINDA (*without turning*): Stefan.

STEFAN: Yes, ma'am.

LINDA: Get Farrell's boy up to go over the shark net thoroughly.

STEFAN: Last week only he did it.

LINDA: Tell him to do it again.

STEFAN: Yes, ma'am.

LINDA (*coming down to the table*): Mrs. Hall-Fenton and her daughters are arriving this evening, also Miss James and a Mr. Welford. Miss James had better have her usual room, the Hall-Fentons, the suite, and you can put Mr. Welford in number seven.

STEFAN: There is a hole in number seven mosquito net.

LINDA: Tell Lola to darn it before to-night; if Lola's too busy, old Mamma Dangan can do it.

STEFAN: Yes, ma'am.

LINDA: And when you next go into town, for God's sake, get some new magazines—these are weeks old.

> *She goes off left.*

STEFAN (*looking after her*): Yes, ma'am.

> *There is again the sound of a Klaxon from the launch, and a faint*

chorus of good-byes and bon voyages from the landing stage. STEFAN
goes off to the kitchen, and the lights fade.

Scene II

The scene is LINDA VALAINE'S *private sitting-room. On the right
there is a doorway hung with a bead curtain. This leads into a
small passage which in turn leads to the left-stage door of the
preceding scene.*

*On the left there is another door with two shallow steps leading
up to it. This opens into* LINDA'S *bedroom. At the back there is a
wide verandah which looks out on to a few rocks in the foreground
and beyond them the open sea. Old-fashioned wooden shutters fold
right across the window opening at night time. The room itself is
not particularly tidy. There are a few chintz-covered cane chairs, a
chaise-longue, a writing desk, and a few pictures and photographs
on the walls. There is a low table by the chaise-longue, and a very
battered basket chair and foot rest on the verandah.*

When the curtain rises it is the afternoon of the same day.
LINDA *is sitting at the desk, writing. She is dressed in the same
clothes as in Scene I.*

There is the sound of an accordion being played in the distance.
LOLA *enters from the right.*

LOLA: Please, ma'am.

LINDA: What is it?

LOLA: Mr. Quinn, ma'am. He wants to see you.

LINDA: Tell him to come in.

LOLA: Yes, ma'am.

> *She goes out.*
> LINDA *shuffles some bills into a pile and puts a paper-weight on
> them, then she takes off her glasses and gets up as* MORTIMER
> QUINN *comes into the room.*

QUINN: Am I disturbing you?

LINDA: Not at all.

QUINN: I want some more information.

LINDA (*smiling*): Very well. Do sit down.

QUINN: Thank you. (*He sits.*)

LINDA (*at table*): Cigarette?

QUINN: Yes, please.

She hands him one and takes one herself. He lights them both.

LINDA: Have you been working all the morning?

QUINN: Yes, but rather aimlessly—it kept on raining and stopping and raining again—very distracting.

LINDA (*sitting on chaise-longue*): This is a distracting time of year.

QUINN: You always appear to be very tranquil.

LINDA: I am. It's monotonous.

QUINN: Why is this time of year so distracting?

LINDA (*vaguely*): Oh, I don't know—the rain, I suppose, and the sudden storms.

QUINN: Everything over-emphasised.

LINDA: Yes.

QUINN: It's a strange life, really.

LINDA: Mine?

QUINN: Yes.

LINDA: What is there strange about it?

QUINN: I don't know actually, but I sort of feel it.

LINDA: You're wrong. My life is perfectly ordinary, a routine—year in, year out—the same routine.

QUINN: Perhaps it's the setting that makes it seem strange.

LINDA: Was the information you wanted about me?

QUINN: Have I been impertinent?

LINDA: No.

QUINN: If I have, will you forgive me?

LINDA: Yes.

QUINN: That's all right, then.

LINDA: Yes, that's all right.

QUINN: When did white people first come to this island?

LINDA: Fourteen ninety-two—I told you that the other day.

QUINN: When did your parents come here?

LINDA: I told you that too.

QUINN: I know—I merely wanted to check up, to be absolutely accurate.

LINDA: Am I in the story you are writing?

QUINN: You may be.

LINDA: You don't know me.

QUINN: An imaginary figure based on fact, what could be better than that?

LINDA: Shall I tell you folk tales about the islanders? I know lots of them.

QUINN: No, thank you.

LINDA: There's Mother Amos and the pirate ship and Captain Laralde's escape from Fever Island, and there's the cave legend——

QUINN: I've read all those in that beastly little book.

LINDA: You're very hard to please.

QUINN: I have no feeling for the past: legends bore me.

LINDA: I wish he'd learn another tune.

QUINN: Stefan?

LINDA: Yes.

QUINN: I like this one.

They both listen for a moment to the distant accordion.

LINDA: Well?

QUINN: Well what?

LINDA: What do you want me to tell you? In what way can I help with this book of yours?

QUINN: I'll tell you a secret.

LINDA: What is it?

QUINN: I'm not writing a book at all.

LINDA: Oh!

QUINN: But don't be disappointed. I shall, eventually. At the moment, however, I'm just sitting and thinking and absorbing and finding out things.

LINDA: I see.

QUINN: One of the greatest advantages of being a writer is the excuse it provides——

LINDA: For not writing?

QUINN (*smiling*): For being alone when you want to.

LINDA: I am alone too much to be able to appreciate that.

QUINN: Yes, you are, aren't you?

LINDA: I heard your typewriter clicking all the morning.

QUINN: Letters, jolly chatty letters to my friends.

LINDA: You needn't be frightened. I don't mind you writing anything you like about me.

QUINN: You're rather unfriendly to-day.

LINDA: I'm sorry. I don't mean to be.

QUINN: What's the matter?

LINDA: Nothing's the matter.

QUINN: New arrivals this evening?

LINDA: Yes. (*With a gleam of malice.*) One of them is coming especially to see you.

QUINN: Who?

LINDA: Hilda James, she wants to interview you for the *Comet*.

QUINN: I don't mind, she can if she wants to.

LINDA: She's a very go-ahead girl, I'm sure you'll like her.

QUINN: Your unfriendliness seems to be changing rapidly to hatred.

LINDA (*softening*): I really did try to put her off, but it was no good.

QUINN: Who else is coming?

LINDA: Mrs. Hall-Fenton and her brood, and a strange man I've never heard of. Someone must have told him about the place: he's coming in to-day from Venezuela on the *Colombie*.

QUINN: New blood for the Birlings. New opportunities for cascades of small talk.

LINDA: Don't you like the Birlings?

QUINN: I worship them.

LINDA: I'm sorry for Elise—her fiancé sailed away and left her in the lurch: that's very seriously mortifying in a small island.

QUINN: All the same, I see his point.

LINDA: That's cruel.

QUINN: I'm all for him. Good luck to him! He was very nearly caught, but he escaped in the nick of time.

LINDA: Woman hater?

QUINN: With reservations.

LINDA: What is it you hate about women?

QUINN: I think I despise most their lack of emotional balance.

LINDA: I see.

QUINN: Do you agree?

LINDA: No.

QUINN: I also dislike their fundamental dishonesty.

LINDA: Poor things.

QUINN: You don't agree with that either?

LINDA: No.

QUINN: Think for a moment of that poor young man who so nearly, so very nearly, married Elise Birling. Could he have loved her, do you suppose? Even for some brief moment in tropical moonlight could he have held her in his arms and found her desirable enough, warm enough, to live his life with, to work for, even to sleep with? Could he have suspected intelligence or integrity in that rattling anæmic little mind? Was the moon so strong? Was the night so enchanted?

LINDA: Perhaps she loved him.

QUINN: Do you believe she did? Come now, honestly, do you believe she could?

LINDA (*turning away*): No.

QUINN: She wanted to be married, she wanted to be clothed and fed and kept.

LINDA: That's quite natural.

QUINN: But hardly honest, to try to turn his young enchantment of her to such cheap account.

LINDA (*rising and speaking with sudden anger*): Nonsense.

QUINN (*startled*): I beg your pardon.

LINDA: I'm a business woman, Mr. Quinn.

QUINN (*smiling*): And I am sure a very excellent one.

LINDA: I'm sorry for Elise, not because she lost a romantic moonlight lover, but because she lost a house of her own and a maid of her own and a position of her own.

QUINN (*quizzically*): Her own?

LINDA: Yes, her own by rights of paying for them. I married a man of small means; it's not all jam by a long way. But it was worth it, every minute of it, just to get away from Mother and home and family.

QUINN: And did you love your man of small means?

LINDA: No.

QUINN: I see.

LINDA (*vehemently*): No, you don't. You see something, perhaps, because you are a writer, and it's your job to make little dramas out of people.

QUINN (*meekly*): I sometimes make little comedies.

LINDA (*ignoring his interruption*): But what you see needn't be the truth. It needn't be anywhere near the truth.

QUINN: It needn't be, but it occasionally is.

LINDA: You see me as being hard and efficient, don't you?

QUINN: At the moment, yes.

LINDA: Well, you're wrong.

QUINN: At least I knew you were going to say that.

LINDA: I expect you despise me for marrying a man I was not in love with.

QUINN: Yes. For you I think it was the wrong policy.

LINDA: It was nothing of the sort.

QUINN: I'm delighted that it all turned out so well.

LINDA: He died.

QUINN: Good.

LINDA: He died in the war.

QUINN: Better and better.

LINDA: Not at all. It would have been nicer for him to die peacefully at home, in Martinique, where he had lived all his life.

QUINN: One can't have everything.

LINDA: Are you ever sorry for people, or are you too clever?

QUINN: I'm certainly too clever to be deceived by your painstaking detachment.

LINDA: You'd like to make me angry, wouldn't you? So that I might say more than I meant to say? It would be good for the book.

QUINN: To hell with the book!

LINDA: I quite agree.

QUINN: Would you like me to go away?

LINDA: Certainly not. You're occupying my best suite. I should like you to stay for years.

QUINN: I feel deeply touched.

LINDA: That was rude, wasn't it? I apologise.

QUINN: Please don't. I asked for it.

LINDA: There are other reasons why I should like you to stay.

QUINN: What are they?

LINDA: You're funny.

QUINN: Funny!

LINDA: Yes, you make people laugh. The other guests, I mean.

QUINN: Good God!

LINDA: You're no trouble. You never make stupid complaints.

QUINN: There was a bat in my room last night.

LINDA: You're nice to talk to in spite of——

QUINN: In spite of being too damned inquisitive.

LINDA: Exactly.

QUINN (*rising*): After that, even if I did go away, I couldn't fail to come back.

LINDA: Don't go for a minute—I'm frightened.

QUINN (*gently*): What are you frightened of?

LINDA: I don't quite know. I really don't quite know. (*There is a spatter of rain on the roof.*) Help me with the blinds, will you?

QUINN: Of course.

They both go out on to the verandah and let down the blinds.

LINDA: That one sticks a bit.

QUINN: I can manage it—there.

LINDA (*violently*): I hate this bloody rain!

QUINN: Very fraying to the nerves.

LINDA: Does it shock you when I swear? I oughtn't to really. It isn't respectable.

QUINN: Respectability is bloody important.

LINDA (*almost breathlessly*): I sit here sometimes and swear all by myself. At the mosquitoes, at those silly screeching little birds. I think of words, all the horrible words I've ever heard, and I say them over and over. I curse the heat, and the thickness of the air, and those dull boring people chattering on the verandah. I'm a missionary's daughter, you see, and missionarys' children take easily to the bad. I was brought up in this very house when it was a mission. There were no motor launches then, and I used to have to row and row backwards and forwards between here and the mainland until my back ached and my muscles cracked, boatloads of snivelling little half-caste children singing hymns, interminable whining hymns to the Lord. I know them all now; every note of them, every word; they're branded on my memory. Mother used to play the harmonium in the evenings while Father roared and bellowed to God till the sweat ran down his kind foolish face. I was brought up to believe that God made this sea and this earth and this sky, so now I swear at God too! God damn him!

QUINN: What do you want? What do you really need?

LINDA: I don't know—that's just it—I don't know.

QUINN: You might marry again.

LINDA: No, I couldn't—I couldn't do that. (*She looks suddenly frightened.*)

QUINN: Why not?

LINDA: I'm too used to being alone. Too happy with my independence.

QUINN: Happy?

LINDA: Contented, then; on the whole, very contented; this is just a mood, that's all—it doesn't go very deep—I get them sometimes when the heat is oppressive, moods like this, but they don't last long.

QUINN: Why did you come back here, once you had escaped and been married?

LINDA: There was nowhere else to go. Mother was all alone, Father had been dead for some years. I was working in Lyons as a stenographer when my husband was killed. I had managed to save a little——

QUINN: A missionary's daughter alone in Lyons.

LINDA: It's a very big town, rich and noisy.

QUINN: I know it well.

LINDA: When I got back here I sent Mother home, back to England—she died eight years ago—and I started this place as a hotel, gradually at first, only just a few guests, planters generally, and a few people from the main island who needed somewhere quiet to convalesce after fever. I cooked most of the meals myself. Then it began to pay—more and more people came for week-ends, and I could afford to make improvements. I made the bathing pool and built extra rooms—all that wing out at the back is new. I engaged extra servants——

QUINN: When did Stefan arrive?

LINDA: Stefan? About six, no, seven years ago.

QUINN: He's very efficient.

LINDA: Very.

QUINN: A long time, seven years.

LINDA: He started as outside boy, just odd jobs; then he helped in the kitchen; and then he became a waiter.

QUINN: And now he runs practically everything.

LINDA (*sharply*): Under my supervision.

QUINN: I intended no slur upon your own efficiency.

LINDA: I think the rain's stopping.

QUINN: Not quite yet. (*He peeps through the blind.*) It's still pretty thick; there'll be another burst before it's through.

LINDA: I hope it will clear before six—I hate people arriving in the rain.

QUINN: He has very strange eyes.

LINDA: Who?

QUINN: Stefan.

LINDA (*lightly*): He's very strange altogether. Russians frequently are. I don't care for him much, but he does his work well.

QUINN (*meditatively*): Honest and industrious.

LINDA: His story would be very useful to you. You must get him to tell it.

QUINN: I have.

LINDA: I congratulate you. He seldom speaks much.

QUINN: I have my own secret way of making people speak.

LINDA (*smiling*): I've noticed that.

QUINN: As a matter of fact, his tale is too melodramatic for me, too obvious. Stowaway voyages in oil tankers—New York docks—South American nitrate mines—revolutions—escapings from prison. Magazine stuff. I prefer more subtle drama, strange little twists in psychology—small unaccountable happenings in people's minds.

LINDA: I hope your afternoon has been profitable.

QUINN: I can see that you are going to be defensive again, so I shall go.

LINDA (*smiling*): Come again—the island legends are very interesting.

QUINN: Thank you. I will.

LINDA: Be nice to Hilda James, won't you? She's very eager.

QUINN: I'll do my best.

LINDA: I'm afraid you won't find any strange little twists in her mind.

QUINN: My first step will be to discover whether or not she has a mind at all.

LINDA: Good luck.

> MORTIMER QUINN *goes out.*
>
> LINDA *wanders over to the desk, sits down at it, and then gets up again irritably. The pattering of the rain swells into a downpour. She stands quite still in the middle of the room with her back to the window. She is trembling a little, and listening intently.*
>
> STEFAN *pushes one of the blinds aside and climbs silently on to the verandah. His white coat and trousers are soaking wet, and his feet are bare.* LINDA *hears him but she doesn't turn. He comes down into the room and stands in front of her, staring at her. She makes no movement. He slips his hand over her body and presses her into his arms with his mouth on hers.*
>
> *The lights fade.*

Scene III

> *The scene is the verandah again. It is about six o'clock on the same day as of the preceding scenes. It is no longer raining, and everything is bathed in strong evening sunlight.*
>
> *When the curtain rises the stage is empty except for* STEFAN, *who is standing with his back to the audience, scanning the sea through the binoculars.* GEORGE *and* TED *come in from the right.*

TED: Two rum punches, Stefan.

STEFAN (*putting down the binoculars*): Yes, sir.

GEORGE: Got any potato chips?

STEFAN: Yes, sir.

GEORGE: Good.

> STEFAN *goes off.*

TED: Funny about the Russians, isn't it?

GEORGE: Damn funny.

TED: That fellow gives me the creeps.

GEORGE: That's because you're over-sensitive, my lad. Just a bundle of nerves, that's all.

TED: Oh, shut up!

GEORGE: Look at the way you got the jitters when you saw that shark.

TED: It was a hammerhead.

GEORGE: The woods are full of them.

TED: I wouldn't swim in the open sea round about here whatever you paid me.

GEORGE: You'd probably be all right in the day-time.

TED: Do you think that yarn's true about the man swimming from here to he main island?

GEORGE: Yes. He never saw so much as a porpoise.

TED: Damn fool.

GEORGE: Mrs. Valaine was good and mad, I believe.

TED: Bad advert for the hotel if he'd got bitten in half.

GEORGE: You bet.

　　MORTIMER QUINN *comes up the steps.*

QUINN: Hallo!

GEORGE: Want a rum punch?

QUINN: Yes, badly.

　　STEFAN *enters with two rum punches.*

GEORGE: Bring another one for Mr. Quinn, Stefan.

STEFAN: Yes, sir.

　　He goes off again.

GEORGE: Here, you have this one.

QUINN: No no, I can wait.

GEORGE: Go on—take it—I'll share Ted's until the other one comes.

QUINN: Thanks.

TED: How was the work?

QUINN: It wasn't.

GEORGE: Rain put you off your stride.

QUINN: Yes, it gave me ideas.

TED: I should have thought that would have been a help.

QUINN: They were unwritable.

GEORGE: I have ideas like that sometimes.

TED: George often gets lecherous in the rainy season. Only this morning he fell in love with a shark.

QUINN: A big one?

GEORGE: I like them big.

QUINN: Did you catch anything?

TED: Two groupers, a few flat-looking things like skate, and a poor little bastard with frills on it.

GEORGE: We put him back, he looked kind of sissy.

QUINN: You mustn't be sexually intolerant.

TED: George would be sexually anything at the drop of a hat.

> STEFAN *enters with the other rum punch.*

QUINN: The next round on me, Stefan.

STEFAN: Yes, sir.

> *He goes off.*

TED: I can't bear that man.

QUINN: Why?

GEORGE: He's a Russian. Ted's got a hate on Russians.

TED: Remember that son of a bitch in La Paz?

GEORGE: He wasn't Russian, he was Polish.

TED: He got drunk in the Strangers' Club and started to fight me.

QUINN: What did you do?

TED: Socked him.

GEORGE: And then we weren't allowed into the club any more.

QUINN: Boys will be boys.

GEORGE *and* TED (*together*): That's what I always say.

> MRS. BIRLING *and* ELISE *come up the steps from the bathing pool.* ELISE *is wearing a bathing costume with a bath robe over it, and pink rubber shoes.*

MRS. BIRLING: Oh, dear, it is hot. I was almost tempted to bathe myself.

ELISE: The water was lovely.

TED: No jellyfish?

ELISE: No—it was beautifully clear, too—you could see right away down to the bottom.

MRS. BIRLING: I must speak to Mrs. Valaine; Elise says there's a splinter in the chute.

QUINN: Still?

> GEORGE *and* TED *laugh.*

MRS. BIRLING: It's very dangerous, you might get blood-poisoning or anything.

> ELISE *takes off her bathing cap, releasing a great deal of damp hair.*

ELISE: Oh, dear, this cap's no use at all.

MRS. BIRLING: Run and get dressed, dear, the launch will be here in a minute.

ELISE: All right, mother.

QUINN: Would you like a rum punch, Mrs. Birling, as you haven't bathed?

MRS. BIRLING: No, thank you, Mr. Quinn. Rum always goes straight to my liver.

QUINN: How horrid of it!

MRS. BIRLING: I feel ill for days if I have so much as a sip—go along, Elise.

> *They both go off upstairs.*

GEORGE *and* TED (*together*): Which only goes to show!

QUINN: You are both sadly lacking in human sympathy.

GEORGE: Yeah, we're tough, we are.

QUINN: At that I don't believe you're either of you one quarter as tough as Mrs. Birling.

> *The launch Klaxon is heard.*

TED: Oh, God! No peace.

GEORGE: Come and sit down.

QUINN: All right.

> *They go up to the back and sit down with their feet up on the rail.* STEFAN *enters from the right with a tray of rum punches. He is folowed by* LOLA *and* MAY, *who go across the verandah and down the steps.* STEFAN *gives* TED, GEORGE, *and* QUINN *their drinks and waits while* QUINN *signs a chit for them; then he also goes down the steps.*
>
> LINDA *comes in from the left. She is wearing a sort of semi-evening dress, very simply made of some cottony material. The three men get up.*

TED: Hallo, Mrs. Valaine.

GEORGE: Have you come to receive?

LINDA: Yes.

GEORGE: Have a rum punch?

LINDA: No, thanks.

TED: Come on, just a sip, to give you courage. (*He hands her his glass.*)

LINDA (*smiling*): Oh, very well. (*She sips a little.*)

QUINN: You look very cool.

LINDA: I've just been swimming.

GEORGE: In the pool? We didn't see you go down.

LINDA: I went off the rocks just beyond my verandah.

TED: Isn't that a bit risky?

LINDA: Not really, in the day-time, it's only at night that the big maurauding fish come in close.

QUINN: It is dangerous all the same.

LINDA: I never swim far out.

> MRS. BIRLING *comes down from the stairs.*

MRS. BIRLING: Elise will be down in a moment.

LINDA: Did she enjoy her bathe?

MRS. BIRLING: Yes, but there was a splinter in the chute; luckily she saw it in time.

TED: In time for what?

LINDA (*quickly*): I'm so sorry, I'll have it seen to.

GEORGE: Here they all come.

> *There is a murmur of voices below the verandah.* LINDA *goes to the top of the steps.* MRS. HALL-FENTON *appears first. She is a buxom, jolly, rather common woman. She is followed by her two eldest girls,* GLADYS *and* PHYLLIS. SYLVIA, *the youngest follows with* HILDA JAMES. *All four girls are unremarkable in appearance.* HILDA, *however, is rather more smartly dressed than the other three.* MARTIN welford *comes last. He is a nice sensitive-looking boy. He wears the usual white tropical suit and a Panama hat. They all come on to the verandah, chattering.* MARTIN *hangs back a little.*

MRS. HALL-FENTON: Here we all are, Mrs. Valaine. The car broke down just near the new bridge, and we nearly as anything missed the launch.

GLADYS: Mother was in the most awful state.

MRS. HALL-FENTON: I wasn't at all. I kept calm.

PHYLLIS: Mother, how *can* you!

SYLVIA: A man went to the petrol station on a bicycle and
    fetched another man. He——

GLADYS: It was one of the sparking plugs.

HILDA: Hallo, Linda.

    She kisses her warmly. All the others have shaken hands.

LINDA: Hallo, Hilda.

MRS. HALL-FENTON (*shaking hands with* MRS. BIRLING): Hallo,
    Mrs. Birling Where's Elise? The girls are dying to see her.

MRS. BIRLING: She's changing. She'll be down in a minute.

MRS. HALL-FENTON (*furtively*): Better?

MRS. BIRLING: Much better, I think; beginning to take more
    interest in things.

MRS. HALL-FENTON: Building up, that's what she needs, building
    up.

LINDA: Mr. Welford?

MARTIN: Yes.

LINDA (*shaking hands*): How do you do?

MARTIN: How do you do?

LINDA: You came on the *Colombie*, didn't you?

MARTIN: Yes.

LINDA: She's a beautiful ship.

    ELISE *comes rushing downstairs.*

ELISE: Phyl—Glad—Syl! How lovely!

    They all kiss.

HILDA: Hallo, Elise, feeling brighter?

ELISE (*a little stiffly*): Yes, thank you, Hilda. I hope you're all
    right.

GLADYS: Isn't that a lovely hat of Hilda's?

PHYLLIS: She got it at Harrison's, a whole new lot came in on
    Tuesday. Trust Hilda to get there first.

LINDA: Mr. Quinn.

QUINN (*coming to her*): Yes.

LINDA: This is Mr. Welford.

QUINN: Hallo. Welcome to the colony.

MARTIN (*shaking hands*): Thanks.

LINDA: Do you mind very much waiting for a few minutes
    before I show you your room?

MARTIN: Not a bit.

QUINN: Come and have a rum punch.

MARTIN: Thanks awfully.

> QUINN *takes him up to the back and introduces him to* TED *and*
> GEORGE. *Meanwhile* STEFAN *and* LOLA *and* MAY *have passed*
> *through with the luggage.* TED *yells for* STEFAN, *who presently comes*
> *on and takes their orders and goes off again.*

LINDA: I've given you the suite, Mrs. Hall-Fenton, and you have
your usual little room, Hilda.

HILDA (*whispering*): Did you tell him?

LINDA: Yes. Wait until after dinner to tackle him.

HILDA: All right—lovely.

GLADYS: Mum, have we got time for a bathe before dressing?

MRS. HALL-FENTON: Yes, if you hurry—go on up.

MRS. BIRLING: Be careful of the chute, there's a splinter in it.

LINDA: I'll take you all up—come along.

ELISE: Oh, Mother, I do wish I'd waited for my bathe.

MRS. BIRLING: Never mind, we can go down to the pool and
watch.

PHYLLIS: Why not bathe again?

ELISE: Oh, I couldn't. I've just changed and everything.

SYLVIA: Come on—do——

MRS. BIRLING (*firmly*): No, Elise mustn't bathe again so soon. She
stayed in too long as it was. We'll see you at the pool. Come
along, dear.

ELISE: Oh, all right.

MRS. HALL-FENTON (*as she goes off with* LINDA): It's so nice being
here again.

GLADYS: Are you going to bathe, Hilda?

HILDA: Of course. Come on—hurry——

> *They all go chattering upstairs.* ELISE *and* MRS. BIRLING *go down*
> *the steps.* STEFAN *enters with another round of rum punches. They*
> *all take them and "Cheerio" each other.*

TED: These are a speciality of the place.

MARTIN: Damn good.

QUINN: Did you stop long in La Guayra?

MARTIN: Only one night, then I went up to Caracas for three
days and came down again and caught the boat.

GEORGE: I know a swell guy in Caracas. Friedman. He's in the Western Union. Did you see him by any chance?

MARTIN: No, I didn't meet anyone really. I was feeling rather ill most of the time.

TED: Fever?

MARTIN: Yes, I had a bad go of it in Brazil.

GEORGE: Are you in coffee or sugar or something?

MARTIN: No, I fly, air survey work. We've been trying to map the Matto Grosso.

TED: Good God! You're not by any chance the chap who got lost, are you?

MARTIN (*smiling*): Yes, I'm afraid I am.

GEORGE: Jesus, what a scoop for Hilda James! This'll take the front page away from you, Quinn.

QUINN: Perhaps he won't want to talk about it.

MARTIN (*looking at him gratefully*): I don't much.

TED: That's all right, we won't say a word.

GEORGE: We read about it, of course. About three months ago, wasn't it?

MARTIN: Yes.

TED: Must have been pretty average bloody.

MARTIN: It was.

GEORGE: How many days?

MARTIN: Thirteen.

QUINN: Shut up, you two. You read the story in the papers. Leave him alone.

TED: Oh, sorry.

MARTIN: Oh, I don't mind telling you about it sometime.

GEORGE: Come out fishing with us to-morrow.

MARTIN: Fine. I'd love to.

QUINN: Have you room in your filthy little boat for a crabbed embittered old writer?

GEORGE: I'll try and use influence with my friend Ted. He pays for the gas.

TED: What about a swim?

QUINN: God! What energy!

GEORGE: All right.

TED (*to* MARTIN): Do you want to swim?

MARTIN: I haven't unpacked my things yet.

TED: I can lend you some trunks, if you like—you can change in our room.

MARTIN: I don't think I will, thanks all the same. I'll wait until to-morrow.

GEORGE: Come on, then, Ted.

TED: Right—see you later.

> GEORGE *and* TED *rush off upstairs.*

QUINN: Have another punch.

MARTIN: Thanks. This lot's on me.

QUINN: Nonsense, you can do the next. Stefan——

MARTIN: It's nice here, isn't it?

QUINN: It would be better without quite so many jolly people.

> STEFAN *enters.*

QUINN: Two more, please, Stefan.

STEFAN: Yes, sir.

> *He goes out.*

MARTIN: I've read a lot of your books.

QUINN (*smiling*): Have you?

MARTIN: I think you're a grand writer.

QUINN: I'm glad.

MARTIN: I suppose you're working on something new here?

QUINN: Just making notes, that's all.

MARTIN: Is it nice being a celebrity?

QUINN: You ought to know. You're a celebrity yourself since your escapade in the jungle.

MARTIN: Oh no, that's just one of those things that happen, mere chance. I mean a real celebrity. Do you like it or does it bore you?

QUINN: I sometimes pretend that it bores me, but really I like it very much.

MARTIN: Have you been here long?

QUINN: About three weeks.

MARTIN: I want to stay a little and rest. They won't let me fly again, you know, for a year. I had blood-poisoning and a lot of fever, and it did something queer to my heart, and my eyes went a bit wrong too. I don't feel like going home just yet.

QUINN: Have you got a family?

MARTIN: A father and a sister. My mother died five years ago.

QUINN: Not married?

MARTIN: Oh no.

QUINN: Do you want to be?

MARTIN: Not a bit. I'm quite happy as I am.

> STEFAN *comes in with the drinks.* QUINN *signs for them.* STEFAN *goes out again.*

MARTIN: He's foreign, isn't he?

QUINN: Yes, Russian.

MARTIN: He moves funnily, doesn't he? Like some sort of animal.

QUINN: He is some sort of animal.

MARTIN: Is she nice?

QUINN: Who, Mrs. Valaine?

MARTIN: Yes.

QUINN: Very nice, rather aloof, rather shut up inside herself, but very nice—I think.

MARTIN: You don't seem quite sure.

QUINN: I'm never quite sure.

MARTIN: Will you have another punch?

QUINN: No, thanks. I think I'll go and change.

MARTIN: I shall too when Mrs. Valaine shows me where my room is.

QUINN: She'll be down in a minute.

MARTIN: Don't worry about me, I'll be all right.

QUINN: Perhaps you'd like to dine at my table as it's your first evening here. You might feel rather strange among all these shrill virgins.

MARTIN: It's most awfully nice of you. I'd like to very much.

QUINN: Fine. See you later.

> *He goes off upstairs.*
>
> MARTIN, *left alone, perches himself on the rail and looks at the view.* PHYLLIS, SYLVIA, GLADYS, *and* HILDA *come running on in bath robes.*

PHYLLIS (*to* HILDA): . . . and when the band stopped, they went on, to the gramophone, until five.

SYLVIA: I was nearly dead, I can tell you.

HILDA: Elise still looks a bit peaky, doesn't she?

PHYLLIS: Oh, I've forgotten my cap.

HILDA: Have mine. I can't dive anyway. I got a bad ear last winter from diving.

PHYLLIS: I hope the chute's working.

> *They run off down the steps.*
>
> STEFAN *comes on and collects the empty glasses. He scrutinises* MARTIN *covertly as he does so. He goes off as* LINDA *comes on, down the stairs.*

LINDA: Oh, Mr. Welford, I'm so sorry to have kept you waiting.

MARTIN (*jumping down from the rail*): It doesn't matter a bit. (*He smiles at her.*) It's lovely here.

LINDA: This is a bad time of year, really. A good deal of rain.

MARTIN: I don't mind rain.

LINDA: Who told you about this hotel?

MARTIN: I met some officers from the H.M.S. *Durban*. They were in Rio for a few days. They told me about it.

LINDA: It's quite primitive, I'm afraid, but I hope you'll be comfortable.

MARTIN (*looking at her intently*): I'm sure I shall.

LINDA (*conscious of his gaze*): You've been ill, haven't you?

MARTIN: Yes. How did you know?

LINDA: You look a little as if you'd been ill.

MARTIN: Fever does pull one down a lot.

LINDA: You must get well and strong again.

MARTIN: I'm feeling much better already. The voyage did me good.

LINDA (*after a slight pause*): Well—will you come with me and see your room?

MARTIN: Rather—thanks.

LINDA: This way.

> *She goes off up the stairs, and he follows her.*

CURTAIN

ACT II: Scene I

The scene is LINDA'*s sitting-room again. It is late afternoon four days later.*

When the curtain rises LINDA *is lying on the chaise-longue. On the low table by her side are a tea tray and a box of cigarettes. She has finished her tea and is reading a magazine and smoking.* LOLA *enters.*

LINDA: What is it, Lola?

LOLA: The list, ma'am, for the town. Stefan made it out.

LINDA: Let me see it.

LOLA (*giving her list*): There is no more Worcester sauce.

LINDA: Is it down here?

LOLA: No, ma'am.

LINDA (*irritably*): Why not? Give me a pencil. There's one on the desk.

LOLA (*fetching pencil*): Yes, ma'am.

LINDA (*reading through the list*): What's this?

LOLA (*giving her pencil*): Eraser, ma'am, for Mr. Quinn. Stefan forgot it last time.

LINDA (*writing*): Night-lights. By the way, Lola, see that Mrs. Birling has two in her room always. She says she saw a bat last night on her verandah, and her light had gone out.

LOLA: Yes, ma'am.

LINDA: Do you always put water in the saucers?

LOLA: Yes, ma'am.

LINDA: And ask Mr. Burchell and Mr. Fox not to take their face towels down to the pool. The rough ones are quite good enough.

LOLA: Yes, ma'am.

LINDA: All right, Lola. You can leave the list here. Tell Stefan to see me about it to-morrow morning before he leaves.

LOLA: Yes, ma'am.

LINDA: And take the tray, I've finished with it.

LOLA *is just picking up the tray when there is a knock on the door.*
Who is it?

MARTIN (*poking his head through the bead curtains*): It's me. Are you busy?

LINDA: No. Come in.

MARTIN (*coming into the room*): Thanks.

He holds aside the curtains for LOLA *to go out with the tray.*

LINDA: Have you had tea?

MARTIN: Yes, thanks.

LINDA: Are you feeling better?

MARTIN: Ever so much better. That's why I came to see you, really, to thank you for being so kind. The bouts don't last very long, but they're beastly while they do. I'm afraid I used up a lot of blankets.

LINDA: That doesn't matter. We have enough and to spare. Fever isn't exactly rare in these parts.

MARTIN: No, I suppose not.

LINDA: Sit down, won't you?

MARTIN: Thanks. (*He sits in a cane armchair.*)

LINDA (*offering him cigarette box*): Cigarette?

MARTIN: No, I don't think I will just now. My head still feels a bit wobbly.

LINDA: Is everybody out?

MARTIN: Yes, all except Mrs. Birling. She's reading on the verandah. Fox and Burchell and Mortimer Quinn are fishing. All the others are in the pool, I think. He's nice, isn't he?

LINDA: Who, Mr. Quinn?

MARTIN: Yes.

LINDA: Very nice.

MARTIN: I envy him.

LINDA: Do you—why?

MARTIN: It must be wonderful, being a writer. To be able to wander around the world and work whenever you like and wherever you like, without being dependent on anybody but yourself. And not to mind being alone.

LINDA: Do you mind being alone?

MARTIN: I hate it, except when I'm flying, but that's quite different. It's grand being alone then.

LINDA: I've always wanted to fly.

MARTIN: You'd love it.

LINDA: Perhaps I should be sick.

MARTIN: No, you wouldn't. Not in an open plane, with the wind in your face, blowing your cheeks out like balloons.

LINDA: That doesn't sound very nice.

MARTIN: It is though, it's marvellous.

LINDA: Have you ever had any accidents?—I mean apart from your jungle adventure.

MARTIN: No, except one, when I was learning, I fell into a turnip field, but that was nothing. How did you know about the jungle business?

LINDA: I recognised your face the day you arrived. Your photograph was in all the papers, you know.

MARTIN: There was a lot of silly fuss about it.

LINDA: And now you're going home?

MARTIN: Yes.

LINDA: I've never been to England.

MARTIN (*surprised*): You are English, though, aren't you?

LINDA: Yes, but I've lived all my life in the Islands. I married a Frenchman and went to France for a year during the war. Apart from that I've been nowhere, seen nothing.

MARTIN: How funny.

LINDA: Funny?

MARTIN: Yes, you don't seem a bit like that, like a person who's stuck in the same place, I mean.

LINDA: How long have you been an—an aviator?

MARTIN: Since I was eighteen. I'm twenty-five now. That's seven years.

LINDA (*ruminatively*): Twenty-five.

MARTIN: Did you think I was older?

LINDA (*with a sudden smile*): No, I didn't.

MARTIN: I've got to waste a whole year, not flying at all.

LINDA: What a shame. But still, you're lucky to be alive, really, aren't you?

MARTIN: Yes, I suppose I am.

LINDA: Did you ever give up hope entirely, all that time you were lost?

MARTIN: Only once, the last day. I was a bit crazy by then, anyway.

LINDA (*suddenly getting up and moving out on to the verandah; she speaks with her back turned*): It's a horrible feeling being lost, isn't it?

MARTIN (*faintly surprised at her tone*): Yes—horrible.

LINDA (*turning*): Why did you crash? What happened?

MARTIN: I didn't crash. I had to make a forced landing because the damn fool mechanic hadn't put in enough petrol. I pancaked on to the trees.

LINDA: Pancaked?

MARTIN: Yes, that means shutting off your engine and dropping, as slowly and gently as you can.

LINDA: I see.

MARTIN: I hardly damaged the plane at all.

LINDA: And then?

MARTIN: Then we climbed out and got down into the jungle.

LINDA: We?

MARTIN: I had a mechanic with me.

LINDA: Oh, I thought you were entirely alone.

MARTIN: I was, after a little while.

LINDA: Why—did he die?

MARTIN: Yes. He went mad and hanged himself with his belt. I'd left him in a clearing for a few hours, because I thought we were near the main river, where I could get help. But it wasn't the main river at all, and when I got back I found him like that, hanging from a tree. It was quite a low tree, his feet were only a few inches from the ground. That was on the sixth day.

LINDA: And you went on?

MARTIN: Yes, I went on. There wasn't anything else to do.

LINDA: What did you eat?

MARTIN: Roots mostly, and leaves. I used to try to catch animals at night, but I never succeeded.

LINDA: You had no gun or anything?

MARTIN: We started with a revolver, and we took the compass

out of the plane too, but we lost them both in the first river we crossed.

LINDA: How did you finally get out?

MARTIN: I got to within about fifty yards of the main river and collapsed—I'd been going for twelve days. I was torn to bits by thorns, and the blood-poisoning had given me a fever. Then suddenly I heard the hooter of a steamer, quite close, and I staggered up and started yelling like mad; then about a quarter of an hour later I heard it again—in the distance. Then I knew I was done for, because steamers only go down that river once or twice a month at most. So I just lay down on the ground.

LINDA: And then?

MARTIN: Then half-way through the next day I sort of came to my senses for a bit, and struggled on to the actual bank of the river, and just by a fluke there happened to be a solitary Indian passing in a canoe. If I'd been five minutes later he wouldn't have seen me. But he did, thank God, and he got me down river to San José, where an old Brazilian priest looked after me until I was well enough to be moved to Sao Paolo.

LINDA: What a dreadful story!

MARTIN: It was pretty awful.

LINDA: You're very young to be so strong.

MARTIN: I'm not particularly strong.

LINDA: I mean strong in spirit.

MARTIN: Oh, I don't know about that.

LINDA: You must be; after all, the mechanic lost courage early, didn't he? He killed himself.

MARTIN: He went out of his mind, poor devil!

LINDA: Did you ever feel that you wanted to kill yourself?

MARTIN: No. I don't think I ever should.

LINDA: I often wonder—— (*She stops.*)

MARTIN: What?

LINDA: I was going to say I often wonder if it isn't braver to kill yourself really, in some circumstances, than to go on living. Then that sounded as though I thought that the mechanic was braver than you, and I don't. I don't at all. I think you must be very brave indeed.

MARTIN: Oh, no, I'm not, really I'm not. I'm scared stiff of a whole heap of things.

LINDA: So am I.

MARTIN: You don't look as though you'd be easily frightened by anything.

LINDA (*smiling*): Don't I?

MARTIN: You seem very calm, and—and still.

The sound of the accordion is heard in the distance.

What's that?

LINDA: Stefan. I allow him to play his accordion at certain hours of the day when nobody's trying to sleep or anything. It gives him a great deal of pleasure.

MARTIN: It's not one of my favourite instruments.

LINDA: He has a passion for music, and that's all he can play.

MARTIN (*laughing*): It's a good long way off, anyhow.

LINDA: He only plays it in his own quarters, down at the very end of the garden. Every now and then he takes it with him when he goes out fishing. I hear it sometimes at night, right out at sea. It sounds rather nice, gay—as though someone were giving a party.

MARTIN: I shouldn't think he'd catch many fish.

LINDA: He does. A great many.

MARTIN: Perhaps the music hypnotises them on to the hook.

LINDA (*absently*): Perhaps it does.

MARTIN: He's an odd-looking bloke.

LINDA (*sharply*): He's a very good head waiter.

MARTIN: Are you angry?

LINDA: Angry! No, of course not. Why should I be angry?

MARTIN: I don't know. I thought your voice sounded a little edgy—(*He rises.*) perhaps I'm boring you——

LINDA: You're not boring me in the least.

MARTIN: I think I'd better be getting along now, anyhow.

LINDA (*with an effort*): Please don't go. It was nice of you to come and talk to me.

MARTIN: I love talking to you.

LINDA (*slightly at a loss*): Oh.

MARTIN: I was a bit afraid of you at first, when I arrived.

LINDA (*with a half smile*): I'm sorry.

MARTIN: But I'm not any more.

LINDA: I'm glad.

They both laugh.

MARTIN: Do I seem awfully young and idiotic to you?

LINDA: No, of course you don't. Why should you think that?

MARTIN: I feel somehow as if I wasn't quite making sense. I expect it's the result of the fever.

LINDA (*gently*): Please sit down again.

MARTIN: All right, if you really don't mind. (*He sits.*)

LINDA (*after a slight pause*): It's hardly rained to-day at all, has it?

MARTIN: No, only a small shower this morning.

LINDA: There'll probably be a storm soon, just to make up for it.

MARTIN: Is your husband dead?

LINDA: Yes. Why?

MARTIN: I only wondered.

LINDA: He was killed in nineteen-seventeen.

MARTIN: Valaine's a pretty name.

LINDA: This island always used to be known as Shark Point. I changed it when I started the hotel.

MARTIN: What's your other name?

LINDA (*after hesitating a moment*): Linda.

MARTIN: That's a pretty name, too. Linda Valaine (*He says it over again.*)—Linda Valaine.

LINDA: I'm glad you like it.

She walks restlessly on to the verandah. MARTIN *follows her with his eyes.*

MARTIN: It is hot, isn't it? Sticky!

LINDA: Yes.

MARTIN: What's the name of that tree—the scarlet one?

LINDA: There are several names for it: Flamboyant, Poinciana— sometimes it's called Flame of the Forest.

MARTIN: I like that best. There are lots of them in Brazil, and some yellow ones too, called "Ipè something".

He rises and comes out on to the verandah.

LINDA: Do you ever get homesick?

MARTIN: Sometimes. Not very often.

LINDA: Most English people do. They sit on the verandah and

talk very sentimentally about grey skies and fogs and Piccadilly.

MARTIN (*laughing*): Piccadilly?

LINDA: Yes, they all seem to miss Piccadilly.

MARTIN: I don't see why they should. It's no nicer than Regent Street, really, or the Mall.

LINDA: I suppose I should miss this very much if I ever went away. But I don't expect I ever shall.

MARTIN: The accordion's stopped.

LINDA (*looking out to sea*): I was right about the storm. Look at those clouds.

MARTIN: They're beautiful, aren't they?

LINDA: Yes, I suppose they are.

MARTIN: It's marvellous when you're flying to go right through a bank like that and come out the other side into clear sky.

LINDA: Then you have to come down again, don't you, after you've seen your clear sky? Down into the thick of it.

MARTIN: Yes, that's not so good.

LINDA (*coming back into the room*): Would you like a drink?

MARTIN (*following her*): No, thanks—I don't think I'd better. (*He puts his hand up to his head.*)

LINDA: What's the matter?

MARTIN: Nothing. I feel a bit dizzy, that's all. I expect it's the heat——

> *He makes a grab at the chair to save himself from falling, but misses it and sprawls on to the floor.* LINDA *runs to him and, kneeling down, lifts his head on to her lap.*

LINDA (*putting her hand on his heart; whispering*): Poor boy—poor little boy——

> *She lifts him up gently and drags him on to the chaise-longue. Then, having placed a cushion under his head, she goes to a corner cupboard and takes out a bottle of brandy and a glass. She pours out some brandy and brings it over to him. With great tenderness she hoists him up and puts the glass to his lips. He opens his eyes and moves his head a little.*

Just drink a little of this, you'll be all right in a moment.

MARTIN (*weakly*): Thanks—thanks awfully——

> *He drinks some of the brandy and relaxes again in her arms. She puts*

*the glass down on the table with her free hand and then strokes his
forehead very gently.*

LINDA: Stay still a minute, stay quite still.

MARTIN: That's lovely.

LINDA: Shh! Don't try to talk.

MARTIN (*very softly*): Linda Valaine.

LINDA: Shhh!

> MARTIN *puts his hand up to hers and pulls it down to his lips. They
> both remain still for a few seconds.* LINDA *then gently disengages her
> hand and rises to her feet, leaning him carefully against the cushions.*

MARTIN: Don't leave me.

LINDA (*brusquely*): Here, finish the brandy. (*She gives him the glass
again.*)

MARTIN (*smiling up at her*): All right.

LINDA: You got up too soon. You should have stayed in bed.

MARTIN: It's not a very comfortable bed. I wish to complain.

LINDA: Don't be silly.

MARTIN: I wish to complain to the management. You're the
management, aren't you?—Linda Valaine!

LINDA: You'd better go to your room and lie down. I'll have
your dinner sent up to you.

MARTIN: I want to have my dinner on the verandah. I've fallen in
love—with Mrs. Birling.

LINDA: Come along now—please come.

MARTIN (*rising rather unsteadily*): Mrs. Birling's liver is in a very
poor state. I think, as the management, you ought to know.

LINDA: Come along. Take my arm——

MARTIN (*simply*): You are a dear.

> *He takes her arm and, leaning on her a little, goes out with her
> through the bead curtains.*
> *The room is empty and silent for a few moments, then there is a
> sudden gust of wind which rattles the shutters and the blinds.*
> STEFAN *comes swiftly in from the verandah. He stands still in the
> centre of the room with his head up, listening. Then he sniffs twice
> and makes an odd little grunting noise like an animal. He begins to
> move about the room, swiftly and silently. He goes into* LINDA'S
> *bedroom and then comes back again. He kneels on the ground by the
> side of the chaise-longue, and smooths the cushions of it with his
> hands. Then he sees the empty brandy glass, picks it up, sniffs at it,*

and puts it down again. Then he slides himself up on to the chaise-longue until he is full length upon it, and buries his face in the cushions. There is another sharp gust of wind, and LINDA's *bedroom door bangs.* STEFAN *jumps to his feet and disappears over the verandah again as the lights fade.*

Scene II

The scene is the verandah again. It is about nine o'clock on the following evening. It is raining hard, and all the blinds are down.

Most of the chairs have been moved away from the balustrade and are placed in groups about the stage. LINDA *and* QUINN *occupy two downstage, with their backs half turned to the audience.* MRS. HALL-FENTON *and* MRS. BIRLING *are sitting together on the right. The portable gramophone is playing a dance record.* MARTIN *is at the table sorting over the records.* TED *is dancing with* SYLVIA, GEORGE *with* HILDA JAMES. PHYLLIS *and* GLADYS *are dancing together. The music comes to an end.*

PHYLLIS: Put on another.

MRS. HALL-FENTON (*rising*): No, dear—we really must go.

GLADYS: But, Mum, it's still pouring.

SYLVIA: Just one more, Mum.

MRS. HALL-FENTON: We shan't be home before midnight as it is, and you know your father's expecting us.

LINDA (*rising*): Is your launch ready? Shall I tell Lola to run down and see?

MRS. HALL-FENTON: He'll be there, he's always punctual.

TED (*pulling aside one of the blinds and looking out*): Yes, he's there—I can see the light.

MRS. HALL-FENTON: Come along, girls.

PHYLLIS: But, Mum, the bags aren't down or anything.

MRS. HALL-FENTON: That won't take a minute.

MAY *enters from the right.*

LINDA: May, take Mrs. Hall-Fenton's luggage down to the landing stage.

MAY: Yes, ma'am.

She goes off upstairs.

MRS. HALL-FENTON: We've had a lovely time, Mrs. Valaine. We shall probably be out again in two weeks' time. My husband has to go up to the plantation.

LINDA: Let me know a day or two before and your rooms will be ready for you.

ELISE *runs in from the night.*

ELISE: I can't find them anywhere, Mother.

MRS. BIRLING: You must have left them on the edge and they got knocked over.

GEORGE: What's lost?

ELISE: My iron jelloids.

LINDA: I expect Stefan found them and put them away.

MRS. BIRLING: You really are very careless, Elise.

LINDA: He'll be back soon, and we can ask him.

PHYLLIS: Good-bye, Elise, Mum's dragging us home.

ELISE: Don't forget Wednesday week.

SYLVIA: Of course not.

GLADYS: Come early, about half-past four, we can have tea at home before we go.

ELISE: All right.

PHYLLIS: You can stay the night if you like, can't she, Mum? It's an awfully long way to drive back.

MRS. HALL-FENTON: Certainly, if Mrs. Birling will let her.

SYLVIA: Will you, Mrs Birling?

MRS. BIRLING: Elise is not strong enough yet to stay up late.

GLADYS: But Wednesday week's a long way off, she'll be much stronger by then. Do say yes.

ELISE: Do let me, Mother.

MRS. BIRLING: I'll think about it.

MAY *comes down with two suitcases and goes down the steps.*

MRS. HALL-FENTON: Come along, there go the bags.

PHYLLIS: Oh, all right. Good-bye, Mr. Welford.

MARTIN: Good-bye.

SYLVIA: Come and see us when you come into town.

GLADYS: Yes, he must, mustn't he, Mother?

MRS. HALL-FENTON: I should be delighted. We're quite easy to find, Mr. Welford. The third house behind the tennis club— you can't possibly miss it.

MARTIN: Thank you very much.

PHYLLIS: Good-bye, Mr. Fox. Good-bye, Mr. Burchell.

GEORGE: Good-bye.

TED: Good-bye.

MRS. HALL-FENTON: Good-bye, Mr. Quinn. It's been so interesting meeting you.

QUINN (*politely*): How nice of you to say so.

SYLVIA: It's been thrilling, hasn't it, Mum?

MRS. HALL-FENTON: Yes, dear.

PHYLLIS: Good-bye, Mr. Quinn.

QUINN: Good-bye.

GLADYS: Good-bye, Mr. Quinn. It was very naughty of you not to dance.

PHYLLIS: I'm sure he really dances beautifully, aren't you, Mum?

MRS. HALL-FENTON: Yes, dear. Hurry up. Say good-bye to Mrs. Valaine.

PHYLLIS: Good-bye, Mrs. Valaine.

LINDA: Good-bye.

SYLVIA: Good-bye, Mrs. Valaine.

LINDA: Good-bye.

GLADYS: We've had a heavenly time. Good-bye, Mrs. Valaine.

LINDA: I'll come down to the launch.

MRS. HALL-FENTON: No, no, you mustn't do any such thing, you'll get soaked.

LINDA: I have my raincoat here.

PHYLLIS: It's not raining as much as it was.

ELISE: It'll stop soon, I expect. Can I go down too, Mother?

MRS. BIRLING: No, dear. I don't want you to catch a chill. You know what you are.

ELISE: Oh, all right.

MRS. HALL-FENTON: Good-bye, Mr. Quinn, Good-bye, Mr. Burchell. Good-bye, Mr. Fox.

TED: Good-bye.

GEORGE: Good-bye.

QUINN: Good-bye, good-bye, good-bye.

ELISE: The book! Don't forget the book.

MRS. HALL-FENTON: Oh, dear. Quick, girls. Write in the book.

PHYLLIS: Where's the pen?

MARTIN (*at table*): Here.

PHYLLIS: What's the date?

TED: Seventeenth.

GEORGE: Eighteenth.

QUINN: Twenty-ninth.

> *They all scramble round the table signing their names in the book.*
> MRS. HALL-FENTON *signs last.*

MRS. HALL-FENTON: There now. Come along.

> *After a fresh chorus of good-byes, they all go off.* LOLA *has previously
> brought in their raincoats.* LINDA *has gone with them. The rest are
> left.* ELISE *runs to the top of the steps and waves.* MARTIN *drops into
> the chair next to* QUINN.

MARTIN: Want a drink?

QUINN: A strong brandy-and-soda.

MARTIN: I'll have the same. Stefan——

QUINN: He isn't here.

MARTIN: Of course not, I keep forgetting.

> MAY *comes up the steps.*

QUINN: May—two brandy-and-sodas, please.

MAY: Yes, sir.

> *She goes off.*

TED (*up at the back*): Where are the cards?

GEORGE: Probably in the bar. I'll get them.

> *He runs off.*

TED (*to* ELISE): Do you want to play hearts?

ELISE: Yes, I'd love to—may I, Mother?

MRS. BIRLING: Just for a little while.

TED: Will you play, Mrs. Birling?

MRS. BIRLING: No, thank you. I've never had a head for cards. I
shall just read my book.

QUINN (*softly to* MARTIN): I do hope she has a head for books.

> MAY *comes in with two brandy-and-sodas.* MARTIN *signs for them.*

TED: Are you coming, Quinn?

QUINN: I'll join in a little later.

TED: Welford?

MARTIN: So will I.

HILDA: Remember your promise, Mr. Quinn.

QUINN: I haven't forgotten.

HILDA: I shan't let you escape.

> GEORGE *comes back with the cards and joins* HILDA, TED, *and* ELISE *at the back. They all sit down at a table.* MRS. BIRLING *goes up and sits near them.*

QUINN (*holding up his glass to* MARTIN): *Salud y amor y pesetas.*

MARTIN: *Gracias. Amor?*

QUINN: *Porque no?* At your age you ought to be thinking of nothing else.

MARTIN: You don't really mean that, do you?

QUINN: I was only just wondering.

MARTIN: Were you? Why?

QUINN: Don't look so stern. It was quite an amiable toast. Health, love, and wealth. What could be fairer than that?

MARTIN: I don't seem to have any of them at the moment.

> LINDA *comes up the steps, taking off her raincoat.*

LINDA: They've all gone, and the rain's stopped.

QUINN: Come and talk to us.

> LOLA, *who has followed* LINDA *on to the verandah, goes round pulling up the blinds.* LINDA *comes over to* MARTIN *and* QUINN *and sits down.*

MARTIN: Drink?

LINDA: No, thank you.

QUINN: Tired?

LINDA: No, not really. But when Stefan has to go into town it leaves us short-handed.

MARTIN: Dinner seemed to go off all right.

LINDA: We had to wait hours between courses. Mamma Dangan's helping in the kitchen, and she dropped a whole tray of hot plates.

MARTIN: I thought I heard a crash.

QUINN: What does Stefan do in the town, carouse?

LINDA: No. He does all the shopping for the week, then he catches the eight o'clock train as far as Baila and bicycles on

from there to the landing stage. Our launch has gone to fetch
him now.

TED (*immersed in their game*): She's trying to jump the moon.

GEORGE: Someone must stop her.

HILDA: I don't believe you can.

MARTIN: Fox and Burchell nearly got drowned this morning.

LINDA: I know. They ought not to use the *Maria*, she's very old,
and the engine's always going wrong.

QUINN: They drifted for two hours. Lucky for them the wind
was right, and lucky for me I wasn't with them. I should have
been sick as a dog.

TED: There's your Queen of Spades.

ELISE (*excitedly*): Oh, do be careful, do be careful!

GEORGE: Whose lead?

HILDA: Mine.

LINDA: They'll have to row to-morrow.

QUINN: Just like you, with your mission children.

LINDA: Yes, without the hymns, and Father's harmonium
wailing after them across the water.

QUINN: There's always the accordion.

LINDA (*looking at him evenly*): Yes. I'd forgotten that.

MARTIN (*laughing*): I wish I knew what you were talking about.

LINDA: It's only that I was telling Mr. Quinn the other day about
my childhood here, when this place was a mission. And he
remembered. He has a very well-trained memory.

MARTIN: It must all have been very different then.

QUINN: The externals were pretty much the same, I expect. The
same storms and insects and stickiness. It's merely the
atmosphere that has changed a bit. (*To* LINDA.) The atmosphere has changed a good deal, hasn't it?

LINDA (*coldly*): Naturally.

TED: She's done it. I knew she would. You could have stopped
her, George, by taking that one trick.

GEORGE: With all those hearts in it? Not on your life.

ELISE: Oh dear! It's my deal now, isn't it?

HILDA: No, it's Mr. Fox's.

TED: Cut for me, somebody.

    LOLA *comes in and comes down to* LINDA.

LOLA: Please, ma'am

LINDA: What is it, Lola?

LOLA: The launch, ma'am.

LINDA: Hasn't it gone? It ought to have gone a half an hour ago.

LOLA: It won't start.

LINDA: Where's Farrell?

LOLA: He's down there now. He told me to tell you.

LINDA: What's wrong with it?

LOLA: I don't know, ma'am.

LINDA: I'll come. (*She gets up.*)

MARTIN (*also rising*): I'll come too, I'm used to engines.

QUINN: I shall stay here because I hate everything to do with them.

LINDA (*to* MARTIN): Please don't trouble.

MARTIN: It's no trouble at all. I should like to.

LINDA (*smiling*): Very well.

QUINN: Bring me another brandy-and-soda, Lola.

LOLA: Yes, sir.

> *She goes off.*
> LINDA *and* MARTIN *go off down the steps.*

GEORGE (*as they go*): Anything wrong?

LINDA (*irritably*): Only the damned launch.

> GEORGE *and* TED *laugh.*

MRS. BIRLING: It always gives me quite a little shock when Mrs. Valaine speaks like that.

QUINN: Pardonable irritation. She's had rather a trying evening.

MRS. BIRLING: Yes, I know, but still——

TED: But it really is a damned launch, Mrs. Birling, though not as bad as the *Maria*. That's God-damned!

MRS. BIRLING: Mr. Burchell, really!

ELISE: He's only teasing you, Mother.

GEORGE: Are we going to play or not?

HILDA: Play this hand without me, I want to talk to Mr. Quinn.

QUINN: Oh, God!

HILDA: Mr. Quinn. You promised.

QUINN: Oh, very well.

LOLA *comes in with his brandy-and-soda. He signs for it.* HILDA
comes over and sits next to him.

Would you like a drink?

HILDA: Yes, please. A crème de menthe.

QUINN (*resigned*): One crème de menthe, Lola. (*To* HILDA.)
Frappé?

HILDA: Yes, please.

QUINN: Frappé.

LOLA: Yes, sir.

She goes off.

HILDA: Now then.

She produces a small writing block and a pencil.

QUINN: Do you like doing this?

HILDA: Yes, I love it.

QUINN: I suppose it must be fun interviewing strange people
you've never seen before in your life.

HILDA: Yes, it is.

QUINN: When did you first start writing?

HILDA: About five years ago. I used to do little articles, you
know.

QUINN: Yes, I know.

HILDA: I suppose you've been writing all your life?

QUINN: Tell me, what did your parents say when you broke
away and got a job of your own?

HILDA: Oh, they were furious at first—at least, Father was, but
he got used to it.

QUINN: I like girls to be independent. I think it's splendid.

HILDA: Oh, I'm so glad.

QUINN: Did you ever think of writing a novel?

HILDA: I started one once, but it didn't get very far. I've written
a play, though.

QUINN: A play?

HILDA: Yes, plays are easier than novels, aren't they? I mean you
don't have to worry about grammar or anything.

LOLA *comes in with the crème de menthe.*

QUINN: Here's your crème de menthe.

HILDA: Oh, thank you.

QUINN *signs for it, and* LOLA *goes off again.*

QUINN: What's your play about?

HILDA: Oh, it's nothing much really.

QUINN: Don't you think it's good?

HILDA: Oh yes, I think it's good, but I don't suppose you would.

QUINN: Drama or comedy?

HILDA: Oh, sort of drama really—you see, it's about this girl who falls in love with a married man——

QUINN: I see.

HILDA: And the wife finds out, and there's a sort of party at Government House, and she gives the whole thing away, and the Governor's absolutely furious and says that the man will have to leave the island and give up his job and everything, and he has an awful scene with the wife and says that she has ruined his career through being so jealous and possessive and all that, and then he goes to find the girl and pour it all out to her, but she's disappeared, and the next morning they find that she's committed suicide!

QUINN: I see that it is a sort of drama, in a way.

HILDA: There are lots of funny bits in it.

QUINN: I'm glad to hear it.

HILDA: After all, you can't have the whole thing on one note, can you? I mean, I always think an audience likes to laugh every now and then.

QUINN: You mustn't pander to that.

HILDA: Yes, but life's awfully funny sometimes, isn't it?

QUINN: Hilariously.

HILDA: Often when the most dreadful things have happened to me, I've suddenly found myself laughing at something that had nothing to do with it at all.

QUINN: That shows lack of concentration but a gallant spirit.

HILDA: Oh, do you really think so?

QUINN: Certainly.

HILDA: It's most awfully sweet of you.

QUINN: Not at all.

LINDA *comes up the steps.*

What news?

LINDA: It seems to have broken down completely. Farrell and Mr. Welford are tinkering at it.

QUINN: That means Stefan won't be able to get back.

LINDA: Not until to-morrow.

QUINN: How annoying.

LINDA: It doesn't really matter. It's often happened before.

QUINN: Where does he sleep? On the beach?

LINDA: No. There's that little clubhouse place by the landing stage. I'd better signal to him. (*She calls.*) Lola—May——

> TED, GEORGE, *and* ELISE *finish their game and come downstage.*

TED: No luck with the launch?

LINDA: I'm afraid not.

GEORGE: Can't he row across?

LINDA (*looking out*): He wouldn't attempt it to-night. It's a long pull at the best of times, and the wind's dead against him.

> LOLA *enters.*

TED: We might go and fetch him. It would be rather fun.

LINDA: I wouldn't hear of such a thing. Lola, get me the flashlight.

LOLA: Yes, ma'am.

> MARTIN *comes up the steps.*

MARTIN: No good. It won't budge.

LINDA: Thank you so much for taking all that trouble.

GEORGE: Poor old Stefan's out of luck.

LINDA: He can get here first thing in the morning in the quarantine launch. It always calls there.

TED: There's always the *Maria*, that's over there.

GEORGE: And likely to remain there for ever.

TED: The man said he could mend it in two days.

GEORGE: That's as good as "forever" as far as Stefan is concerned.

> LOLA *comes in with a flashlight.*

LOLA (*giving it to* LINDA): Here's the light, ma'am.

LINDA: Thank you.

> *She goes over to the balustrade and flashes the light three times.*

QUINN: Perhaps he isn't there yet.

QUINN: He's sure to be.

HILDA (*to* MARTIN): It's awfully romantic, isn't it? Being on an island and having to flash signals across the sea?

MARTIN: Yes, awfully.

ELISE: There—I thought I saw a light.

QUINN: Does he always have one handy for occasions like this?

LINDA: He'll use his bicycle lamp.

> *She flashes the light again. Everybody waits, gazing out to sea in silence.*
> *Suddenly a pin-point of light appears on the main island.*

TED: That's him.

HILDA: Is it moving?

LINDA: Hand me the glass.

> GEORGE *picks up the glass from the rail and gives it to her.*
> *Take the light and give three short flashes, then two long ones, and then three more short ones. I'll watch.*

ELISE: Let me! Oh, do let me!

LINDA: All right.

ELISE (*brandishing the flashlight*): Say when.

LINDA: Go on. Three short—now wait—now two long—now wait again—now three short. That's right.

MARTIN: Can you see?

LINDA: Yes, there, he's waving the lamp. (*She puts down the glasses and comes downstage.*) That's that.

TED: It's blowing up again.

QUINN: It's always blowing up again.

MRS. BIRLING: Come along, Elise. Bedtime.

ELISE: Oh, Mother, not yet.

MRS. BIRLING: It's after half-past ten.

HILDA: Mr. Quinn kept his promise, Linda.

LINDA: Did he? I'm so glad.

HILDA: He gave me a lovely interview.

TED: What about a drink?

GEORGE: All right.

TED: Welford?

MARTIN: Thanks.

TED: Quinn?

QUINN: No more for me, thanks.

TED: Any good asking you, Mrs. Valaine?

LINDA: No, I must go into the kitchen and arrange about breakfasts.

MRS. BIRLING: Come along, Elise. Good-night, Mrs. Valaine. Good-night, everybody.

> LOLA *comes in and takes the drink orders from* TED.
> MRS. BIRLING *and* ELISE *go off upstairs after saying good-nights to everyone.*

HILDA: Will you talk to me again to-morrow, Mr. Quinn?

QUINN: I'm afraid I shall be working all the morning.

HILDA: Just five minutes.

QUINN: We'll see.

HILDA: Well, thank you ever so much, anyhow. Good-night.

QUINN: Sleep well.

HILDA: Good-night, everybody. See you all in the morning.

TED: I hope so.

> HILDA *goes off laughing.*
> MAY *comes in.*

LINDA: You'd better put the blinds down again, May, we don't want everything to get wet.

MAY: Yes, ma'am.

LINDA (*going off to the kitchen*): Has Mamma Dangan gone home yet? I shall need her in the morning.

MAY: She's still in the kitchen, ma'am.

> LINDA *goes off.*
> MAY *begins to pull down the blinds.* LOLA *comes in with drinks.* TED *and* GEORGE *come downstage and join* QUINN. MARTIN *stands with his back turned looking over towards the main island until* MAY *lets down the blind; then he comes down and joins the others.*

TED (*to* QUINN): Are you sure you won't have a drink?

QUINN: No, thanks. I'm going to bed.

TED: Here you are, Welford. (*He gives him drink.*)

MARTIN: Thanks.

GEORGE: Poor old Stefan.

TED: I don't suppose he minds.

GEORGE: That old clubhouse is a bit gloomy, hasn't been used for years.

QUINN: It will probably fit nicely with his mood.

GEORGE: A few scorpions and vampire bats, and it'd be home from home. Cheerio, everybody.

MARTIN: Cheerio!

QUINN: Well, good-night.

TED: Did you enjoy your interview with La Garçonne?

QUINN: I now have no secrets from her.

TED: There's the sort of girl you ought to marry, Quinn.

QUINN: I know. I've been thinking very seriously about it.

GEORGE: Imagine the headlines in the *Comet*. "Local girl makes good!" "Local girl makes eminent novelist!"

TED: Now's your chance, Quinn. Her room's quite near yours. Now's your chance to clinch it. You must be pretty lonely thrashing about under that big mosquito net all by yourself.

QUINN (*severely*): I am willing to exchange banter with you boys. I am willing, even at the expense of a little dignity, to prove to you that the gulf between intellect and mere brawn is not necessarily unbridgeable. I have been at pains, during the last week or so, to make you feel at ease in my company. I have laughed, God help me, at your jokes. But there are some subjects upon which I cannot bring myself to jest. One of them is marriage. Marriage is a beautiful thing. A sacrament.

GEORGE: Nuts, Mr. Quinn!

QUINN: Thank you very much.

He goes off upstairs.

TED (*laughing*): Good old Quinn.

GEORGE: That's a swell guy.

MARTIN: Yes. He laughs at everything, doesn't he?

GEORGE: Yeah. That's what I like about him.

MARTIN: I expect he's quite right.

TED: At that he'll get caught one day. You mark my words.

MARTIN: Caught?

TED: Some dizzy little blonde will get under his skin.

MARTIN: I wonder?

TED: I've seen it happen time and time again. These cynical chaps without any illusions, they get bowled out quicker than anyone.

GEORGE: If you ask me, I believe he's got a bit of a yen for Mrs. Valaine right now.

MARTIN: Mrs. Valaine!

GEORGE: Yeah, why not? He goes and visits her most afternoons. They talk and have tea and admire the view.

MARTIN: I don't see that that means——

GEORGE: Maybe it does, maybe it doesn't, but she's not a bad looker when she's got her glasses off—just the right age for him. Red hair, too——

MARTIN: What's that got to do with it?

GEORGE (*humming*): "When a red-haired momma gets ants in the pants——"

MARTIN: Oh shut up!

GEORGE (*surprised*): What's wrong?

MARTIN: She's nice, Mrs. Valaine. It sounds rather rotten, talking about her like that.

GEORGE: I never said she wasn't nice.

TED: Don't take any notice of George. He's got a mind like a drain.

MARTIN (*forcing a smile*): All right.

GEORGE: Have another drink?

MARTIN: No, thanks.

GEORGE: Come on, just to show there's no hard feeling.

MARTIN: Just a half, then.

GEORGE: Lola!

TED: The bar's shut, I expect.

GEORGE: I'll go to the kitchen.

> *He goes off.*

TED: He's a funny chap—George. He doesn't mean half he says.

MARTIN: I feel a bit on edge to-night anyway.

TED: You're right about Mrs. Valaine. She is damned nice.

MARTIN: She was awfully kind to me when I was ill the other day.

TED: I bet she was. No nonsense about her. That's what I like.

MARTIN: You've been here before, haven't you?

TED: Yes, last year. George had an overseeing job in British Guiana and got a couple of weeks' leave, so I wangled ten days and joined up with him. It's a good spot.

MARTIN: Must be a bit monotonous all the year round.

TED: Yes.

MARTIN: I expect she's lonely.

TED (*looking at him quickly*): Yes, I expect she is.

> GEORGE *comes back with three drinks.*

GEORGE: May was just closing down.

TED: Fine.

MARTIN (*taking drink*): Thanks.

GEORGE: Well, here goes.

MARTIN: Cheerio!

TED (*to* MARTIN): Good luck!

> *They all drink.*

GEORGE: Well, that's that.

TED: No fishing to-morrow.

MARTIN: Why not?

TED: Poor old *Maria's* having her face lifted.

GEORGE: We can go a bit of a way out in the rowboat.

TED: Thank you for nothing. I wouldn't care to land anything bigger than a prawn in that little tub.

GEORGE: No spirit, that's your trouble. No guts.

TED: We might throw a line off the rocks and just sit and wait.

GEORGE: Why trouble to throw the line? Let's just sit and wait.

TED: Bed for me, anyway.

GEORGE: All right.

TED (*to* MARTIN): Coming?

MARTIN: No, I don't feel like sleeping yet.

TED: I always allow a half an hour extra. George likes bedtime stories.

GEORGE: The hell I do! Good-night.

MARTIN: Good-night.

TED: See you in the morning.

MARTIN: Fine. Good-night.

TED: Good-night.

> TED *and* GEORGE *go off upstairs.*
> MARTIN, *left alone, settles himself into his chair and lights a cigarette. A shower starts, swells rather louder and then dies down again.* LINDA *comes in from the kitchen.* MARTIN *jumps up.*

LINDA: Oh, I thought everybody had gone to bed.

MARTIN: So they have, except me.

LINDA: I see that.

MARTIN: I felt I couldn't sleep just yet.

LINDA: Do you feel all right?

MARTIN: Fine.

LINDA: Good.

MARTIN: That's an awfully pretty dress.

LINDA (*brusquely*): I'm glad you like it.

MARTIN: It looks so cool.

LINDA: It is.

MARTIN: Have you forgiven me for being so silly yesterday afternoon?

LINDA: Silly?

MARTIN: Yes. Fainting about all over your room.

LINDA: Well, you could hardly help that, could you?

MARTIN: I felt idiotic afterwards.

LINDA: Anyway, I'm glad you're all right again now.

MARTIN: I still feel a little foolish.

LINDA: You've no reason to. Good-night.

MARTIN: Good-night.

     LINDA *goes towards her room.*

MARTIN (*desperately*): I suppose you must go to bed.

LINDA (*turning*): Yes, I'm tired.

MARTIN: It's been a hard day for you, hasn't it?

LINDA: Very.

MARTIN: I wish it hadn't.

LINDA: How do you mean?

MARTIN: If you weren't so tired, you might have stayed and talked for a little.

LINDA: You ought to be in bed yourself. You need all the sleep you can get, at your age.

MARTIN: What's my age got to do with it?

LINDA: You're young, and you've been ill.

MARTIN: I'm not so terribly young.

LINDA: Aren't you?

MARTIN (*smiling*): And you're not so terribly old, if it comes to that.

LINDA: Thank you.

MARTIN: Why do you pretend to be?

LINDA: I don't pretend.

MARTIN (*offering her his case*): Will you have a cigarette?

LINDA: Very well.

> *She takes one.*

MARTIN (*lighting it*): And then will you sit down for a minute?

LINDA: Very well.

> *She sits down.*

MARTIN: It's most awfully sweet of you. I'm feeling rather miserable.

LINDA: Why?

MARTIN: I don't know, just a mood.

LINDA: You ought to get away from the tropics. You ought to go home.

MARTIN: I know.

LINDA: You need cold winds and fresher air.

MARTIN: That's not enough to go home for.

LINDA: Isn't there anyone you want to see?

MARTIN: Only my father and sister. Father's all right, but we're not exactly companions, and Edith's married. She's going to have a baby soon, I think.

LINDA: No one else?

MARTIN: No. No one else.

LINDA: I should have thought at least that you'd have a fiancée waiting to welcome you.

MARTIN: No. I was engaged once, though.

LINDA: What happened?

MARTIN: We used to quarrel rather, over little things, then I was mad about flying, and she wasn't interested in it at all, and then, just before I went out to Brazil, she broke it off.

LINDA: Did you love her?

MARTIN: I thought I did.

LINDA: Were you unhappy?

MARTIN: Yes, at first, but I got over it after a while.

LINDA: One can get over anything providing one can get away— escape.

MARTIN: Yes, I suppose one can.

LINDA: Were you her lover?

MARTIN (*startled*): What?

LINDA (*distinctly*): Were you ever her lover?

MARTIN (*after a slight pause*): Yes—once.

LINDA (*gently*): I'm sorry—please forgive me—I didn't mean to be inquisitive.

MARTIN: It wasn't because of that the engagement was broken off, it had nothing to do with it—it just sort of happened; and then, afterwards, I felt rather beastly about it and——

LINDA: Did she? Feel beastly about it, I mean.

MARTIN: No, I don't think she did.

LINDA: You're romantic, aren't you?

MARTIN: Yes, I think I must be.

LINDA: It's dangerous to be romantic.

MARTIN: Dangerous?

LINDA: Yes. It lets you down.

MARTIN: That can't be helped, can it? If you're made like that, you've just got to put up with it. I often feel it would be nice to be like Fox or Burchell—they don't seem to worry at all, they don't seem to want anything——

LINDA: What do you want?

MARTIN: I don't know. That's just it. That's what's so silly.

LINDA: Marriage?

MARTIN: No, not really. I don't think I want to be married.

LINDA: You said the other day that you hated being alone.

MARTIN: Don't let's talk about me any more.

LINDA: Why not?

MARTIN: It's dull.

LINDA: I don't find it so.

MARTIN: That's because you're kind. You are tremendously kind, you know.

LINDA (*getting up suddenly*): No, I'm not.

MARTIN: Don't go away.

LINDA: I must.

MARTIN: Just to prove that you're not kind?

LINDA: Come and have tea with me to-morrow. We'll talk some more then.

MARTIN (*rising slowly to his feet*): All right.

LINDA: Go to bed now, like a good boy.

MARTIN (*very quietly*): I'm not a boy.

LINDA (*lightly*): I'll try to remember.

MARTIN: You can't go away now, just at this moment.

LINDA: Why not?

MARTIN: It's too important.

LINDA: What do you mean?

MARTIN: You know, you know perfectly well.

LINDA: You're talking nonsense.

MARTIN: Perhaps I am. It hasn't anything to do with words
anyhow. It doesn't matter what you say or what I say.

LINDA: Good-night.

MARTIN: Good-night.

> *They stand still looking at each other.*

You see I was right, Linda Valaine.

LINDA: Even if you were right, what then?

MARTIN: Please come a little nearer.

LINDA: No.

MARTIN: Please.

> LINDA *walks up to him and very gently kisses him. His arms go
> around her, they stand there very still for a few moments. The rain is
> steadily growing louder on the roof.* LINDA *moves a little away from
> him.*

LINDA (*looking away from him*): That's all.

MARTIN: No. No, it isn't. It couldn't be.

LINDA: It must be.

MARTIN: Why do you say that?

LINDA: Please go away.

MARTIN: How can I—possibly?

LINDA (*miserably*): You don't understand.

MARTIN: What is there to understand? I love you. Isn't that
enough?

LINDA: Love.

MARTIN: Yes. There isn't any other word. When you put your
hand on my forehead yesterday, I knew it then. I knew that I
loved you. It isn't just that I want to go to bed with you, really
it isn't. It's much more. Please believe that—it's so necessary
that you should believe that.

LINDA (*with an effort*): Why is it so necessary?

132

MARTIN: And don't try to be hard any more. I heard it in your voice then. It didn't sound real a bit.

LINDA: How could you love me? You don't know anything about me.

MARTIN: Yes, I do. I know all that I want to know. Facts don't matter anyhow. One knows things inside, deep down.

LINDA (*looking at him*): Yes—that's true.

MARTIN: I know how you feel about me too.

LINDA: Do you?

MARTIN: Yes. It's part of the whole thing. It's through myself that I know you. I couldn't feel like this about anybody—about anybody in the world—if they didn't feel the same about me. You do love me, don't you?

LINDA (*softly*): Yes.

MARTIN: Linda——

> *He makes a movement towards her.*

LINDA (*holding up her hand*): No, no—please don't.

MARTIN (*stopping*): All right.

LINDA (*speaking quickly*): You said I was kind a little while ago, and it sounded, when you said it, a very lovely thing to be.

MARTIN: I think it is.

LINDA: If I let you love me it wouldn't be kind at all, it would be cruel.

MARTIN: Why? Why do you say that?

LINDA: There are too many things between us. Too many things in the way.

MARTIN: Do you love anybody else?

LINDA (*violently*): No, no—I don't. I've never loved anybody else—never in my life. And now it's too late—it's too late——

MARTIN: What do you mean? Why is it too late?

LINDA: Fifteen years ago, ten years ago, I might have been able to hold this for a while. Long enough at any rate to have made it worth while. But now it's too late. It's too late, I tell you. It's all right for you, you're young, whatever happens, however deeply you may suffer, you have time ahead of you, time to forget and change and build something new. But I have no time at all——

MARTIN: None of this is what you really mean.

LINDA: It is. I swear it.

MARTIN: You're being kind again. Kind to me. Why?

LINDA: I'm trying to save you.

MARTIN: From what?

LINDA: Humiliation.

MARTIN: What on earth do you mean?

LINDA: The humiliation of realising afterwards that you have given so much for so little. That's what I want to save you from. With all my heart I want to, but I don't believe I'm strong enough.

MARTIN: I'm not scared. I'll take the risk.

LINDA: It's my risk too.

MARTIN: You don't trust me at all, do you?

LINDA: Remember what I said just now. Promise me that whatever happens you'll remember it.

MARTIN: I promise.

LINDA: If only you'd go away, go upstairs to bed now, loving me as you do, then to-morrow leave, leave the island for good—I should be so deeply grateful.

MARTIN: You know I can't do that.

LINDA: Very well.

MARTIN: I do love you terribly. Honestly I do.

LINDA: I know. That's why I want you to go.

MARTIN: That sounds foolish to me, unreasonable.

LINDA: Yes. I expect it does.

MARTIN: This should be so wonderful, this moment. So thrilling. And yet somehow there's something wrong. I wish I knew what it was. I wish you'd tell me. You're frightened—I can see that—I'm a little frightened too. Perhaps it's the strangeness of the whole thing that's scaring us both, the suddenness of finding how we feel about each other. It's like a sort of dream to me, it has been ever since the first moment when I arrived, when you introduced me to Quinn and the others and I had several rum punches, and then you came back and showed me my room and you made a joke about the mosquito net—do you remember?

LINDA: Yes. I remember.

MARTIN: My heart was thumping, and I didn't know why a bit. I hadn't the least idea. The whole place and everyone in it seemed unreal. You seemed the most unreal of all. You see, I expected Mrs. Valaine to be an old half-caste woman with brass ear-rings. Then, when I got ill and you came to see how I was and were so sweet, and gentle, then I began to know, I began to realise. It isn't casual, this. It isn't just meeting an attractive woman and wanting to have an affair with her—I swear it isn't. You do believe that, don't you?

LINDA: Yes. I believe it.

MARTIN: It's twisted me up a good deal. I can't even look at you steadily, without trembling, and just now, a few minutes ago, when you came over to me, it was as though the world had come to an end, as though there wasn't anyone anywhere but just you and me.

LINDA: I should have liked that moment to be all. That moment when I kissed you. If you could have gone away then, suddenly, for ever, there would never be anything to prevent you loving the memory of me always.

MARTIN: I don't understand. I can't see why you're so sad, so dreadfully troubled about us loving each other. Why shouldn't it be happy? Even if only for a little while, why shouldn't it be happy?

LINDA (*very quietly—almost whispering*): Even if only for a little while.

MARTIN: Dearest—dear love.

LINDA: Yes.

MARTIN: I want you so.

LINDA: I know.

MARTIN: It's all right, isn't it?

LINDA: Yes. It's all right.

> *He takes her in his arms and kisses her, gently at first, then with more and more passion. The downpour of rain on the roof reaches a crescendo as the lights fade on the scene.*
>
> *When the lights come up again it is a few hours later. The rain has stopped, and brilliant moonlight is shining thrugh the chinks in the blinds. The verandah is empty.*
>
> MORTIMER QUINN *comes down from the stairs. He is in his pyjamas and a dressing-gown. He walks about the verandah aimlessly for a moment or two, then, observing the moonlight through the blinds, he*

goes round pulling them all up. The night outside is brilliant and still except for the ceaseless chirruping of tree frogs. He draws a chair up to the balustrade and, after lighting a cigarette, settles himself comfortably in it with his feet up on the rail. Suddenly he becomes alert and listens intently for a moment. Then, jumping to his feet, he picks up the binoculars and scans the sea between the island and the mainland. He puts down the binoculars again and looks sharply over towards LINDA's *apartments. He snaps his fingers indecisively for a second, then, very quietly and swiftly, he goes off upstairs again. The stage remains empty for a little while; then, gradually, above the noise of the insects and frogs, the chug-chug of a motor launch is heard.*

CURTAIN

ACT III: Scene I

It is LINDA'S *sitting-room. The time is about 4 a.m.*

The moonlight is still strong and is streaming into the room. The rocks just beyond are silhouetted black against the sea.

When the curtain rises the room is empty. Presently STEFAN *comes stealthily in through the bead curtains. He is carrying his accordion, slung round his shoulders. He stands silently in the centre of the room, gazing at* LINDA'S *bedroom door, then, savagely and wildly, he begins to play. There is no melody in his playing. Just a series of crashing discords. He stops dead for a moment or two, and then goes on again.*

LINDA *comes out of the bedroom. She is wearing a dressing-gown over her nightgown. She switches on the light by the door. She stands staring at him, and he stops playing.*

LINDA (*quietly*): Stefan! Have you gone mad?

> STEFAN *plays a little run on the accordion.*

Please go out of my room.

> STEFAN *laughs and plays another little run.*

Go at once. Do you hear me!

> STEFAN *laughs louder and plays some more chords.*

(*Going up to him.*) You're drunk!

> STEFAN *shakes his head and goes on playing.*

(*Her voice rising.*) Go away—go away!

> STEFAN *walks about the room playing louder and louder. Suddenly he comes up close to her, still playing, and spits full into her face. She wipes her face slowly with the sleeve of her dressing-gown. Finally he comes to a standstill opposite her, stops playing, and quietly unstraps the accordion from his shoulders. They stand silent, looking at each other for a few moments.*

STEFAN: I will stay.

LINDA (*tonelessly*): Very well.

STEFAN: We will talk, eh?

LINDA: I am very tired.

STEFAN: Poor Linda. Poor tired Linda.

LINDA: Oh God! (*She rubs at her face again with her sleeve.*)

STEFAN: You thought to be very clever, didn't you? To leave me alone over there, with no boat.

LINDA (*in a high matter-of-fact voice, obviously calculated to reach the bedroom*): The launch broke down, Stefan.

STEFAN: You are lying.

LINDA: You must not speak like that, Stefan. I won't have it.

STEFAN: No, ma'am. No, ma'am. I am sorry, ma'am. Yes, ma'am. I am indeed sorry.

LINDA: I've warned you before about being drunk. The next time it happens I shall dismiss you.

STEFAN (*with a sneer*): It will never happen again, ma'am. Never, never again.

LINDA (*with a gesture of supplication, imploring him to go*): Very well, Stefan. Now take that ridiculous accordion away and go to bed.

STEFAN: I think I will stay.

LINDA: Go at once, and you'd better make yourself some strong black coffee in the kitchen on your way.

STEFAN: You are frightened now. I have never seen you frightened before. Perhaps it is because you are so tired.

LINDA: Please go immediately, Stefan.

STEFAN (*patting the chaise-longue*): Sit down here, like you always do, quiet and still, then you will not be tired any more.

He takes her by the arm. She shrinks away from him.

LINDA: Please don't touch me.

STEFAN (*gripping her wrist*): Why should I not touch you? Why should I not touch you as much as I wish?

He forces her down on to the chaise-longue and stands over her, still holding her wrist.

LINDA (*whispering*): You're hurting me.

STEFAN: I am sorry.

He suddenly releases her hand and, seizing her in his arms, forces his mouth on to hers. His eyes, all the time, are staring fixedly at the bedroom door. LINDA *struggles for an instant in his arms and then lies still. He throws her back on to the cushions and stands away from her.*

STEFAN (*clearly and loudly*): Now go back to your lover. Your young baby lover. Hold his body tight and close, as you have held mine so often——

LINDA (*agonised*): Stop, stop—please—I implore you——

STEFAN: Young love is very thrilling, isn't it? For a woman who is tired! For a woman who is no longer young herself——

LINDA (*whispering frantically*): Go away—Stefan—go away——

STEFAN (*still louder*): I have a right to be here.

LINDA (*getting up and coming to him*): Stefan—Stefan——

STEFAN: All these years. So many hours of so many years I have been here with you. Why should I not be here now?

LINDA *clings to him and tries to put her hand over his mouth. He pushes it away.*

Why do you not have the shutters closed, my Linda dear? It is so quiet and good in here with the shutters closed. Do you remember that night——

LINDA (*urgently*): I'll do anything you say. I'll never see him again. I swear it—I swear I'll never see him again if only you'll go away now.

STEFAN: Why are you whispering, Linda? Who is there near to hear what we say to each other?

LINDA: Go away now—please, please—be kind—just this once—come back in a little while—ten minutes only—come back in ten minutes and I'll be alone—I swear I will. See, I'm on my knees to you——

She slithers down on to her knees at his feet.

STEFAN (*pulling her up*): I remember the first time you wore that pretty dressing-gown. It was when I had been away—just like to-night—but then you wore it to welcome me back.

LINDA (*whispering frantically*): Please, please, Stefan—for God's sake—don't—don't——

STEFAN: He is a lucky little boy. Lucky to find a woman so warm, so tender, who knows so much of love. Be gentle with him at first, my dear—do not show him too much delight—he will only faint again. His poor young heart will stop beating, he will be lost in your arms as he was lost in the jungle. The scent of your hair will give him a fever, a fever too strong for a nice young Englishman. Do take care with him, my Linda. Let him think sweetly of you. Let him feel you a little cold, just at first, a little surprised at his passion. This will be only kind because he is such a nice young lover. He would not understand you as I know you, as I have known you for so long. He would shudder away from you——

LINDA (*the tears are running down her face*): I see—I see what you're doing.

STEFAN: He would like to feel in his inside that you were lonely, a lonely woman without love, that by giving you his body, his brave, nice young body, he was doing for you a favour. That is how Englishmen like to feel, because it makes for them a romance. He would like to go away from you with a sadness and write back letters to you from his home—not very many, just a few, to show that he was a gentleman, just as he would give me a tip and perhaps shake my hand. Then after a little he would write once more and say good-bye because he was going to be married, and that he would never forget you, and that he hoped very much that you would be happy.

LINDA (*quietly, in a dead voice*): That is enough now, Stefan.

STEFAN: You are a fool, my Linda.

LINDA: That is enough now, Stefan.

STEFAN (*violently*): Come here.

LINDA: No.

> STEFAN *drags her into his arms again and kisses her brutally. She stands rigid. Then he shoves her with all his force in the direction of the bedroom. She staggers against the chaise-longue and just manages to save herself from falling.*

STEFAN (*almost shrieking*): Go back to him! Go back to your little English gentleman. Slip into his arms. Press him on to your breast, with my kisses on your lips and my spittle on your face——

> *He spits at her again. She moves, and it goes on her dressing-gown. She stands still for a moment with her head down; then she sinks on to the chaise-longue.*

> STEFAN *is standing trembling and watching the bedroom door.* MARTIN *comes out. He is wearing only a shirt and trousers and*

slippers. He is carrying his coat in his left hand. It trails on the three steps as he comes down them. His face is lifeless, and he moves slowly across the room as though he were walking in his sleep. He goes out without looking once at either LINDA *or* STEFAN. *The bead curtains jangle into place behind him.*

LINDA *sits dully looking after him.* STEFAN *snatches up the accordion and plays a wild fanfare of chords.* LINDA *gets up very wearily and goes towards the bedroom.* STEFAN *flings down the accordion with a crash and darts after her. He catches her just as she reaches the door.*

STEFAN (*breathlessly, almost grunting*): Linda—Linda——

LINDA (*looking at him*): I wish that you were dead.

STEFAN (*clutching her hand*): No—you must not say that—Linda——

LINDA (*without emotion*): I wish that you were blind and dead and deep down under the earth. Out of sight for ever.

STEFAN (*pressing her hand to his face*): No, no—Linda——

LINDA: Let go of my hand.

STEFAN *lets go of her hand. She comes down the steps, brushing past him as though he weren't there, and walks over to the corner cupboard. She takes out the brandy bottle and a glass and pours herself out a little. She drinks it thoughtfully, and then puts the bottle back in the cupboard and the glass on the desk.* STEFAN *watches her miserably. She walks over to the accordion and taps it with her foot.*

LINDA: Take this away.

STEFAN: I will take it, Linda.

LINDA: Thank you.

STEFAN: I have loved you so much, Linda.

LINDA: Please go away. You have done what you wanted to do. You can go to bed now.

STEFAN: Linda—please, Linda——

LINDA: What do you want?

STEFAN: You will forgive me. Not now, perhaps you will not forgive me now—but soon——?

LINDA (*looking at him wonderingly*): Forgive you?

STEFAN: I was crazy, Linda—I was crazy with pain that you did not love me any more. It has been going round in my head for days.

LINDA: I have never loved you.

STEFAN: You say that because you are so angry.

LINDA: No. It is quite true.

STEFAN: For seven years we have been together.

LINDA: I have never loved you.

STEFAN: You belong to me. We belong to each other.

LINDA: No, Stefan.

STEFAN: What was it, then? This that has been between us for so
long?

LINDA: Something that I needed. Something that I needed, or
thought I needed, enough to sacrifice my pride for. Something
that has humiliated me deeply and for ever.

STEFAN: No, no—that is not true.

LINDA: Yes. I can see it clearly now.

STEFAN: This young Englishman. It is he who has made you
think that way.

LINDA: Yes.

STEFAN: Do you love him then so much?

LINDA: Yes.

STEFAN: You are a fool.

LINDA: Yes, I see that too.

STEFAN: He will go away and leave you.

LINDA: He will never look at me again.

STEFAN: If I had not come to-night. He would still have gone
away.

LINDA: Yes.

STEFAN: You are too old for him. Too old in love.

LINDA: This is the first time I have ever loved anyone.

STEFAN (*wildly*): That is not true! That is a lie you are saying!

LINDA: Would you like me to tell you how much I love him?
How much he means to me?

STEFAN: No, no——

He makes a movement towards her.

LINDA: Stay where you are. Stay quiet. You have made enough
noise to-night.

STEFAN (*nearly breaking down*): You will forgive me one day—
please say you will forgive me.

LINDA: I only asked for a little while, because that was all I could
possibly have. I told him it was only for a little while.

STEFAN (*flaring up again*): Did you tell him about me? Did you tell him about you and me? The nights we've been together? The love words we've said?

LINDA: No. I was too ashamed.

STEFAN (*pitifully*): Ashamed! So ashamed?

LINDA: I couldn't have looked into his eyes and even thought of you without my heart turning sick inside me.

STEFAN: I know you cannot mean these things. It is only because you are so angry. I know it is only because you are so angry.

LINDA: I am not angry.

STEFAN: If you are not angry, then you will understand. You will understand a little how I felt. Why I was so bad——

LINDA: How could I have ever let you touch me!

STEFAN (*wretchedly*): Oh, Linda——

LINDA: I didn't know. I thought that was all there was.

STEFAN: There is no more, for me.

LINDA (*contemptuously*): You?

STEFAN: You are all I have. You are all I love in the world.

LINDA: How horrible! How loathsome!

STEFAN: It is true that I love you.

LINDA: As a dog loves a bitch in the gutter.

STEFAN (*wildly*): Do not say that! Do not say things so wicked!

LINDA: For God's sake, get out!

STEFAN: This Englishman. Is he so noble? So pure in his heart? So much finer than me? When so quickly he runs to your bed——

LINDA: Don't you see? Can't you understand that this is something deep and tender and dear to me, something that you've smashed, destroyed utterly? I love him. Listen carefully, if you can ever hear. I love him. I love him. I love him.

STEFAN: You will never forget him?

LINDA: Never. Until the day I die.

STEFAN: He will be here always, between us?

LINDA: He will be here always.

STEFAN (*appealingly*): Linda—please, Linda——

LINDA: If I could forget him, I would. I would give everything I have in the world if I could be able to forget him. If he had

died it would be easier. If he had loved me for a little and
grown tired it would be easier. But now never—never——

Her voice breaks.

STEFAN (*tenderly*): Perhaps that is not quite true—perhaps in
time— long time, Linda—it will be better——

LINDA: It was when he fainted that I knew—when I took him in
my arms. It was as though the world had come to an end—
that's what he said to-night—To-night! Is it still to-night?

She starts to wander about the room. STEFAN *watches her silently.*
She goes on talking, to herself, as though he were not there at all.

I tried so hard to be honest—to warn him that there was
something strange and horrible quite near, all round us, that it
would never possibly be as he wanted it—as I wanted it—I wasn't
strong enough to keep him away, and I should have been. I
should have pretended I didn't care a bit, that it was only just
amusing, a sort of silly little flirtation. Then when he went away
nothing would have been spoiled. I should have been able to love
his love for me, alone, hold it to myself always. But now it's too
late—it's too late. He's lying up there in his room cutting me out
of his heart, cutting me out of his memory. He's calling himself a
fool, a bloody fool. Laughing bitterly at himself for getting mixed
up with a cheap middle-aged hotel keeper, who's the mistress of
her own head waiter——

She stops still for a moment and looks at STEFAN; *then she laughs*
harshly.

Poor Stefan. Asking to be forgiven. (*She pauses for a moment.*) I will
see that your wages are paid up until the end of the month, but
you had better leave to-morrow.

STEFAN (*warningly*): Linda——!

LINDA (*her voice rising*): Go away to-morrow, do you hear? Go
back to the mines, to the prisons, to the scum you came
from——

STEFAN: I will kill you if you speak like that!

LINDA: Go away and die.

STEFAN: Do not hurt me so. I will kill you if you hurt me so.

LINDA: Go away and lick your wounds like the senseless animal that you are. Get out of my sight. Get out of my sight, I tell you. Go away and die!

She walks swiftly into the bedroom and shuts the door behind her. There is the sound of the key turning in the lock.
STEFAN *gives a loud cry and rushes up to the door. He batters on it with his fists, whimpering and crying. Presently he sinks down on to the top step, weeping hopelessly.*

STEFAN (*whispering brokenly through the door*): Please, Linda, you will forgive me one day. You are all I have—all I love in the world——

He drags himself to his feet and comes slowly down the three steps. He comes to the centre of the room and then turns and stands there looking out to sea. He looks once more, despairingly, at LINDA'S *door. He takes his coat off and lays it gently on the bottom step. He looks all round the room as though he were trying to memorise every detail of it. He picks up the accordion and lovingly plays a few notes on it; then he puts it down again, giving it a little pat with his hand as he does so. He gives a small shudder as though he were suddenly cold, then, very swiftly, he goes out on to the verandah and climbs over the balustrade. For a moment he can be seen standing on the rock, silhouetted against the sea; then he jumps and disappears from sight.*
The lights fade.

Scene II

The scene is the verandah again. It is about eight o'clock in the morning. The blinds are all up, as it is not raining. The breakfast tables are all ready laid along by the left-hand balustrade.

MORTIMER QUINN *comes down from upstairs, smoking a cigarette. He goes over and perches himself on the rail, looking out over the sea.* LOLA *enters from the kitchen with a tray of cruets. These she places methodically on the different tables.*

QUINN: Good morning, Lola.
LOLA: Good morning, sir.
QUINN: Nobody down yet?

LOLA: Mr. Fox and Mr. Burchell, sir. They are in the pool.

QUINN: Did Stefan get back all right?

LOLA: No, sir.

QUINN: What about the Quarantine launch? That should have got him here by half-past seven, shouldn't it?

LOLA: It passed by on the way to Baila. It did not stop.

QUINN: Oh, I see.

> LOLA *goes out.*
>
> TED *and* GEORGE *come up the steps in swimming trunks and bath robes.*

TED: Hallo!

GEORGE: Why didn't you come and swim?

QUINN: Too much effort. How was it?

GEORGE: Fine.

TED: We've got news.

QUINN: News?

TED: Strange doings.

QUINN: Good God! What?

GEORGE: The old *Maria's* back.

TED: Nobody knows why she came. Nobody knows how she came. We asked Farrell—he's still tinkering at the big launch. The poor old girl must have done the trip all by herself in the middle of the night.

GEORGE: I always said that dame had spirit.

TED: We left her yesterday, a derelict, over on the other side, having done her damnedest to drown us——

GEORGE: And here she is at anchor, bouncing up and down as though nothing had happened.

QUINN: Very mysterious.

TED: Have you had breakfast?

QUINN: No, I'm just going to.

TED: Come on, George—I'm hungry.

GEORGE: Was it you banging about in the passage last night?

QUINN: Certainly not. I slept like a new-born babe.

GEORGE: Sounds lousy.

TED: We thought we heard——

GEORGE: *I* thought *I* heard—you were snoring like a hog—I thought I heard someone fall down——

QUINN: Why you should imagine I spend my nights falling down in the passage, I can't think.

TED: No offence. No offence. We only thought you might have been drunk again.

QUINN: Go away, both of you.

GEORGE: Come on, Ted, Uncle's a bit grouchy.

They both run off upstairs.

LOLA *comes on again, this time with* QUINN'S *coffee and orange juice. She puts it down on his table.*

QUINN: Thank you, Lola.

He flicks his cigarette over the rail and sits down at the table.
LOLA *goes off again.*

MARTIN *comes down from upstairs. He is carrying a suitcase in either hand. He puts them down by the door. His face looks agonised, but he is obviously making every effort not to display any emotion at all.*

QUINN: Hallo!

MARTIN: Hallo!

QUINN: You're not leaving, are you?

MARTIN: Yes.

QUINN: Oh, I'm so sorry. I didn't know.

MARTIN: This place doesn't agree with me, really—it's too hot and sticky—I'm frightened of the fever coming back again—I think I'd be better at home.

QUINN: Cooler winds and fresher air.

MARTIN (*jumping*): What!

QUINN: What's the matter?

MARTIN: Nothing.

QUINN: Why did you start like that?

MARTIN: I don't know. I feel a bit jumpy this morning. I didn't sleep very well.

QUINN: Come and sit down and have some coffee.

MARTIN: No, thanks, I don't want any.

QUINN: I think you'd better, really. It'll pull you together.

MARTIN: I'm all right.

QUINN: You look far from all right.

MARTIN (*desperately*): I've got to go. I must go.

QUINN: The launch doesn't leave until nine-thirty, anyhow, and it's broken down. They've probably made some arrangements about getting one over from the mainland, but it certainly won't be here yet, even if they have.

MARTIN (*trying to control himself*): Oh—oh, I see.

QUINN: So you'd much better come and sit down and relax.

MARTIN: Perhaps I could get a little boat and row or something.

QUINN: It would be very foolish to attempt it in your present condition.

MARTIN (*quivering*): I'm all right, I tell you.

QUINN (*gently*): Come on. Stick by me.

> *He gets up quickly and goes to* MARTIN. MARTIN *shrinks away from him.* QUINN *puts his arm round his shoulders and leads him to the table.*

MARTIN (*sinking down at the table*): Thanks.

QUINN (*pouring him out some coffee*): Here.

MARTIN: Thanks awfully—I'm sorry to be so stupid—I do feel rather rotten.

QUINN: Do you know if there's a boat sailing to-day.

MARTIN: No.

QUINN: I'll come over to the main island with you, and we'll find out.

MARTIN: No, no—please don't trouble—I can manage——

QUINN: I have to go anyway. I have to send some cables and buy carbon paper and collect some prints at the Kodak place—I've been putting off going for days—too lazy—this is a very good excuse.

MARTIN: It's very decent of you.

QUINN: If there isn't a boat, we'll make a night of it and stay at the Royal. We'll dine and go to a cinema. (*He sees that* MARTIN *is on the verge of breaking down.*) Here—have a cigarette.

MARTIN (*taking one*): Thanks.

QUINN: Between you and me I'm getting a bit sick of this place myself. It's rather nerve-racking. The rain and the insects and the feeling of being shut away from everywhere.

MARTIN: Yes—I——

QUINN (*quickly*): Don't trouble to answer, I'll go on talking. Just concentrate on your coffee and getting yourself well in hand. Stick at this table with me when the others come down. I never speak to anyone at breakfast anyhow, if I can help it. I have a writer's privilege of being slightly disagreeable. I'll keep them away.

MARTIN (*with his head down*): I'm very grateful.

QUINN: Never mind about that.

MARTIN (*still not looking up*): You know a lot, don't you?

QUINN: Yes, I know a lot.

MARTIN: You know that it's nothing to do with fever or heat or insects that I'm leaving?

QUINN: Yes, I know that.

MARTIN: I've been a bloody fool.

QUINN: Perhaps you have, a bit, but you'll get over worrying about it in a little while.

MARTIN: Not for a long time.

QUINN: I can't be much of a comfort, I'm afraid, although I'd do all I could to make you mind a little less. I could reel off a few philosophical phrases, stinking with wisdom. Being a dealer in words, that sort of thing comes naturally to me, but they wouldn't be any use.

MARTIN (*with an attempt at a smile*): No, I'm afraid they wouldn't.

QUINN: I could kick myself, though, for not having warned you.

MARTIN: Warned me?

QUINN: I knew how things were.

MARTIN: Does everybody know?

QUINN: I shouldn't think anybody even remotely suspected.

MARTIN: How did you find out?

QUINN (*smiling*): Good luck always pursues me in my researches. I happen on strange chancy little clues. Small unconscious gestures, an over-casual intonation, the dead blandness of people's eyes when they have some tawdry secret to conceal. . . . It's all very interesting, if faintly discouraging.

MARTIN (*looking down again*): Discouraging?

QUINN: Yes. You see I always affect to despise human nature. My role in life is so clearly marked. Cynical, detached, unscrupulous, an ironic observer and recorder of other people's passions. It is a nice façade to sit behind, but a trifle bleak. Perhaps I am misunderstood! I often toy with that idea.

Perhaps I have suffered a great deal and am really a very lonely, loving spirit.

MARTIN: You're certainly very considerate.

QUINN: When you are as fundamentally selfish as I am, you have room to be considerate.

MARTIN (*trying to smile again*): I see.

QUINN: What discourages me most is confusion.

MARTIN: Confusion?

QUINN: The dreary capacity of the human race for putting the right labels on the wrong boxes. People go blithely on their little journeys with all the things they really want in the hold. Right down in the bottom of the ship where they can't possibly get at them without a great deal of trouble. So they just don't take the trouble and make do with what they've got in the cabin. That's why most people's minds are dressed wrong for every situation they encounter.

MARTIN: How did you find out?

QUINN: About Stefan and Mrs. Valaine?

MARTIN: Yes.

QUINN: I wander about at night. I have a very unpleasant character.

MARTIN: I see.

QUINN: It's a tragic story, for them both.

MARTIN: It's horrible.

QUINN: Don't think about it. Wait until you can view it in clearer perspective. You're too close now. Too tied up. Try to put it out of your mind.

MARTIN: If only I could. Why didn't you warn me?

QUINN: Would it have been any use?

MARTIN: I don't know.

QUINN: It didn't seem to be any of my business.

MARTIN: It wouldn't have made such a good story anyhow, if I'd known——

QUINN (*with a little laugh*): Splendid! That's much better.

MARTIN: I'm sorry—that was beastly of me.

QUINN: Don't be silly. I'm here for you to kick against. I'm invulnerable, undentable! Kick away all you like. Snap out of your deep romantic despair and be a man, my son. Take the mood from me. Even if it isn't quite true, it will carry you a little way on your journey. Cry later on, when you're alone. We can all cry when we are alone. But you're not alone now. I'm here, full of resource. I'll entertain you, jolly songs and stories—I'll keep your mind clicking until I get you on to that boat if it kills me!

MARTIN (*very quietly*): I think you're the nicest man I've ever known.

QUINN (*sharply*): Shut up.

MARTIN (*with sudden anger*): Why should it be like this? Is everything that looks lovely and true on the surface so vile and rotten underneath?

QUINN: Don't romanticise unduly. Look at the truth. Never mind about her. Never mind about him. Look at the truth in yourself. What was it that was so lovely and true? The natural physical longing inside yourself for an emotional outlet. You are, I should imagine, temperamentally fastidious. Too fastidious to be able to enjoy the unglamorous sexual buccaneering indulged in by most boys of your age. There's nothing so lovely and true in that particular restraint. It's just a biological fact. Don't kid yourself. Look at facts first, clearly and without illusion, before you dress them and paint them up and set them in romantic highlights. Take stock of the circumstances and the atmosphere that fooled you into feeling so deeply. Strong moonlight. A small island, so easily enchanted if you care to forget the disadvantages. The scents and sounds of a tropical night. A lonely woman richly endowed with all the qualities your senses need. Ripe, perhaps a little over-ripe. Warm and wise in experience. A trap for the young and unwary——

MARTIN: Please don't say any more——

QUINN: Every nerve in your body is aching with unhappiness, I know that perfectly well, you have been shocked and humiliated unbearably. But it has nothing to do with love. Love has different pains, deeper agonies. You have the capacity for loving with all your heart one day. Don't betray that by even remembering this confused, sordid little episode.

MARTIN: It was more than that. I swear it was. It could have been more than that.

QUINN: Never. The time values were wrong. Time is a very important factor. She knew that, I expect, somewhere at the back of her mind—she's not a fool. But she allowed herself to be swept away too easily. She was confused too. She lost her head and snatched too eagerly. Poor thing.

MARTIN: I hate her.

QUINN: Not even that. In quite a little while you'll be able to afford to be sorry for her. Then you'll forget her.

MARTIN: Will it be as easy as that?

QUINN (*firmly*): Yes. If you're wise.

MARTIN: I'm not wise.

QUINN: You will be, after this.

MARTIN: I wonder.

QUINN: Next time, be sure of what you want. Go out only for what you know you can get. Don't try to smear your physical desire with luminous paint. It rubs off too quickly, and then the whole thing looks cock-eyed, supremely ridiculous, like a pleasure park in the early morning: orange peel and paper bags and garbage.

MARTIN: I'll do my best.

QUINN (*smiling*): Second best is frequently better, and far less exhausting.

> LOLA *comes in with two plates of eggs and bacon. She brings them to the table.*

QUINN: Mr. Welford is having breakfast at my table this morning.

LOLA: Yes, sir.

QUINN: Bring some fresh coffee, will you?

LOLA: Yes, sir.

> *She goes out again as——*
> MRS. BIRLING *and* ELISE *come down from upstairs.* MRS. BIRLING *goes straight to her table and sits down.* ELISE *goes to the top of the steps and looks up at the sky.*

MRS BIRLING: Good morning.

QUINN: Good morning.

MRS BIRLING: Good morning, Mr. Welford.

MARTIN: Good morning.

QUINN (*softly to* MARTIN, *with a smile*): Well, that's over.

ELISE: There isn't a cloud, it's going to be lovely.

MRS BIRLING: Come and sit down, dear.

ELISE (*coming over to the table*): I wish I'd got up earlier now and bathed before breakfast.

MRS BIRLING: You know what happened last time you bathed before breakfast.

ELISE (*petulantly*): Oh, Mother——

MRS BIRLING: You went all to pieces for the rest of the day.

> LOLA *brings in the* BIRLINGS' *breakfast.* HILDA JAMES *comes in brightly.*

HILDA: Good morning, everybody.

MRS BIRLING: Good morning.

HILDA: I've been up for hours. I went for a walk, right along that path on the way to the caves. How are you, Mr. Quinn?

QUINN: Liverish, thank you. Very liverish.

MRS BIRLING: There now. There *is* something liverish about this place.

HILDA (*coming to* QUINN's *table*): I've changed my mind after talking to you last night.

QUINN: Completely?

HILDA (*whispering*): I mean about my play.

QUINN: Oh, I see.

HILDA: She's not going to commit suicide at all.

QUINN: Perhaps you're right.

HILDA: She's going to have a scene with him, saying good-bye and everything, and then she's going away all alone.

QUINN: Poor thing.

HILDA: It's better, isn't it? I mean it's sort of more like real life?

QUINN (*drily*): Much more.

> *There is a slight pause.* QUINN *devotes himself to his breakfast.*

HILDA: How are you this morning, Mr Welford?

MARTIN (*with an effort*): Fine, thank you.

HILDA (*moving away to her own table*): We must all have a lovely swim later on.

> LOLA *enters with her breakfast at the same moment that* GEORGE

and TED *come down from upstairs. They have dressed in shirts and trousers and smarmed their hair down.*

TED: Good morning, good morning, good morning.

MRS BIRLING: Good morning.

GEORGE: Lola. Bring us food. A lot of food.

LOLA: Yes, sir.

    She goes off.

TED: Hallo, Welford!

MARTIN: Hallo!

GEORGE: Mr. Quinn, would you be very kind and write in my autograph book?

QUINN: No.

GEORGE: Thank you so much, I haven't got Mussolini either.

TED: He hasn't even got an autograph book.

ELISE (*laughing*): Oh dear, you are silly, you really are.

HILDA: Is the launch mended yet?

TED: Farrell's still working on it. He plans to have it ready by August Bank Holiday.

GEORGE: God, that's only two months. I shall be able to have my baby in the old country after all.

    They both sit down at their table. MAY *comes in from the kitchen and goes down the steps to the landing stage.* LOLA *comes in with breakfast for* GEORGE *and* TED.

HILDA (*conversationally*): It was fun last night, wasn't it?

TED: How do you mean?

GEORGE: Did we miss anything?

HILDA: I mean the dancing and everything, like a party.

MRS BIRLING: I hope Mrs. Hall-Fenton and the girls got home all right.

ELISE: Oh, I'd forgotten. Is Stefan back?

TED: Haven't seen him.

GEORGE: It must have been him that brought back the *Maria*.

TED: I never thought of that.

GEORGE: Well, if it was, where is he?

HILDA: We'll ask Lola.

MRS BIRLING: Don't eat so quickly, Elise. It'll only give you indigestion.

ELISE: Oh, Mother!

*Suddenly from the direction of the landing stage there comes a loud
shriek. Everybody jumps.*

GEORGE: What the hell's that?

TED (*jumping to his feet*): Someone's hurt!

There is another loud shriek. At this everybody jumps up. MAY *comes
running wildly up the steps, screaming violently. Her face is distorted
with terror. She rushes off into the kitchen, still shrieking.* GEORGE
and TED *dash off down the steps, followed by* HILDA JAMES.

MRS BIRLING: What on earth is it? What on earth has happened.

ELISE: Come on, Mother.

ELISE drags MRS. BIRLING off down the steps after the others.
QUINN *and* MARTIN *stare at each other.*

MARTIN (*making a movement to go*): Oh God! You don't think——

QUINN (*sharply*): Stay where you are. Sit down.

He pushes him into his chair. LINDA *comes on from the left. Her face
is dead white and quite expressionless.*

LINDA: What's the matter? What's happened?

She goes swiftly towards the steps. QUINN *intercepts her.*

QUINN: Don't go.

LINDA: Let me pass, please.

QUINN (*firmly*): Don't go. (*He catches her arm.*) Don't go. Whatever it is, it has nothing to do with you. Stay here until I come
back.

LINDA: But I must——

QUINN: You must not! It has nothing to do with you. Remember
that. It has nothing whatever to do with you. Stay here.

He goes quickly down the steps.
LINDA *stands still, looking after him, then she turns towards*
MARTIN. *She stares at him beseechingly for a moment, but he does
not look up. She comes slowly down to his table.*

LINDA: Martin.

MARTIN *doesn't answer.*

(*Pitifully.*) Martin—please——

*She moves slowly away from him again. Her eyes are filled with
tears. She stands by the balustrade and leans her head wearily
against one of the poles supporting the roof. She has her back to him
and is looking out to sea.*

(*In a whisper.*) Good-bye, Martin.

> MARTIN *at last looks up, but she doesn't see him.* QUINN *comes up the steps. He goes to* LINDA.

QUINN (*gently*): I think you'd better go back to your room.

LINDA (*tonelessly*): What is it?

QUINN: Stefan has been drowned.

LINDA: Drowned!

> *She starts to go towards the steps.* QUINN *again stops her.*

QUINN: I shouldn't go if I were you. Really I shouldn't. The sharks have torn him to bits. It's pretty horrible.

LINDA (*slowly*): Oh—I see.

QUINN: Please go to your room, before they all come up.

LINDA: Yes. Perhaps that would be better. Thank you. Thank you very much for being so considerate.

> *She goes towards the door on the left; then she turns and sees* MARTIN'S *suitcases. She looks once more at him. He is still sitting at the table with his hand over his eyes.* LINDA'S *face suddenly hardens. She speaks in a harsh cold voice.*

LINDA: I must see about engaging a new head waiter.

> *She goes out.*

CURTAIN

SOUTH SEA BUBBLE

A comedy in three Acts

To

VIVIEN

with my love

NOËL

South Sea Bubble was first produced in London at the Lyric Theatre, Shaftesbury Avenue, on 25 April 1956. It was presented by H. M. Tennent Ltd, with the following cast:

JOHN BLAIR-KENNEDY ("Boffin")	Arthur Macrae
CAPTAIN CHRISTOPHER MORTLOCK	Peter Barkworth
SIR GEORGE SHOTTER	Ian Hunter
LADY ALEXANDRA SHOTTER	Vivien Leigh
PUNALO ALANI	Alan Webb
SANYAMO	William Peacock
EDWARD HONEY	John Moore
CUCKOO HONEY	Joyce Carey
ADMIRAL TURLING	Nicholas Grimshaw
MRS. TURLING	Daphne Newton
ROBERT FROME	Eric Phillips
HALI ALANI	Ronald Lewis

Directed by WILLIAM CHAPPELL
Settings by PETER SNOW

The action of the play passes on the island of Samolo, a British possession in the Pacific Ocean.

TIME: The Present.

ACT I

Scene I. *The verandah of Government House. Evening.*
Scene II. *The same. A few minutes later.*

ACT II

Scene I. *The same. A few hours later.*
Scene II. *Hali Alani's house. Later the same night.*

ACT III

Scene I. *The verandah. The next morning.*
Scene II. *The same. A few hours later.*

ACT I: Scene I

The verandah of Government House, Pendarla.

On the audience's left are double doors leading to the hall and the main living-rooms of the house. On the Right, the verandah continues at an angle. At the far end of this angle, out of sight, there are steps leading down into the garden.

The view of the bay and the mountains is spectacular and the tops of tropical trees and foliage can be seen below the verandah rail. The verandah is furnished with luxurious garden furniture in bright colours.

When the curtain rises it is evening, a little while before sunset.

CAPTAIN CHRISTOPHER MORTLOCK, *the Governor's A.D.C., comes on, followed by* JOHN BLAIR-KENNEDY.

CHRISTOPHER *is a nice-looking young man in the late twenties.* BLAIR-KENNEDY (Boffin) *is a novelist of some repute. He is an attractive man and might be anywhere between thirty-five and forty-five.*

CHRISTOPHER: I expect you'd like a drink before you see your room?

BOFFIN: I most certainly should. I'm still shaking like a leaf after that landing.

CHRISTOPHER: Coming in over those mountains is always a bit tricky.

BOFFIN: It's an eccentric little airfield, isn't it? The first one I have ever seen with corrugated runways.

CHRISTOPHER: H.E.'s been agitating for them to do something about it for months. The Samolans aren't very good at engineering.

BOFFIN: So it would seem.

CHRISTOPHER (*at the drinks table*): What would you like? There's gin, whisky, rum or kala-kala.

BOFFIN: What's kala-kala?

CHRISTOPHER: It's a sort of native vodka. They make it out of plantain roots. They tread the roots into a pulp, which they mix with coconut water and then ferment the whole thing.

BOFFIN: I think that for the moment I would prefer some ordinary whisky that nobody's trodden on. I don't believe in going native too soon.

CHRISTOPHER: Right. (*He proceeds to mix a whisky and soda.*) Lady Alexandra will be furious that your plane was on time. She hoped that it would be delayed so that she could get to meet you herself.

BOFFIN: It was a sweet thought, but one more hour with all those vomiting Chinese children and I should have shot myself.

CHRISTOPHER: Children are a nuisance in a plane, aren't they?

BOFFIN: Frankly—yes. These, being Chinese children, were a little special. Their general behaviour convinced me that all that well-known Oriental imperturbability must be a habit acquired in later life.

CHRISTOPHER (*handing* BOFFIN *his drink, then glancing at his watch*): The Women's Federation meeting must be over by now. She should be here at any minute.

BOFFIN: She has to do a great deal of that sort of thing, I suppose?

CHRISTOPHER: Oh, yes. She made a flying tour of all the other islands a few weeks ago—no less than twenty-nine speeches in four days, it was a terrific success. At one place they nearly tore the aeroplane to pieces just before the take-off.

BOFFIN: Very gratifying. Have you been out here long?

CHRISTOPHER: Three years. I was here with Sir Hilary and Lady Blaise for the last part of their term.

BOFFIN: What were they like?

CHRISTOPHER: Quite nice really, but a bit sticky. Sir George and Lady Alexandra are very different.

BOFFIN: Is Sir George popular?

CHRISTOPHER: He's wonderful on the administrative side, down-to-earth and no nonsense. The Samolans like that. They don't quite approve of his politics of course, but they respect him all the same.

BOFFIN: I gather that this island is a Conservative stronghold.

CHRISTOPHER: On the whole, yes. There are some subversive elements of course, but most Samolans are still Empire minded. You see, they've been happy and contented under British rule for so many years that they just don't understand when they're suddenly told that it's been nothing but a corrupt, capitalist racket from the word go.

BOFFIN: I trust that it is not His Excellency who tells them that.

CHRISTOPHER: Oh good Lord, no. But he is a bit Leftish in his views, isn't he? In the nicest possible way of course.

BOFFIN: Of course.

CHRISTOPHER: And sometimes, some of the things he says, sort of shakes 'em up a bit. If you know what I mean.

BOFFIN: I do, I do indeed, I do.

CHRISTOPHER: The Samolans are sweet people, in many ways, and they have a lot of charm, but they're a bit backward politically.

BOFFIN: Like the Irish.

> *At this moment* SIR GEORGE SHOTTER *comes in from the hall. He is a cheerful man of about fifty. His figure is stocky but in good order. He exudes friendliness and is far from being a fool.*

GEORGE: Boffin! I thought I heard the car—why didn't somebody tell me? (*He shakes hands with* BOFFIN.) How was the flight?

BOFFIN: Ghastly.

GEORGE: It's generally a bit bumpy between here and Yara. Have any trouble coming in?

BOFFIN: Yes. We bounced like a tennis ball.

GEORGE: It's that damned runway. They just won't fix it.

BOFFIN: I shall leave by sea.

GEORGE: You can't talk about leaving when you've only just arrived. Did the Press get you at the airport? They've been ringing up all day.

CHRISTOPHER: Wheeler was there from the *Examiner*, and poor old Kabu-Anu. Mr. Blair-Kennedy said he'd give them interviews to-morrow morning.

GEORGE: We don't often have celebrities on this island. I'm afraid you'll have to do your stuff to a certain extent. You won't mind, will you?

BOFFIN: That "certain extent" has a sinister ring. What have you been up to?

GEORGE (*airily*): Nothing much—ask Sandra—she has it all taped.

BOFFIN: Oh God!

GEORGE: Cheer up. A lecture or two here and there never hurt anybody.

BOFFIN: A lecture or two! You know perfectly well I couldn't give a lecture if my life depended on it.

GEORGE: Nonsense.

BOFFIN: It isn't nonsense. I can't even say a brief speech of thanks without stammering and stuttering and making a cracking fool of myself.

GEORGE: The Samolans will love that—they're very easily amused.

BOFFIN: Perhaps they'd like me to do a few conjuring tricks.

GEORGE: You're a famous author and all famous authors are expected to give lectures as a matter of course. If you're smart enough to write all those damned words it oughtn't to be all that difficult to spout a few of them.

BOFFIN: I'll never forgive you for this, George, or Sandra either.

GEORGE: Well, you fix all that up with her, it's nothing to do with me.

BOFFIN: I am not going to give any lectures, George, and that's final. I am willing to agree to a couple of Press interviews, I might even consider reading a short address over the local radio, but beyond that I will not budge.

GEORGE: You'll have to open the new wing of the University Library whether you like it or not.

BOFFIN: I do not.

GEORGE: It's all laid on for Tuesday the twenty-fourth.

BOFFIN: Then it must be all laid off again.

GEORGE: They're offering you a degree.

BOFFIN: I don't want a degree.

GEORGE: Give him another drink, Chris, he's getting petulant.

> At this moment LADY ALEXANDRA SHOTTER *comes in at a run. She is exquisitely dressed, gay, charming, and at the moment, rather breathless. She flings herself at* BOFFIN *and hugs him.*

SANDRA: Oh darling Boffin—I can't believe you're really here at last—I've been counting the days, so has everyone else for the matter of that—the whole island is in an absolute uproar about your arrival. And there was I in the middle of that beastly meeting and unable to get to the airport. I've been in a frenzy—I heard your plane fly over the institute and I nearly lost control and rushed outside to wave—and then, to my horror, just as everything was finished, that awful Mrs. Paouna got up—you know, George, the one with the goitre the size of a grape fruit—and she droned on and on for ever like a buzz saw. Chris dear, for Heaven's sake give me a straight kala-kala with ice. (*To* BOFFIN.) How was the flight?

BOFFIN: Unspeakable.

SANDRA: And how was England when you left?

BOFFIN: Bathed in sunshine as usual.

SANDRA: Did you see Marjorie?—Is it true about Bertie and Freda? And how is Sylvia's baby?

BOFFIN: Yes—No—Hideous.

SANDRA: There are a million things I want to ask about—I don't know where to start.

GEORGE: Press on, my love. You're not doing badly.

CHRISTOPHER (*giving her a glass of pink liquid*): Here's your drink, Lady A.

He goes.

SANDRA (*as he disappears*): Thank you, Chris. (*She sips her drink and looks at* BOFFIN *and* GEORGE.) That's better. You look rather dim, Boffin—Has George been bellowing at you?

BOFFIN: No. Just giving me a brief outline of my itinerary.

SANDRA: Oh George, you promised to leave that to me. (*To* BOFFIN.) There's nothing to worry about, really there isn't— just one or two tiny appearances here and there—for the sake of morale and prestige more than anything else. You see we've only had two English writers out here in three years and both of them were Rosita Forbes.

BOFFIN: I am not going to give any lectures, Sandra.

SANDRA (*gaily*): Of course you're not—whoever suggested such a thing?—lectures are Hell. I wouldn't let you give one even if you were aching to.

BOFFIN: Good.

SANDRA: One or two little cosy informal talks perhaps about the state of the modern novel or the Sitwells or something——

BOFFIN: No, Sandra. No little cosy informal talks about the state of anything whatever.

SANDRA: You'll have to open the new wing in the University Library whether you like it or not.

BOFFIN: As far as I am concerned, Sandra, the new wing of the University Library will remain for ever bolted and barred.

SANDRA: But they're planning to give you a degree.

BOFFIN: I don't care if they're planning to give me a Peerage. The answer is No.

SANDRA: This is all your fault, George. You jumped at him before he had time to get his breath and now he's dug his feet in.

BOFFIN: I certainly have.

SANDRA: Old Professor Wali-Anu will be heartbroken.

BOFFIN: He'll have to rise above it.

SANDRA: I simply can't face him with the news that you won't come after all the trouble he's taken. He absolutely worships everything you've ever written.

BOFFIN: Then he must be a very immoral old gentleman.

SANDRA: As a matter of fact I think he is rather, but all the students adore him.

GEORGE: Think it over, Boffin, my boy. The Pendarla University may not mean much in your life, but it stands for a great deal out here. It has carried aloft the torch of English learning through the jungles of heathen ignorance for generations—it has——

SANDRA: Don't overdo it, darling, it was only built in 1909.

BOFFIN: You had no right to arrange things like that without consulting me first.

SANDRA: How could we possibly consult you? You've been flipping about the Pacific for months. Besides, it's perfectly natural that whenever someone as famous as you comes to an out-of-the-way place like this that we should want to make much of you. It's a tremendous compliment really and you ought to be very proud, instead of turning up your nose and being pompous.

BOFFIN: All right—all right—have it your own way.

SANDRA: Oh that's wonderful of you, and I take back what I said about you being pompous. I didn't mean to let you in for a lot of nonsense, really I didn't, but it would help us so tremendously if you'd co-operate just a tiny little bit.

BOFFIN: No lectures.

SANDRA: We'll discuss those later.

BOFFIN: There will be none to discuss.

SANDRA: Darling Boffin—we'll see.

BOFFIN: I've come out here with a purpose, Sandra, and that purpose is to collect data and make notes for a satirical novel about British Colonial Administration.

GEORGE: Not too satirical, I hope, Boffin. I don't want to be forced to resign.

BOFFIN: And I really can't waste time making a series of personal appearances like a movie star. I want to relax and absorb atmosphere and find out about things and talk to people.

SANDRA: That's exactly what we're asking you to do.

BOFFIN: Yes, but not about the Sitwells.

SANDRA: It doesn't necessarily have to be about the Sitwells. What's the matter with the Brontës?

BOFFIN: A great deal I should imagine, judged from the standpoint of modern psychology, but I don't happen to be particularly interested in them. What I am interested in is what's going on here, on this island, this remote, far-flung outpost of Empire.

GEORGE: Commonwealth.

SANDRA: As a matter of fact, it's not nearly as far-flung as it used to be, all the principal trans-Pacific airlines call here, and in a year or two, when we get the jet planes, we'll be as get-at-able as Wimbledon.

BOFFIN: Have I made myself clear?

SANDRA: It's no use, George—we shall have to give in. No lectures.

BOFFIN: Thanks.

SANDRA: You'll have to put up with a bit of lionising, though. A couple of cocktail parties and one literary lunch—how's that?

BOFFIN: All right.

SANDRA: At any rate, you won't have to worry about dinner to-night. It will be as dull as ditchwater.

BOFFIN: I can't wait.

SANDRA: We thought you'd like to be quiet on your first evening.

BOFFIN: I'm surprised that you hadn't organised a civic reception.

SANDRA: Don't be mean. After all, you've won, except about the University Library. As a matter of fact, we ought to have asked the Professor to-night, George—but Cuckoo's always so beastly to him.

BOFFIN: Who's Cuckoo?

SANDRA: Cuckoo Honey. She's the wife of the Colonial Secretary. I don't suppose you'll take to her, nobody does much at first.

BOFFIN: Why?

GEORGE: She's a rather over-typical Colonial type—Anglo-Indian background, you know—prides herself on saying what she thinks.

SANDRA: Poor Cuckoo. It's the mixture of Bangalore and Earl's Court that makes everything so difficult really, but she's not bad once you get below the surface.

BOFFIN: I'll wear an aqua-lung.

SANDRA: Her husband's quite sweet and a great help to George, but he has asthma.

GEORGE: Hay fever.

SANDRA: Well, whatever it is, it makes him rather snuffly. Then there are the Turlings. They're a sort of institution on the island. He's a retired Admiral and they've lived here for years.

GEORGE: He's an amiable old snob, a push-over for a title. Talk about your aunt, Lady Gravesborough—she was a Marchioness, wasn't she? He'll eat out of your hand.

BOFFIN: I'm not sure that I'd quite want him to do that.

GEORGE: Well, have a try anyway—you see—it'll work like a charm.

BOFFIN: There's nothing much to say about my aunt really, except that she died of drink in San Remo.

SANDRA: That's all except for the Chief of Police and Hali.

BOFFIN: What's that?

SANDRA: It isn't a thing, darling, it's a political leader. He's the head of the P.I.P.

BOFFIN: What does that mean?

GEORGE: People's Imperial Party. They're very powerful and, to my way of thinking, damned retrogressive.

SANDRA: George naturally supports the S.S.N.P. The Samolan Socialist Nationals. I did so hope that when he gave up politics and became a Governor that he'd stop being a man-of-the-people, but he hasn't quite.

GEORGE: I'm proud of being a man-of-the-people.

SANDRA: You're a rip-snorting old careerist, darling, and you always have been ever since you left that dreadfully over-publicised grocer's shop in Huddersfield.

GEORGE: Never you mind about Huddersfield.

SANDRA: I don't very much.

BOFFIN: What does the S.S.N.P. stand for?

GEORGE: Self-government for the native population and Dominion status.

BOFFIN: Are they ready for that yet?

SANDRA: That's the whole point. Hali Alani says they're not and Koga Swalu says they are.

BOFFIN: Who the devil is Koga Swalu?

SANDRA: The Opposition leader, and I must say he's a horror. Covered in warts and stinks like a badger.

GEORGE: Come now, Sandra, fair's fair, he can't help that.

SANDRA: Oh yes, he can. He could wash more, to start with, and have his warts treated with what-d'you-call-it acid.

BOFFIN: Is he coming to dinner too?

SANDRA: No, thank God, he came last week. We have to have them alternately. Whenever they meet they snap and snarl at each other and the servants get jumpy and hand people all the wrong things. Of the two I naturally prefer Hali. He's frightfully good-looking in rather a bogus sort of way—you know—long coffee-coloured hands and gleaming teeth. George can't stand him.

GEORGE: It isn't him I object to, it's his politics.

SANDRA: Hali's political views are perfectly sound. He just

doesn't believe in progress. Personally, I find it very refreshing. He's also absolutely devoted to me and pays me the most lovely compliments. Naturally I'm on his side through thick and thin.

GEORGE: You know, the trouble with you, love, is that you talk the most arrant nonsense.

SANDRA: Be that as it may, Hali is a very fascinating man, and even though you do say you wouldn't trust him an inch . . .

GEORGE: I wouldn't trust any of them an inch. Hali is a tricky proposition, fascinating or not, and so is his father, who's a mischievous old intriguer. They can both make a lot of trouble with the elections coming on in a few weeks' time. I'm depending on you to see that they don't.

SANDRA: On me? You must be out of your mind. What on earth could I do?

GEORGE: Charm Hali. Get round him. Persuade him to change his views, or at least to modify them. You're an attractive woman, aren't you? Trained in the old-world school of aristocratic diplomacy?

SANDRA: All I ever learned at Roedean was the school song. I might sing him that. It's very rousing.

BOFFIN: That's a thoroughly immoral suggestion, George.

GEORGE: I don't see why. I should be the last to underrate the importance of woman's influence on politics—if properly directed.

SANDRA: "Disguise our bondage as we will, 'tis woman, woman rules us still," Thomas Moore. Born 1779. Died 1852.

BOFFIN: Good Lord, you can still do it!

SANDRA: "Thro' all the drama—whether damned or not—Love gilds the scene, and women guide the plot".

BOFFIN: Congreve?

SANDRA: No. Richard Brinsley Sheridan. Born 1751. Died 1816.

GEORGE: Don't encourage her, for heaven's sake. She'll go on for hours.

SANDRA: I do it better really when I'm in my cups. How would you like me to begin, George?

GEORGE: Begin what?

SANDRA: Influencing Hali, of course. I'm entranced with the

whole idea. Shall I lure him into the garden in the moonlight and pop a tuberose into his buttonhole and murmur loving little slogans about the Samolan Socialist National Party?

GEORGE: Don't rush it. Get him in the right mood first.

BOFFIN: This may end in tears.

SANDRA: But I don't approve of the S.S.N.P. I think they're a lot of stinkers.

GEORGE: That's neither here nor there. I do approve of them, and you are representing me.

SANDRA: Oh George, how sweet and generous of you. Am I really?

GEORGE: None of that sarcastic stuff, now. You're my wife, aren't you?

SANDRA: Yes, dear, but I hoped that it was a love match and not a political gambit.

GEORGE: You're my helpmate. You share my joys and sorrows. You smooth away my cares with your gentle womanly hand——

BOFFIN: "When pain and anguish wring the brow, a ministering angel thou."

SANDRA: Sir Walter Scott. Born——

GEORGE: Never mind about Sir Walter Scott for the moment, dear. Just concentrate.

SANDRA: All right. But I draw the line at the Samolan Socialist Nationals.

GEORGE: You want these island people to have the right to govern themselves, don't you? To emancipate themselves from the hideous yoke of Imperialistic oppression—to be free to shoulder the responsibility of their own destiny?

SANDRA: You know perfectly well I don't want any such thing. Neither do they.

GEORGE: I suppose you'll be saying next that they're perfectly happy as they are.

SANDRA: But they are—blissfully. They sing from morning till night. They weave away and make the most lovely waste-paper baskets and never stop having scads of entrancing children who swim before they can walk and have enormous melting eyes like saucers. And whenever they feel a bit peckish all they have to do is to nip a breadfruit off a tree or snatch a yam out of the ground.

GEORGE: What about education?

SANDRA: Well, what about it? They learn automatically all they need to know. They hunt and dive and swim and fish and make the most wonderful things with their hands. You can't do anything with your hands. You can't even mend the gramophone.

GEORGE: So we're back again at that, are we?

SANDRA: And as for swimming. (*To* BOFFIN.) Have you ever seen George swim? He goes churning up and down doing a sort of Margate breast stroke.

GEORGE: I like to see where I'm going. What's the fun of having your head under the water all the time?

BOFFIN: I must say I'm on George's side there.

GEORGE: Anyway, what's my swimming got to do with self-government?

SANDRA: Everything. It gives you an inferiority complex and your inferiority complex makes you have the wrong views. I've always said that, ever since I married you. You've no idea what the tiniest little inferiority complex can do to people. I've been reading all about it in an American book about sex.

BOFFIN: All American books are about sex.

SANDRA (*pursuing her theme*): Look at the Kaiser and his withered arm and all the trouble it caused. And Marat with that awful skin disease, and Richard the Third and his hump. I believe there was something rather peculiar about Saint Teresa too, but I can't remember what it was at the moment.

GEORGE (*patiently*): Listen, my love. All I asked you to do was to use your well-known woman's wiles discreetly and coax Hali Alani round to being a little more progressive in his ideas. I didn't look for an unprovoked argument about inferiority complexes, Richard the Third's hump and my swimming.

SANDRA: Never mind, darling. I'll do what you say. It's against my principles but I'll try my best. How far would you like me to go?

GEORGE: On second thoughts, I'd rather you didn't say anything at all. You'll only bewilder him and make matters worse.

SANDRA: Nonsense. I'm all set now. I intend to fascinate him within an inch of his life. And if it ends in the divorce courts you have only yourself to blame. You'd better have a notebook handy, Boffin. This evening might turn out to be an eye-opener for the Colonial Office.

GEORGE: Sandra—listen——

SANDRA: Not another word. The die is cast.

> CHRISTOPHER *comes in, having changed for dinner.*

Oh Chris, how correct of you to be dressed so soon. I knew this would happen and it's all my fault. Deal with everyone for me and for heaven's sake tell Sanyamo to tidy the verandah, it's a shambles.

CHRISTOPHER: I've already told him. Everything's under control.

SANDRA: What about the appetisers?

BOFFIN: What a disgusting word!

SANDRA: Yes, isn't it? I know a lot of others too. They're all part of the progressive modern trend. I can say "Lounge" and "Phone" and "Let's have a small one before we buzz".

CHRISTOPHER: Punalo Alani is here, Your Excellency. He says he has an appointment.

GEORGE: Damn! I completely forgot he was coming. Is he in the office?

CHRISTOPHER: Yes, sir.

GEORGE: Well, I'll see him out here, it's cooler. You show Boffin his room, Sandra. I shan't be long.

SANDRA: Can't we stay a minute? I should love to show Boffin Punalo Alani. (*To* BOFFIN.) He's the father of the one George wants me to fascinate at dinner. He's a terrific old boy and looks like a wizened ivory nut.

GEORGE: Run along, dear, Punalo is here to talk business. Boffin can meet him some other time. Go and fetch him, Chris.

CHRISTOPHER: Yes, sir.

> *He goes.*

SANDRA: Why on earth does he want to see you at this time of day? Do you suppose there's anything wrong?

GEORGE: As far as Punalo Alani is concerned, everything I do is wrong. He's a class-conscious, prejudiced old Die-Hard, and a damned nuisance into the bargain.

SANDRA: Well, don't let him work you into a bad temper for the whole evening, there's a dear, and don't be too beastly to him either. He's very old indeed and I'm madly in love with him. Come on, Boffin, I'll show you your room. It's quite hideous and full of ants but the view's wonderful. Let's buzz.

BOFFIN: I don't mind if I do.

> SANDRA *and* BOFFIN *go off.*
> GEORGE *helps himself to a whisky and soda and lights a cigarette.* CHRISTOPHER *returns, ushering in* PUNALO ALANI. PUNALO *is a dignified, distinguished old man. His age might be anywhere between sixty-five and eighty-five.*

CHRISTOPHER: Mr. Punalo Alani, sir.

GEORGE: Tell Sanyamo I don't want to be disturbed for the next ten minutes.

CHRISTOPHER: Yes, sir.

> *He goes.*

GEORGE (*shaking hands*): Good afternoon, Punalo Alani.

PUNALO: Good afternoon, Your Excellency.

GEORGE: Would you like a drink?

PUNALO: No, thank you. I know how busy you are, and I don't want to detain you longer than is necessary.

GEORGE: Sit down at any rate.

PUNALO: It would go against the grain for me to sit while Your Excellency is standing.

GEORGE (*with a smile*): This is an informal interview, Punalo Alani. However, have it your own way. (*He sits.*)

PUNALO (*also sitting*): Thank you. As a matter of fact, Your Excellency has the sublime gift of making all interviews informal. It is most refreshing.

GEORGE: I'm glad you think so.

PUNALO: Although, for us of the older school, it can, at times, be a trifle disconcerting.

GEORGE: I suspect that it would take a great deal to disconcert you, Punalo Alani. You are a very shrewd man.

PUNALO: Your Excellency is most kind. But at the moment I am more than disconcerted; I am profoundly worried.

GEORGE: Why—what's wrong?

PUNALO: A great deal. I come to you as a suppliant. It is not a role that I like, for I am a proud man, but there is no alternative.

GEORGE: What on earth is the matter?

PUNALO: I love my country, and I love my people.

GEORGE: Yes. I am aware of that.

PUNALO: And it is a great sadness to me that you, our Governor, should so palpably be in sympathy with the aims and policies of the Samolan Socialist Nationals, who, in my opinion, are our enemies.

GEORGE: I really cannot discuss party politics with you, even informally. As Governor, I am entirely impartial. I have no bias in either direction.

PUNALO: Officially that is so, Your Excellency. But your opinions are well known and, in your high position, your opinions, even unofficially, carry considerable weight.

GEORGE: Please come to the point, Punalo Alani.

PUNALO: May I remind you that it was largely owing to your influence last year that the Inter-Island Boat Service abolished first and second class accommodation in favour of an over-all Tourist class.

GEORGE: And a damned good thing, too. The time for archaic class distinctions has passed.

PUNALO: So has the Inter-Island Boat Service. Into liquidation.

GEORGE: That was the fault of bad organisation and inefficient management.

PUNALO: I beg to disagree, Your Excellency. The reason the company is on the verge of bankruptcy is because the wealthier Samolan and Chinese families have ceased to travel in the steamers and have, on their own initiative, inaugurated a system of private launches.

GEORGE: Industrial profiteers have never been remarkable for their sense of patriotism.

PUNALO: It was not their sense of patriotism that was involved. It was their sense of smell.

GEORGE: What absolute nonsense.

PUNALO: On the contrary. A perfectly logical demonstration of cause and effect.

GEORGE: Cause and effect?

PUNALO: The introduction into the first class cabins and saloons of goats, pigs, chickens and an occasional mongoose wrought considerable havoc in a remarkably short space of time. In addition to which, all luxury fittings, curtains, rugs and smaller articles of furniture entirely disappeared; not only were all the buttons gouged out of the cushions, but by the end of November there weren't even any cushions. I understand that, with the exception of the occasional mongoose, much the same problem confronts your own nationalised British Railways.

GEORGE: I am willing to admit that the re-grading of the Inter-Island Boat Service has been badly bungled, but I still maintain that in theory it was, and is, an admirable idea. Fully in keeping with democratic principles.

PUNALO: It is sad, is it not, that the gulf between theory and practice is so often unbridgeable?

GEORGE: In a progressively-minded island with a properly organised education system, these things would never occur.

PUNALO: However progressive Samolo became, I fear we should still find it difficult to educate our goats and pigs and chickens.

GEORGE: What's all this leading up to, anyway?

PUNALO: It has come to my knowledge that the Samolan Socialist Nationals are planning to introduce a new bill into the House of Representatives.

GEORGE: Well, they have a perfect right to do that if they wish to.

PUNALO: The bill concerns Public Conveniences.

GEORGE: Public Conveniences?

PUNALO: The object of it is to dispense with the penny-in-the-slot system at present in force in the principal public buildings, shops, hotels, cinemas and night-clubs, and make all lavatories on the island entirely free.

GEORGE: It sounds an excellent idea. Why shouldn't they?

PUNALO (*patiently*): Again we are faced with that unbridgeable gulf. It may sound excellent in theory, but in practice it would be disaster.

GEORGE: Why?

PUNALO: In the first place the loss of revenue from the penny-in-the-slot system would create a serious economic problem. In the second place, the social repercussions from such an arbitrary measure would be appalling.

GEORGE: I can't see for the life of me why they should be.

PUNALO: Your Excellency's point of view may be biased by the fact that you are seldom required to use Public Conveniences yourself.

GEORGE: That is beside the point.

PUNALO: Again I beg to differ. In your position as Governor you automatically enjoy certain privileges and rightly so. Even in the most Utopian Welfare States, privilege is accepted as a natural perquisite of authority. In the Soviet Union itself, that Marxist Paradise of Left-Wing intellectuals, there is no recorded instance of the late Mr. Stalin queueing up for a public lavatory.

GEORGE: I fail to see what the Soviet Union has to do with the present discussion.

PUNALO: The Soviet Union has a great deal to do with the Samolan Socialist Nationals, whom Your Excellency tacitly encourages with your support.

GEORGE: You have no proof of that.

PUNALO: Come, come, Your Excellency. It is a well-known fact that Koga Swalu and three of his chief supporters are, or were, acknowledged members of the Communist Party.

GEORGE: I have no wish to discuss the matter any further.

PUNALO: I am sorry if my words have offended you. But Samolo, thank God, is not yet a Welfare State, and it is still permissible to speak freely without fear of reprisals.

GEORGE (*glancing at his watch*): If you have anything more to say, Punalo Alani, please say it. As you yourself admitted at the beginning of this interview, I am a very busy man.

PUNALO: I ask you most humbly, Your Excellency, but most urgently, to veto the Public Convenience bill.

GEORGE (*irritably*): Why the devil should I? To begin with, I have not even considered the matter and also, as I have already explained, my official influence does not extend to imposing vetoes on either party.

PUNALO: You have your prerogative of a casting vote in the House of Representatives.

GEORGE: And you seriously expect me to exercise it over a triviality like this?

PUNALO: Public Conveniences are far from being trivialities, Your Excellency. They are, if you will forgive the play upon words, of fundamental importance. Many issues are involved, notably the question of prestige.

GEORGE: Prestige?

PUNALO: Prestige means much to the Samolan people. It provides an incentive to work and encourages progress. An industrious citizen who has, through his own gumption, worked his way up from the cane fields or the banana plantations and become a successful merchant, naturally expects to enjoy the perquisites of his improved social status. One of these is the privilege of being able to spend a penny when he feels like it.

GEORGE: You are wasting my time and your own, Punalo Alani.

PUNALO (*ignoring the interruption*): But it is not only for himself that he covets this minor accolade: it is for his wife and family. Take old Chim Paouna, for instance, the proprietor of the Pendarla Furnishing Company. Mrs. Paouna, his wife, is one of the most respected and majestic members of the community. Imagine her fighting and struggling with her own employees to force her way into a free lavatory in her own building. The humiliation would kill her.

GEORGE: Mrs. Paouna is quite wealthy enough to instal an entire floor of private toilets if she is so over-sensitive.

PUNALO: Have you envisaged, from the point of view of hygiene alone, the state of the water closets after a week's gratis promiscuous occupation?

GEORGE: No, I most certainly have not.

PUNALO: They will be a grave menace to public health and there won't be a chain or a plug left.

GEORGE: As I said before, you are wasting my time.

PUNALO: I see you are quite adamant.

GEORGE (*rising*): Quite.

PUNALO (*also rising*): Then there is nothing more to be said.

GEORGE: I am sorry, Punalo Alani.

PUNALO: I too am sorry, Your Excellency. You are a stubborn man and, like so many of your countrymen, incurably romantic.

GEORGE: I don't know what you mean.

PUNALO: Your conviction that extreme socialism necessarily implies progress is romantic to the point of fantasy. I know that you have the interests of my country at heart——

GEORGE (*interrupting testily*): In that case, why not accept the fact that over certain matters of policy we do not see eye-to-eye?

PUNALO: As a private individual, I would be willing to accept that unhappy fact, but as a loyal Samolan and a representative of a large number of the Electorate, I cannot.

GEORGE: I understood that you retired from public life some years ago?

PUNALO: That is so. But my son Hali has not retired. He represents the People's Imperial Party. It is on his behalf and on the behalf of the whole country that I came to see you this evening.

GEORGE: Why not let your son speak for himself? He's quite capable of it.

PUNALO: His command of English is not so clear as mine. He, alas, had not the ineffable good fortune to be educated at Eton.

GEORGE: Just as many fools emerge from Eton as from any other school.

PUNALO (*with dignity*): I am not one of them, Your Excellency.

GEORGE (*more gently*): I didn't mean to imply that you were. But, as you know, I have not much faith in the mystic properties of the "Old School Tie".

PUNALO: The "Old School Tie" is not, I admit, as important as many consider it to be, but old school ties are very important indeed. I myself have many of them. They bind me both emotionally and intellectually to the England I knew when I was a boy. An England which in many respects was far more peaceful and better ordered than it is to-day.

GEORGE: England has fought two wars since you were a boy.

PUNALO: I am well aware of that. I served in one of them myself.

GEORGE: Progress is inevitable, Punalo Alani. Why don't you face up to it?

PUNALO: Progress?

GEORGE: Certainly. No one who was not blindly prejudiced could deny that from the point of view of housing, education, employment and general well-being the ordinary working Englishman to-day is far better off than he was fifty years ago.

PUNALO: That may be so, but may I point out that the population of England alone is forty times larger than that of the entire Samolan Archipelago. Also England is an industrial country and Samolo is not. We are a backward race, Your Excellency, so backward, old-fashioned and reactionary that we still like British Rule.

GEORGE: I see that you are romantic, too, Punalo Alani.

PUNALO: Realistic at the same time, Your Excellency. And, with all due respect, I think I have a clearer knowledge of my country's temperament than you have. I know that your friends the Samolan Socialist Nationals wish to emancipate us from the cosy Imperialism that has gently guided us for so long. They wish us to "Stand Alone", to have "Self-Government", to endure, unprotected, the fearful discomforts of State-controlled democracy, which are racking Western civilisation. Believe me, we are too young yet for such brave experiments. Too young and gay and irresponsible to be able to do without our old Nanny.

GEORGE: What has all this sentimental nonsense to do with Public Conveniences?

PUNALO (*with sudden sharpness*): A great deal, Your Excellency. As you may discover to your cost.

GEORGE (*icily*): Is that a threat?

PUNALO: Not a threat, Your Excellency. Merely a warning. Good evening.

> PUNALO ALANI *bows austerely and——*
> *——walks out.*

GEORGE (*alone*): Well, I'll be damned!

THE LIGHTS FADE

Scene II

The time is a few minutes later.

    CHRISTOPHER *is wandering about, filling up cigarette-boxes.*

    SANYAMO, *the Samolan butler, enters, carrying two trays of "Appetisers". He is a handsome man in the late thirties and wears the traditional sarong and a white coat.*

CHRISTOPHER: How's your wife, Sanyamo?

SANYAMO: Which one, Captain?

CHRISTOPHER: The one that had the baby.

SANYAMO: Very well, Captain, but the baby is terrible.

CHRISTOPHER: In what way terrible?

SANYAMO: It makes wicked sounds in the night.

CHRISTOPHER: Does it look like you?

SANYAMO: Oh no, Captain. It looks like Mr. Rochester.

CHRISTOPHER: Who on earth's Mr. Rochester?

SANYAMO: He was here last year with the Oil Company. He was very kind.

CHRISTOPHER: I see.

    CUCKOO *and* EDWARD HONEY *come in.* EDWARD *is rather dim, earnest and painstaking.*

    CUCKOO *is pure Kensington with an Anglo-Indian background.*

CUCKOO: Good evening, Chris. Are we the first?

CHRISTOPHER: Yes. Lady A.'s only just gone to dress.

CUCKOO: There now. What did I tell you, Edward? We needn't have hurried after all.

EDWARD: I want a few words with H.E. before dinner, anyhow. (*To* CHRISTOPHER.) Is he in his room?

CHRISTOPHER: Yes. He's dressing.

EDWARD: I think I'll go along. He won't mind.

CUCKOO: You didn't forget to bring a spare handkerchief, did you?

EDWARD: No, dear.

CUCKOO: And keep well away from the window. You were caught by that bougainvillæa before.

EDWARD: Yes, dear.

CUCKOO: We don't want a repetition of what happened at the Bradley-Coburns, do we?

EDWARD: No dear, we don't.

CUCKOO: And don't keep H. E. too long, you know what you are.

EDWARD: Yes, dear.

He goes.

CHRISTOPHER: Would you like a drink?

CUCKOO: No, thank you. I'll wait a little. What's he like?

CHRISTOPHER: Who?

CUCKOO: John Blair-Kennedy, of course.

CHRISTOPHER: Very nice.

CUCKOO: Everybody seems to be making an awful fuss about him coming here. Personally I don't care for his books much— too talky.

CHRISTOPHER: I'm afraid I've only read the one about the West Indies.

CUCKOO: Oh, that's a sort of travel book. I mean his novels. They're awfully cynical, you know, and none of his characters seem to believe in anything. They're amusing I suppose, in a flippant way, but I must say I prefer books that have a little more grip, more reality. Do you know what I mean?

CHRISTOPHER: Oh yes—rather.

CUCKOO: Of course I know that there *are* people who go through life having affairs with everybody they see and making jokes and laughing at everything but I can't feel that they really *contribute* very much.

CHRISTOPHER: No. I suppose they don't.

CUCKOO: He's *her* friend more than his, isn't he?

CHRISTOPHER: How do you mean?

CUCKOO: I mean he's known Lady A. longer than he's known H.E.

CHRISTOPHER: I'm afraid I don't know. I didn't ask him.

CUCKOO: I believe he was one of her beaux before she was married.

CHRISTOPHER: I didn't ask him that either.

CUCKOO: Don't be silly, of course you didn't. Lady A. was very gay in her younger days, you know.

CHRISTOPHER: She occasionally smiles, even now.

CUCKOO: It was a great surprise to everyone when she married H. E. Nobody ever thought she'd ever settle down.

CHRISTOPHER: I wouldn't call being a Governor's wife and organising Women's Federation meetings and making public speeches, settling down exactly.

CUCKOO: You know perfectly well what I mean. After all, everybody knows she belonged to rather a wild set in London. One of her greatest friends was Lady Caroline Trouncer.

CHRISTOPHER: What did *she* do?

CUCKOO: My dear, she was notorious! She married three husbands one after the other.

CHRISTOPHER: She couldn't very well have married them all at the same time.

CUCKOO: Then she ran off to East Africa with a jockey, leaving behind her two sweet little girls, and then she went to Vienna and had her face lifted.

CHRISTOPHER (*laughing*): Really, Cuckoo!

CUCKOO: It's true. There was a tremendous craze for it at one time. There was even a rumour that Lady A. had had hers done.

CHRISTOPHER (*angrily*): Damned nonsense!

CUCKOO: Naturally I don't believe it, but that was the rumour. Quite definitely.

CHRISTOPHER: If you don't believe it and it's only a rumour, why spread it?

CUCKOO: Why, Chris—you're getting quite hot under the collar. You're not falling in love with her, are you?

CHRISTOPHER: Of course I'm not.

CUCKOO: There's no "of course" about it. It would be quite natural for a young man of your age to conceive a romantic passion for Lady A. She's still a very attractive woman and I'm sure she wouldn't mind in the least.

CHRISTOPHER: Lady A. has been very kind to me and I like her very much. I like H.E. too. He's a wonderful man.

CUCKOO: My dear, you needn't be so aggressively loyal. I'm absolutely devoted to them both myself.

CHRISTOPHER: You don't speak as if you were.

CUCKOO (*putting her hand on his arm*): Why, we're almost squabbling, aren't we? How too ridiculous. Don't be cross.

CHRISTOPHER: I'm not in the least cross.

CUCKOO: You know I can't help saying what I think. It's part of my nature.

CHRISTOPHER: Yes, I know.

CUCKOO (*after a slight pause*): Are we friends again?

CHRISTOPHER: Of course.

CUCKOO: I wanted to talk to you seriously, and confidentially.

CHRISTOPHER: What about?

CUCKOO: You won't fly off the handle again, will you?

CHRISTOPHER: If it's about Lady A. and H.E., I might.

CUCKOO: Well, it is—and you mustn't. It's too important—and I'm worried.

CHRISTOPHER: Why?

CUCKOO: They have too many mixed parties here at Government House. I've never been to one without at least a few coloured people present, and generally there are dozens. Believe me, the British are beginning to resent it.

CHRISTOPHER: There have to be mixed parties at Government House. It's part of the job. And a very important part too.

CUCKOO: Of course it is. I know that. But there is such a thing as going too far. I tell you, people are beginning to criticise, and I don't like it. Neither does my husband.

CHRISTOPHER: Why doesn't he say something to H.E., then? After all, he is the Colonial Secretary.

CUCKOO: It wouldn't be any use. You know Edward isn't a very forceful character and H.E. can be as stubborn as a mule when he likes. Anyhow, it's Lady A. they're talking about most. She's hob-nobbing too much.

CHRISTOPHER: Rubbish.

CUCKOO: Look what happened at the races last Tuesday. She spent nearly the whole afternoon with those awful Amabooas.

CHRISTOPHER: Choom Amabooa is the great grandson of one of the native princes here in the old days before the revolution. He's a nice boy.

CUCKOO: What about his wife? Why, she's half Chink!

CHRISTOPHER: What difference does that make?

CUCKOO: Of course, if you're determined not to understand——

CHRISTOPHER (*irritably*): Look out—somebody's coming.

> ADMIRAL *and* MRS. TURLING *come in. He is square and stocky with bristling eyebrows. She is faded, gentle and rather vague.*

MRS. T.: We're not late, I hope? The car went wrong and we had to keep stopping.

CHRISTOPHER: Not a bit. Lady A. and H. E. are still dressing.

ADMIRAL: There's a rattle somewhere and I can't locate it.

MRS. T.: How are you, Cuckoo? (*She kisses* CUCKOO *absently.*) What a pretty dress.

CUCKOO: You must have seen it before.

MRS. T.: Of course I have, dear, several times. But I'm very fond of it. How are the children?

CUCKOO: Cynthia's all right, but I left poor Susan in floods.

MRS. T.: What's the matter?

CUCKOO: They won't let her play Prince Charming in the pantomime because that horrid Rogers girl insists on doing it.

MRS. T.: What a shame. What's Susan going to be, then?

CUCKOO: The Fairy Godmother, and a wolf in the forest scene. The last time she was an animal she came out in a terrible rash all over.

MRS. T.: It's having to crawl about in a hot skin in this climate.

CHRISTOPHER: Martini, Mrs. Turling?

MRS. T.: (*accepting it*): Thank you.

CHRISTOPHER: Admiral—pink gin as usual?

ADMIRAL: Thanks, Chris—best drink in the world—can't bear mixtures—never could. Did this writer chap, Blair-Kennedy, arrive safely?

CHRISTOPHER (*handing him his pink gin*): Yes. He got in about two hours ago.

ADMIRAL: His aunt was Lady Gravesborough, you know. I met her once in Malta years ago. She danced a Scottish Reel like a two-year-old.

MRS. T.: Malta was such fun in those days.

ADMIRAL: It was in old Crutchworth's time. He used to be called "Crossbones".

CUCKOO: Why?

ADMIRAL: Rammed a Chinese junk in Hong Kong harbour—
sank it like a stone—terrible hullabaloo.

CHRISTOPHER: Ready for a drink yet, Cuckoo?

CUCKOO: Yes—a dry Martini, please.

CHRISTOPHER (*handing her one*): Here you are.

> BOFFIN *comes in. He is wearing a white dinner-jacket.*

BOFFIN (*to* CHRISTOPHER): There was a strange insect in my
bathroom, brown and rather beastly, like a small lobster.

CHRISTOPHER: Sounds like a scorpion.

BOFFIN: That's what I feared.

CHRISTOPHER: We often get them in the dry season.

BOFFIN: We must pray for rain.

CHRISTOPHER (*introducing*): Admiral   Turling—Mrs.   Turling—
Mrs. Honey—Mr. Blair-Kennedy.

BOFFIN: How do you do?

ADMIRAL (*shaking hands*): Have a good flight?

BOFFIN: From the aeronautical point of view, yes. Socially, it left
a good deal to be desired.

MRS. T.: The last time we flew home there was a whole family
of the most enchanting Chinese children in the plane.

BOFFIN: They must have season tickets.

ADMIRAL: I once met your aunt, Lady Gravesborough, in Malta.

BOFFIN: Was she sober?

ADMIRAL (*slightly nonplussed*): Yes—I think so.

BOFFIN: Then it must have been a very long time ago. She took
to the bottle in her later years, you know, and kept on
marrying very young Italian counts with sweeping eyelashes
and too many bracelets.

MRS. T.: Just fancy.

BOFFIN: They all turned up in Bugattis for the reading of the
will. It was most impressive.

MRS. T.: It must have been.

> SIR GEORGE *comes in, wearing an immaculate white suit.* EDWARD
> HONEY *follows him with his handkerchief to his nose.*

GEORGE: Sorry I'm late, everybody. Your husband started
sneezing again, Cuckoo. We had to take the flowers out of the
room and close all the windows. Boffin—this is the Colonial

Secretary—he looks a bit under the weather at the moment but it will pass off. Give him a drink, Chris.

EDWARD (*shaking hands, miserably*): How do you do?—must apologise for this.

BOFFIN: Not at all—I sympathise. It always happens to me at race meetings. I'm allergic to horses.

CUCKOO: How extraordinary it is—about being allergic, I mean—it's quite a new thing, isn't it?

BOFFIN: Doctors find it very useful. It simplifies diagnosis.

> ROBERT FROME *comes in. He is a large, sunburnt man in the late thirties. He is Chief of Police for the Pendarla district.*

GEORGE: Good evening, Bob.

BOB: I'm afraid I'm a bit late, sir. But another car robbery case came up just as I was leaving. Grigsby's away in the hills and I had to deal with it.

GEORGE (*introducing*): Captain Frome, our Chief of Police—Mr. Blair-Kennedy. You know everyone else.

BOB: Rather. (*Shaking hands with* BOFFIN.) Hope you had a good journey?

CUCKOO: It's becoming quite an epidemic, all these car robberies. Do you think it's a gang?

BOB (*accepting a Martini from* CHRISTOPHER): No—not as serious as that really. This time it was the Lashmores' new Buick.

ADMIRAL: Surely that can be traced fairly easily. There are very few American cars on the island.

BOB: We shall probably get it back in a day or two, providing we can locate it before they break it up.

MRS. T.: Break it up?

BOB: Yes—it's a new racket. They take them up to the hills, dismember them completely and then smuggle the bits over to one of the other islands and sell them.

BOFFIN: What on earth do the people that buy them do with them?

BOB: All manner of things. Make them into ornaments and pots and pans. The natives are extremely clever with their hands, you know.

BOFFIN: Yes. Lady Alexandra explained that to me only a little while ago, didn't she, George?

BOB: Radiator caps fetch a big price.

BOFFIN: Why?

BOB: The women wear them.

BOFFIN: Don't tell me where—let me guess.

BOB (*to* GEORGE): Hali is dining here tonight, isn't he, sir?

GEORGE: Yes.

BOB: I'll have a little talk to him. His organisation has ways and means of finding out things that we poor policemen can't compete with.

CUCKOO: I wouldn't trust Hali farther than I could see him.

EDWARD (*warningly*): Now then, dear——

CUCKOO: He's too smooth and I don't believe he means a word he says. I can't bear people who don't mean what they say. Can you, Mr. Kennedy?

BOFFIN: I don't mind them. It's the people who only say what they mean who frighten the life out of me.

CUCKOO (*with a little laugh*): How cynical! That's just like a line out of one of your books.

BOFFIN (*agreeably*): Yes, isn't it? No wonder they're so successful.

LADY ALEXANDRA *comes in. She is, as usual, a trifle breathless.*

SANDRA: I'm so sorry, everybody. I do wish I could just once be on time for something, but everything went wrong—George, ought the bath water to be such a very dark brown? It looks like Mulligatawny.

ADMIRAL: It's the drought.

SANDRA: Good evening, Cuckoo. How nice and cool you look. I love that dress. Edward, dear—how's the sinus?

GEORGE: Hay fever, my love.

EDWARD: Not very good, I'm afraid.

SANDRA: It is beastly for you, I *am* so sorry. Perhaps a Benzedrine inhaler would be a help, I believe I've got one somewhere. Admiral, how nice to see you—(*To* MRS. TURLING.)—Grace, I must talk to you later. You are on the Unmarried Mothers sub-committee and so it's more your dish than mine.

MRS. T.: What has happened?

SANDRA: It's the cashier in Woo Chung's Emporium. She's been at it again.

MRS. T.: Oh dear—how unfortunate.

SANDRA (*to* BOFFIN): Illegitimacy is one of our major problems here. This girl is an absolute fiend. She never stops having children all over the place and nothing will induce her to get married. We even had her baptised at Easter but it was no good.

BOFFIN: Funny—I always thought that was a sure cure.

SANDRA: The trouble is I can't help rather liking her. She's quite lovely in a louche sort of way and she has a beguiling sense of humour and the most tremendous vitality.

BOFFIN: I should think she'd need both.

SANDRA: Then, of course, there's the cross-breed question. If only the Samolans would be content to hop into bed with each other it would all be so much simpler. But they will fraternise.

MRS. T.: They're a friendly people, you know, and immensely hospitable.

SANDRA: Nothing has ever been able to convince them that sex is wrong. To them it's just as simple as eating mangoes.

BOFFIN: Only less stringy and indigestible.

CUCKOO: There's an appalling amount of mixed blood on this island, Mr. Kennedy, and it's increasing alarmingly. Before we know where we are we shall find ourselves in the same position as South Africa.

BOFFIN: Or Brighton.

GEORGE: I think we've had enough of this sort of conversation now. Hali will be arriving in a minute and we don't want him to catch us all chattering away about miscegenation. He mightn't quite like it.

SANDRA: It's all my fault—I started it. But I did want Boffin to get some idea of what goes on.

BOFFIN: I'm doing fine.

SANDRA: Bob! I never said good evening to you. What's happened about the sex murder?

GEORGE: Here we go again.

BOB: Nothing so far, I'm afraid.

SANDRA: Any clues?

BOB: Only a screwdriver and a rather tattered copy of *Lady Chatterley's Lover*.

SANYAMO *comes in.*

SANYAMO (*announcing*): Mr. Hali Alani.

SANYAMO *steps aside to allow* HALI ALANI *to enter, and then disappears.* HALI *is tall, distinguished and impeccably dressed. He is wearing a white European dinner-jacket over a brilliantly coloured Samolan sarong. On his feet are gold sandals.*

HALI: I fear very much that I am the latest to arrive.

SANDRA: Don't give it another thought. You've only beaten me by a short head, anyhow.

HALI *bows and shakes hands with* GEORGE *and then kisses* SANDRA'S *hand.*

GEORGE: Good evening, Hali. I missed you at the races on Tuesday. What happened to you?

HALI: I had to attend a family funeral.

SANDRA: Oh, how sad for you. I'm so sorry.

HALI: Please do not be sorry. It was splendid fun. There was a dance afterwards.

GEORGE: Not a very close relative, I gather?

HALI: Oh no. Only a cousin once and for all removed. He was very old and very disagreeable, and it was what you would call high time.

SANDRA: I see. I want to introduce you to Mr. Blair-Kennedy. He has just arrived.

HALI (*bowing to* BOFFIN): The island welcomes you.

BOFFIN: Thank you.

HALI: Your books are an unfailing delight to me. I have them all and every one and I read them without ceasing. You are a most admirable and cheerful fellow.

BOFFIN: Thank you again.

HALI: It would ease my heart of much of its grateful burden if you would permit me to show you some of our island customs. There may be a great deal to enchant and astound you and provide you with copies. I will therefore, with His Excellency's permission, give you a buzz in the morning.

BOFFIN: That will be delightful.

SANDRA: Admiral and Mrs. Turling you know—The Colonial
Secretary—Mrs. Honey——

CUCKOO: Good evening, Mr. Alani.

HALI: I am so sad about your daughter being again a wolf this
year, Mrs. Honey.

CUCKOO: How on earth did you know? It was only decided this
afternoon.

BOB: Hali knows everything.

HALI: It is nothing mysterious! This afternoon I rushed into Mr.
Robbins the bank manager by chance. His little daughter with
the funny teeth is also to be a wolf.

BOFFIN: It sounds most suitable, but I'm afraid I have rather lost
the thread of the conversation.

SANDRA: It's the pantomime, Boffin dear. They do one every
year. It confuses the natives dreadfully.

CUCKOO: How can you, Sandra! It was a tremendous success last
time.

SANDRA: Not with the students, Cuckoo. They thought it was
propaganda and resented it. (*To* BOFFIN.) Mrs. Togstone, who
is an ardent supporter of the Samolan Socialist Nationals,
played Dick Whittington. It nearly caused a riot.

MRS. T.: Poor Mrs. Togstone—that native hut—and all those
brooches.

GEORGE: This year they're doing *Cinderella*, less controversial. All
class distinctions nicely adjusted. None of that inflammatory
stuff about men-of-the-people becoming Lord Mayors. Just
honest, straightforward snob value.

SANDRA: I don't think they really believed for a moment that
Mrs. Togstone was a man-of-the-people. They just got
thoroughly muddled by the whole thing and rather irritable.

GEORGE: What will you drink, Hali?

HALI: Some plain soda-water, if you please.

SANDRA: Oh dear—how unconvivial of you.

HALI: If I drink strong liquor before food, I am liable to become
immeasurably gay and make loud noises.

BOFFIN: I should have thought that plain soda-water would
induce even louder ones.

SANDRA: There's a kala-kala cocktail all ready for you. It's a Government House speciality. We call it "Westward Ho".

GEORGE: Come on, Hali—let yourself go and relax—no politics tonight. You don't have to be careful what you say.

CUCKOO: I am sure that Mr. Alani is always careful what he says.

HALI: How kind of you, Mrs. Honey. It is true that I try to be, but my English sometimes betrays me into foolishness. I have not, alas, my father's supreme mastery of the language, but then, he went to Eton.

GEORGE: That's more than I did.

SANDRA (*warningly*): Now then, George—no inverted snobbism——

HALI: My father learnt many other things at Eton beside language.

BOFFIN: Could be.

HALI: And he wore a black shiny hat. We have it still in our library.

SANDRA: Mr. Alani, please weaken and have one little drink. I shall feel utterly miserable if you don't.

HALI: How can I not weaken at such sweet and tempting words.

SANDRA: Chris. Give Mr. Alani a "Westward Ho" immediately, and give me one too, and then we can all make terrific noises and have a wonderful time.

HALI (*with a smile*): I am overruled.

SANDRA: British Colonial Administration in a nutshell.

     CHRISTOPHER *hands* SANDRA *and* HALI *two cocktails.*

SANDRA (*raising her glass*): To your self-control, Mr. Alani.

GEORGE (*raising his glass*): To your ultimate self-government, Hali.

SANDRA: George, dear, there are moments when your subtlety quite overwhelms me.

HALI (*raising his glass*): To you, Lady Alexandra. I drink this one little toast to you because of your great kindness and understanding of my people; because for our island it is sweet that you are here; because you make so light the good work you do; because you always laugh at serious things and make the little swift jokes to ease away the difficulty of living, and above all, Lady Alexandra, to use the vulgar slang that flies too easily to my tongue, because you do not miss a bloody trick! (*He drinks his cocktail in one gulp.*)

SANYAMO (*entering*): Dinner is served, Your Excellencies.

SANDRA: Thank you, dear Hali Alani. That was a most charming toast and it has touched me very much. Come along, everybody—Boffin—Cuckoo—Admiral—Grace— (*She ushers the women off in the direction of the dining-room. Just as she is going, she turns to* GEORGE *and says softly.*) How am I doing, darling?

CURTAIN

ACT II: Scene I

The scene is the same and the time is about three hours later.
When the curtain rises, BOFFIN *is lying in a long chair with a
whisky and soda beside him on a small table.* CUCKOO HONEY *is
seated near him. She is working on an embroidery frame.*

CUCKOO: —and of course they're dreadful about animals—no
imagination whatever. The way they belabour those poor
unfortunate mules would make your blood boil. I've always
been funny like that, you know—I just can't bear to see
animals ill-treated.

BOFFIN: Perhaps you should consult a psychiatrist.

CUCKOO: No, but seriously—they're not nearly as civilised as
they think they are. Of course, some of them, the more
educated types like Hali Alani, have a sort of veneer, but it's
only skin-deep, I assure you. Just you try scratching that
veneer, and see what happens.

BOFFIN: I doubt if a suitable opportunity will occur.

CUCKOO: I sometimes wonder if dear Sandra really understands
that.

BOFFIN: What?

CUCKOO: How primitive they still are—underneath.

BOFFIN: I think we're all fairly primitive underneath. I know that
I am constantly having to crush down the most appalling
urges.

CUCKOO: I expect you see life quite differently from ordinary
people—I mean, being a world-famous writer and having
people making a fuss of you all the time.

BOFFIN: They occasionally let up.

CUCKOO: I'm afraid you must have found this evening very dull.

BOFFIN: Not at all. I've enjoyed it immensely.

CUCKOO: You know, I have a dreadful confession to make.

BOFFIN: Confession?

CUCKOO: You'll probably think me absolutely awful, but I can't bear false pretences and playing up to people—it's just not in my nature.

BOFFIN: Very commendable.

CUCKOO: And anyhow, you're so brilliant and successful that what I say couldn't matter to you one way or the other, could it?

BOFFIN: That depends what it is.

CUCKOO: Well, it's this—I've read all your books and, frankly, I didn't care for them.

BOFFIN: Did you buy them or get them from the library?

CUCKOO: I bought them of course. We have all our books sent out from Hatchards.

BOFFIN: Well, that's all right then, isn't it?

CUCKOO: Honestly, I don't think they're worthy of you.

BOFFIN: How do you know?

CUCKOO: Do you—really and truly—like them yourself?

BOFFIN: Tremendously. I just can't put them down.

CUCKOO: Of course, I know they're frightfully clever and all that, but you must admit they don't "contribute" very much, do they?

BOFFIN: They contribute a hell of a lot to me.

CUCKOO: I wasn't speaking commercially.

BOFFIN: I was.

CUCKOO: With the world in its present state there are so many really important things to write about.

BOFFIN: Name three.

CUCKOO: I know I'm not very good at expressing myself and I expect you think I'm an awful fool——

BOFFIN: The idea had occurred to me.

CUCKOO (*with a flustered little laugh*): I asked for that—didn't I?

BOFFIN: Yes.

CUCKOO: But a man with your gifts and your experience of the world and people, don't you think you have a sort of responsibility, a sort of duty, to the public?

BOFFIN: In what way?

CUCKOO: You could do so much to help.

BOFFIN: Who?

CUCKOO: All sorts of people.

BOFFIN: How?

CUCKOO: I see it's no use saying any more. You're just deliberately misunderstanding me.

BOFFIN: I wouldn't be sure of that.

CUCKOO (*with dignity*): You must forgive me if I have been impertinent.

BOFFIN: Why?

CUCKOO: I'm sure I'm very sorry if I spoke out of turn. I should have thought a man in your position would be big enough to be able to take a little honest criticism.

BOFFIN: Why?

CUCKOO (*angrily, shoving her embroidery into her bag*): But I see I was wrong.

BOFFIN: Then you're making giant strides, Mrs. Honey.

> CHRISTOPHER *comes in.*

CHRISTOPHER: I've just packed the Turlings into their car. Their battery's dead and they have no lights, so Bob Frome is leading them home. Where's Lady A.?

CUCKOO: She's still in the garden with Hali Alani. They went out a long time ago.

CHRISTOPHER: Edward has finished with H. E. He's gone to his own office to sign some letters. He asked me to tell you to pick him up there when you go.

CUCKOO: It's getting very late.

CHRISTOPHER: I can drop you home if you like. I've got to go to Mitzi's party at the Opula Club.

CUCKOO: No. I'd better wait for Edward. Oughtn't you wait until Hali Alani goes?

CHRISTOPHER: No. H. E. said it would be all right. Mr. Kennedy, would you explain to Lady A. that I've gone on to Mitzi's?

BOFFIN: Certainly. Who is Mitzi?

CHRISTOPHER: Mitzi Radlett. She's quite a character. I'll get Lady A. to ask her up to dinner one night and we'll make her do her imitations. She takes off everyone in the Colony.

CUCKOO: Personally I can't stand her. Of course in our position here we have to be outwardly nice to everyone. I mean to say, it's part of the job, isn't it?

BOFFIN: Presumably.

CUCKOO: I said to my husband only the other day, "Have her to the house if you must—officially. But no more than that."

BOFFIN: Was he planning a more intimate association?

CUCKOO: No, Mr. Kennedy. He was not.

CHRISTOPHER: Poor old Mitzi. You have got it in for her, haven't you?

CUCKOO: Certainly not. I just don't happen to like the way she goes on. Of course, I know she has money and entertains a lot, and Heaven knows I'm not a snob, but one either knows how to behave or one doesn't. (*To* BOFFIN.) Don't you agree?

BOFFIN: With every fibre of my being.

CHRISTOPHER: She's very popular on the island.

CUCKOO: Only with a certain set. Actually, she is a very bad influence. Pam Hewlenn said that the last party she gave was an absolute brawl, all colours and classes mixed up.

CHRISTOPHER: *I* think Mitzi's parties are great fun. Good-night, Cuckoo. Good-night, sir.

BOFFIN: Good-night. I hope you have a good time.

CHRISTOPHER: Thanks.

   He goes.

CUCKOO: Poor Chris.

BOFFIN: Why poor? He seems remarkably cheerful to me.

CUCKOO: We're all rather worried about him. He gads about far too much.

BOFFIN: Why shouldn't he when he's not on duty?

CUCKOO: In a small island like this, any of us who have the slightest connection with the Government are always on duty.

BOFFIN: I think you shoulder the White Man's Burden quite splendidly, Mrs. Honey. You must be exhausted.

CUCKOO: I know you're laughing at me and I suppose it's my own fault.

BOFFIN: You have the most disconcerting habit of making statements to which there is absolutely no reply.

CUCKOO: I just can't help feeling strongly about certain things. I was brought up in India you see, and I expect a sense of the importance of British prestige is more or less ingrained in me.

BOFFIN: Time marches on.

CUCKOO: My father was stationed at Darjeeling when I was born.

BOFFIN: Nice place, Darjeeling.

CUCKOO: Do you know it?

BOFFIN: No. But a friend of mine shot himself through the foot there once. He spoke very highly of it.

CUCKOO: I always think that India gives one an entirely different viewpoint, particularly with regard to our relationships with native populations.

BOFFIN: It's certainly done its best.

CUCKOO: I know that the modern democratic idea is that we should treat them all as equals, but I must say——

BOFFIN: Allow me to correct you. The really modern idea is that we should treat them all as superiors.

CUCKOO (*with a gay laugh*): I see we agree at last.

BOFFIN: It's been a grisly struggle.

CUCKOO: You mustn't think from the way I go on that I don't like the Samolans. As a matter of fact I'm very fond of them. They're like children in some ways but what I really feel is that they are becoming rather spoiled children. That's why I'm worried about Sandra.

BOFFIN: Oh—are you worried about *her* too?

CUCKOO: Not worried exactly—but a little bit perturbed.

BOFFIN: Why?

CUCKOO: Well, I don't think she quite realises a lot of things, all the ins and outs of the situation.

BOFFIN: She'll probably win through in the end. Give her time.

CUCKOO: You've known her for years, haven't you?

BOFFIN: Yes. We're old friends.

CUCKOO: She must have been lovely as a girl.

BOFFIN: No. As a matter of fact she was quite hideous.

CUCKOO: Oh!

BOFFIN: Fat and ungainly, you know—always knocking things over.

CUCKOO: You can't expect me to believe that.

BOFFIN: You can believe anything if you have enough faith. Wishful thinking works wonders.

CUCKOO: You could help her.

BOFFIN: In what way?

CUCKOO: By talking to her.

BOFFIN: About the ins and outs of the native population?

CUCKOO: Well, more or less—I mean——

BOFFIN: That's exactly what I would be fascinated to find out. What *do* you mean?

CUCKOO: Everybody adores Sandra. She's so enthusiastic and so vital and she works terribly hard, but she *is* inclined to be a trifle indiscreet.

BOFFIN: Indiscreet?

CUCKOO: You must have seen for yourself at dinner to-night how she was laughing and joking with Hali Alani to the exclusion of everyone else and now she's been out in the garden alone with him for hours. I know there isn't anything in it *really* and that it's just thoughtlessness, but you know how people gossip in a small place like this.

BOFFIN: That is becoming increasingly clear to me.

CUCKOO (*stiffly*): I'm afraid I rather resent your tone, Mr. Kennedy.

BOFFIN: Well, that's quite fair. I've been resenting yours for the last ten minutes. (*He rises and goes to the drink table.*) Would you like a drink?

CUCKOO: No, thank you.

BOFFIN: I think I'll have one if you don't mind.

CUCKOO: I wouldn't like you to misunderstand my motives in speaking as I have.

BOFFIN (*mixing a drink*): Don't worry. I understand your motives perfectly.

CUCKOO: I thought I could talk to you confidentially, as a friend.

BOFFIN: Surely that was rather an erratic assumption, considering that we only met this evening for the first time?

CUCKOO: I'm aware that I am entirely to blame for the fact that we're not hitting it off. I should never have made the foolish mistake of criticising your books.

BOFFIN: Your real mistake lay in imagining that I should be interested.

CUCKOO: That was downright rude, Mr. Kennedy.

BOFFIN: Yes, it was, Mrs. Honey, and, unlike your own rather

inept achievements in the same field, it was fully intended to
be.

CUCKOO (*bridling*): Well, really! Good-night, Mr. Kennedy.

BOFFIN (*raising his glass*): The skin off your nose, Mrs. Honey.

> CUCKOO *sweeps out.*
> BOFFIN *looks after her with a slight smile and sips his drink.*
> SANDRA *and* HALI ALANI *come in from the garden.* HALI *is wearing
> a tuberose in his buttonhole.*

SANDRA: Boffin, darling. Your first evening in Samolo and here
you are sozzling all by yourself in the moonlight. Where's
everybody gone?

BOFFIN: I can tell you categorically, but I warn you it will be
dull.

SANDRA: Where's Chris?

BOFFIN: With dear old Mitzi. She's giving some killing imitations
at the what's-a-name club.

SANDRA: You must meet Mitzi. She's one of those people one
loves out here but rather dreads having to lunch in London.

BOFFIN: Heaven knows I'm not a snob but one must draw the
line somewhere.

SANDRA: I see you've been talking to Cuckoo.

BOFFIN: Cuckoo has been talking to me. There's a subtle
distinction.

SANDRA: There's something about Cuckoo that I like but I can
never think what it is. Has she gone home?

BOFFIN: She flounced off in a rage to collect her allergic husband.

SANDRA: Were you beastly to her?

BOFFIN: Fairly. But she certainly asked for it.

SANDRA: Oh dear! There's been a drama—I can feel it in the air.
Hali, do help yourself to a drink and sit down. You look so
impermanent standing about like that.

HALI: It is getting late, Lady Sandra. It is time for me to tootle off
home.

SANDRA: Don't tootle quite yet, just relax for a minute after
pounding up and down all those garden paths. (*To* BOFFIN.)
He's been teaching me the Samolan names for everything—
absolutely fascinating. The night-scented jasmin's out on
account of the moon. I've forgotten the name for that already.

HALI: Solali Lalua Lugi.

BOFFIN: That ought to fix Beverley Nichols.

SANDRA: Give me some orange juice, Boffin. There's some in that jug. Hali—would you like whisky, brandy, kala-kala or what?

HALI: I, too, will take orange juice.

SANDRA: Oh dear, it's awfully difficult to influence people who only drink orange juice. Won't you at least have a nip of gin in it?

HALI: If you will, Lady Sandra.

SANDRA: Of course I will.

HALI: Is it me that you wish to influence?

SANDRA: Oh, yes. Didn't you know? I've been tearing myself to shreds in the garden for hours.

HALI: On what part of me is it that you wish the influence to work? My character or my political views?

SANDRA: I think you have a charming character, Hali. I wouldn't try to tamper with it for the world.

HALI: Was it for the politics, then, that you gave me the tuberose?

SANDRA (*smiling*): I gave you the tuberose because it smells very nice and looks very nice. You really should have a hibiscus behind your ear. I can't imagine why I didn't think of it.

BOFFIN: You must be slipping.

HALI: A red flower behind the ear in this country makes a great significance.

BOFFIN: It would be fairly significant in Uxbridge.

HALI: Where is that?

BOFFIN: A dear little village near Arthur Rank.

SANDRA: Boffin—be a dear and give us our drinks and go right away somewhere.

BOFFIN: I've only just unpacked.

SANDRA: You know perfectly well what I mean. Haven't you got a nice book to read?

BOFFIN: Yes. It's called *To-morrow is the End*. But I don't feel in the mood for it to-night. (*He hands them their drinks.*)

SANDRA: Go and play the piano, then. Just let your fingers roam lightly over the keys—not too lightly though, because the climate makes them stick. Improvise—something romantic and nostalgic. (*To* HALI.) He improvises beautifully.

BOFFIN (*going into the house*): Don't we all?

He goes.

SANDRA: Isn't Boffin charming? He's one of my dearest friends.

HALI: In that he is most splendidly fortunate.

SANDRA: Have you really read his books or were you merely being polite?

HALI: I have read every one. They have made me laugh like drains.

SANDRA: Just one drain, Hali. Not a whole lot.

HALI: I find the English idiom difficult to grip.

SANDRA (*settling herself in the chaise-longue*): Now then—where were we?

HALI (*sitting on the verandah rail*): When?

SANDRA: When I said it was time to come in.

HALI: We were speaking about the Samolan children and how like fishes they swam. You also mentioned His Excellency your husband and the hump of Richard the Third.

SANDRA: You probably thought I was dotty. But I must have been leading up to something.

HALI: You were looking most pretty while you spoke.

SANDRA: Was I really? How gratifying.

HALI: I am very susceptible to the beauty of ladies.

SANDRA: Very right and proper. Your parents must be so relieved.

HALI: In any country, Lady Sandra, you would be most lovely. But here in Samolo it is even more clear.

SANDRA: How do you account for that geographical distinction?

HALI: The light on this island is different—particularly when the stars are out. When we were standing by the big jacaranda tree and looking up at the sky—your eyes were shining.

SANDRA (*scrutinising her face in her compact*): Well, my nose is shining now like a lighthouse. (*She powders it vigorously.*)

HALI: You make the mock of my words?

SANDRA: Well, no—not exactly—but I never quite know what to do when people pay me compliments. It rather embarrasses me.

HALI: Most ladies like the compliments no end.

SANDRA: Yes, I'm sure they do, but——

HALI: I do not quite understand. When we walk in the garden you are most sweet and soft, but here on the verandah you are suddenly sharp as nails. I find myself at sea.

SANDRA (*helplessly*): Oh, dear!

HALI: Have I, without knowing, said something beastly rude to offend you?

SANDRA: No, Hali. Of course you haven't.

HALI: Then why is the mood of growing friendship suddenly in the smithereens?

SANDRA: The mood of growing friendship is quite all right—really it is—only I would just like it to stay like that and not become complicated in any way.

> At this moment BOFFIN, indoors, begins to play sentimental music on the piano. There is a slight pause.

HALI: Did His Excellency ask you to talk to me in the garden?

SANDRA (*with a smile*): The tuberose was my own idea entirely.

HALI: Did he, Lady Sandra?

SANDRA (*listening to the music*): There now—that sounds lovely, doesn't it? He has such a light touch. A light touch, Hali, is one of the most important things in the world. You will remember that, won't you?

HALI: I will try. (*He turns away.*)

SANDRA: Are you angry with me?

HALI: Yes.

SANDRA: Oh—please don't be. There isn't anything to be angry about—really there isn't.

HALI: I am a man of great pride in my heart and I do not like to be thought the bloody fool.

SANDRA: No one would ever think you that, Hali.

HALI: I wish to be a friend both to you as a lady, and to your country, which I love much although I have never been there. I wish to be trusted.

SANDRA: There was no question of not trusting you.

HALI: His Excellency does not trust me, or my father.

SANDRA: Of course he does. Why shouldn't he?

HALI: Because he thinks we are behind times and make the bad influence on people.

SANDRA: I don't think he considers you a bad influence exactly. He just feels that your ideas for the future of the country are a little—a little retrogressive.

HALI: What is that?

SANDRA: Well—the opposite of progressive. Going backwards instead of forwards.

HALI: I thought that "progressive" meant going to the left.

SANDRA: Well, in a political sense I suppose it does really; at any rate that is what a lot of people seem to think.

HALI: His Excellency, also?

SANDRA (*firmly*): Yes, Hali. My husband is a socialist and an idealist. He believes that all men should be equal and independent and free to do what they want to do. That is why he wishes to help the Samolans to break away from British Colonial authority and learn to govern themselves.

HALI: But they do not want to. They are most contented as they are.

SANDRA: Yes, I know, but you must see that it would be better for them in the long run.

HALI: Why?

SANDRA (*foundering a little*): Well—because they would ultimately have Dominion status and be their own masters like Canada and Australia and South Africa.

HALI (*horrified*): South Africa?

SANDRA: Oh dear, perhaps I shouldn't have mentioned South Africa. I'm not very good at this sort of discussion. Do let's talk about something else.

HALI (*smiling*): You are a very sweet lady.

SANDRA: That's better. Now we know where we are.

HALI: And that is a beautiful, beautiful dress.

SANDRA: Thank you, Hali. I'm so glad you like it. It came from Paris.

HALI: Does Paris have self-government?

SANDRA: Yes, every Tuesday.

HALI: I have never in my life made the travels. I have never seen any of the world's glorious wonders, Mount Vesuvius, the Arc de Triomphe, the Albert Hall.

SANDRA: Well, when you do, take my advice and make a bee line for the Arc de Triomphe.

HALI: There are so many questions I would wish to pose to you.

SANDRA (*smiling*): Pose away.

HALI: For instance, is it true that in England all the Public Conveniences are free?

SANDRA (*startled*): Public Conveniences? Do you mean buses and taxis and tubes?

HALI: Oh no. I mean Public Conveniences.

SANDRA: What an extraordinary question. Why on earth do you want to know?

HALI: Both my father and I think most deeply about Public Conveniences.

SANDRA: Then you should really try to snap out of it.

HALI: What is snap?

SANDRA: Never mind. It doesn't matter.

HALI: You have not given the answer to my question.

SANDRA: It rather took me by surprise.

HALI: Are they then free for rich and poor alike?

SANDRA: Well, if you must know, some of them are and some of them aren't. In most of them you pop a penny in the slot and hope for the best.

HALI (*clapping his hands*): Hurrah! Bravo! Good egg!

SANDRA: This is one of the most baffling conversations I have ever had.

HALI: Was it about the Public Conveniences that His Excellency wished that you would influence me?

SANDRA: No. Strange as it may seem to you, the subject never came up.

HALI: I am most glad.

SANDRA: I think I am too, really. It's not a particularly edifying topic.

HALI: Was it perhaps that he wished you to persuade me to turn to the left?

SANDRA: No, Hali, it was not. Please don't let's talk about it any more. It was just foolishness.

HALI: You will perhaps let me say one more tiny thing?

SANDRA: If you insist.

HALI: It is this. In the political affairs in which I have power, I believe that I know, and that my father knows, what is best for our people, and no beautiful woman, even you, Lady Sandra, in the moonlight and under the bright stars, would make me change the idea. No siree. Not for all the rice in China.

SANDRA (*laughing*): Oh, Hali—you really are very beguiling.

HALI: Is it at me you laugh now—or my bad English?

SANDRA: A little of both—but it isn't unkind laughter.

HALI: Have I not made you a little ashamed with what I have said?

SANDRA: Yes—as a matter of fact you have.

HALI: That then is to the good.

SANDRA: You must accept your victory gracefully, Hali. There's no necessity to rub it in.

HALI: We are friends?

SANDRA: Of course we are. I really am sorry—I wouldn't have hurt your feelings for the world.

HALI: Whoopee! You make my heart light.

SANDRA: Good. You haven't finished your drink.

HALI: I drink little. It is not well for me when I drink. Sometimes in my life I have been badly drunk and made great trouble.

SANDRA: You have that in common with several of my dearest friends.

HALI: Once at a party in the hills, I broke two people's heads— boum—like that—they crack together.

SANDRA: I've often wanted to do that, even when stone-cold sober.

HALI: What is this music he plays now?

SANDRA (*listening*): A very old song—I haven't heard it for ages.

HALI: It is pretty.

SANDRA: It was tremendously popular years ago—it was played by barrel organs and dance orchestras—once it was even done by massed bands at the Aldershot Tattoo.

HALI: What please is that?

SANDRA: A lot of soldiers marching about for a week in Hampshire.

HALI: You will dance with me, please?

SANDRA (*startled*): Oh—do you really think that would be a good idea?

HALI: Why not?—I dance with much grace and ease.

SANDRA: I'm sure you do, but don't you think we should look rather silly swirling about out here all by ourselves?

HALI: Who would see us?

SANDRA: Well, almost anybody really—Sanyamo might come in—he's a very correct butler—it might fluster him.

HALI: Sanyamo is himself a most alert dancer—ever since he was a little boy he has danced—did you not know that?

SANDRA: No—actually the subject never happened to come up.

HALI: Please, Lady Sandra. It would be such pleasure to me.

SANDRA: Very well, Hali—if you insist.

> *She dances with him. While they are doing so,* CUCKOO *comes in. She sees them and stands transfixed with horror.*

CUCKOO: Lady Alexandra!

SANDRA (*disengaging herself from* HALI'S *arms*): Why, Cuckoo—I thought you had gone ages ago.

CUCKOO: I've been waiting for Edward. He's getting the car. I came back for my bag.

HALI (*picking it up from a chair*): Is this it?

CUCKOO (*taking it—icily*): Thank you—it is.

SANDRA (*to* HALI): You know, if we are going to take to dancing seriously on this verandah we must do something about the floor. It's like nougat.

CUCKOO: I apologise for intruding.

SANDRA: Please don't, it couldn't matter less. Mind you, if we had been doing something really complicated, such as Hali whirling me round his head like an Indian club, a sudden interruption might have been fatal, but as it is there's no harm done.

> EDWARD *comes in.*

EDWARD: Ah, there you are, Hali Alani. You've parked your car just in front of mine and I can't get out. If you'll give me your keys I can move it.

HALI: I will come myself—I am so sorry. Excuse me, please, Lady Sandra?

HALI *and* EDWARD *go out.*

There is silence for a moment. SANDRA *takes a cigarette and lights it.*

SANDRA (*handing* CUCKOO *the box*): I'm so sorry—cigarette?

CUCKOO: No, thank you.

SANDRA: What's the matter, Cuckoo? You look depressed. Has Edward got the snuffles again?

CUCKOO: I am not depressed, but I am a little upset.

SANDRA: Did you get into an argument with Boffin?

CUCKOO: I think Mr. Kennedy is the rudest man I ever met.

SANDRA: What nonsense, Cuckoo. He's perfectly charming. You must have provoked him. What on earth did you say to make him take against you?

CUCKOO: Whether Mr. Kennedy takes against me or not isn't of the faintest interest to me. It's not that that's upsetting me.

SANDRA: Perhaps it was those crayfish at dinner? George loves them but personally I can never get at them—to me they're a form of occupational therapy.

CUCKOO: It's nothing to do with the crayfish.

SANDRA: It couldn't have been the lamb. It was dull, I grant you, but there was nothing malign about it.

CUCKOO: You are purposely misunderstanding me.

SANDRA: Perhaps, Cuckoo. It's sometimes quite a wise plan, you know.

CUCKOO (*with a rush*): I must say what's on my mind, Sandra. And if you think I'm interfering, it can't be helped. I'm like that and always have been.

SANDRA: Like what?

CUCKOO: If anything's worrying me I just have to come straight out with it.

SANDRA: That must make your life rather convulsive socially.

CUCKOO: I'm your friend, Sandra, you really must believe that.

SANDRA: It may be idiotic of me, but I always believe that everyone is my friend until I have definite proof to the contrary.

CUCKOO: I've lived in the Colonies much longer than you have and I know—I really know.

SANDRA (*quietly*): What do you know, Cuckoo?

CUCKOO: Where to draw the line.

SANDRA: That particular knowledge seems temporarily to have forsaken you.

CUCKOO: I know you think I'm interfering but it can't be helped.

SANDRA: You said that before.

CUCKOO: You must not do these things, Sandra—you really must not!

SANDRA: What things?

CUCKOO: Hali Alani is all very well in his way.

SANDRA: That's all we can any of us hope to be.

CUCKOO: In fact, I'm sure he's very fascinating and attractive——

SANDRA: If this is your idea of coming straight out with something, I have news for you.

CUCKOO: What I mean to say is—that in your position here you cannot afford to—to hob-nob with the natives. You really cannot.

SANDRA (*with a sigh*): Oh, Cuckoo. You are making the most cracking fool of yourself. Do please stop.

> GEORGE *comes in. He is carrying his coat over his arm.*

GEORGE: Hallo, my love. I thought everyone had gone.

SANDRA: They nearly have. Hali is moving his car so that Edward can take Cuckoo home.

GEORGE (*sensing that all is not well*): Have I interrupted a little private chat?

SANDRA: Cuckoo has been advising me on the technique of Colonial social procedure. She has an unerring grip on inessentials.

> BOFFIN *comes in.*

BOFFIN: Has anyone thought of doing anything about that piano?

SANDRA: It's tuned regularly.

BOFFIN: I meant something more drastic than that, like throwing it into the sea.

SANDRA: Thank you for playing it anyway, dear Boffin. You've been a great comfort.

GEORGE (*going to the drink table*): How about a nightcap?

> EDWARD *and* HALI *come back.*

EDWARD (*to* CUCKOO): I'm ready when you are, dear.

GEORGE: Won't you have a drink before you go?

EDWARD: No, thank you, sir.

HALI: I must say good-night, Your Excellency. It has been an evening of great delight.

GEORGE: I hope my wife has been looking after you all right?

HALI: Lady Sandra, like always, has been most kind.

SANDRA: We've been walking in the garden, George. It was all highly romantic, and I gave him a tuberose, and later we had a fascinating little chat about Public Conveniences.

EDWARD (*in horror*): A tuberose—oh dear! (*He sneezes.*)

SANDRA: Now that must be mental suggestion, Edward. You couldn't possibly have smelt it from right over there.

HALI (*advancing to* SANDRA): Lady Sandra——

SANDRA (*with sudden decision*): Just a moment, Hali. (*She gives a swift look at* CUCKOO.) George.

GEORGE: Yes, dear?

SANDRA: Hali has very kindly said that he would take me to Mitzi Radlett's party at the club. You know she invited us both and I never did a thing about it.

GEORGE: It's a bit late to drive all that way, isn't it?

SANDRA: Not really late—and I don't feel in the least like going to bed.

GEORGE: Well, I do, I must say.

SANDRA: Ah, darling, but you've been working, while I've merely been enjoying myself. As a matter of fact I still am.

GEORGE: I still think it's a bit late to go careering about the island.

SANDRA: You can't call just going to the dear old Opula club careering about the island.

GEORGE: Are you going, Cuckoo?

CUCKOO: I certainly am not.

GEORGE: Oh, of course, I forgot, you and Mitzi had a bit of a dust-up, didn't you?

CUCKOO: Not at all—it is merely that . . .

EDWARD: Never mind all that now, dear . . .

GEORGE: Do you feel like going, Boffin?

BOFFIN: Well—I . . .

SANDRA: I've been trying to talk him into it for hours but he was adamant. He says his head is still splitting from the plane and he thinks he's starting a summer cold. How is your head now, dear?

BOFFIN: Just turning round and round.

GEORGE: Try some Phensic.

SANDRA: I've had some put by his bed.

BOFFIN: You think of everything, dear.

SANDRA: Hali will look after me and drive me back all right— won't you, Hali?

HALI: For me it will be the great pleasure to drive you anywhere you wish, Lady Sandra.

SANDRA: How sweet of you—thank you so much. As a matter of fact, Chris is at the party already and he can bring me home quite easily. Anyhow, I shall only stay a little while, just to make a politeness. (*She kisses* GEORGE.) Good-night, darling.

GEORGE: Well, if you must go you must, I suppose. Run along and enjoy yourself.

SANDRA: Don't forget to have a light breakfast in the morning because there's curry for lunch. Good-night, Edward—do try to wipe from your mind anything in the least floral. Boffin, darling, I do hope you sleep well and wake up feeling smooth and ironed out. The room you're in is rather stuffy, I'm afraid—you'd better do what I do and throw everything wide open.

BOFFIN: You're telling me!

SANDRA: Come along, Hali—we really must not dawdle any more—we should have been there hours ago. (*She snatches up her cloak and bag and slips her arm through* HALI'S.) Good-night, Cuckoo. I'm afraid you've had a beastly evening what with one thing and another. She's in rather a state, Edward, so you'd better keep your eye on her—and for heaven's sake see that she doesn't hob-nob with anyone peculiar on the way home.

> SANDRA *and* HALI *go off*.

THE LIGHTS FADE

Scene II

SCENE: *The scene is Hali Alani's house.*

TIME: *About three hours have elapsed since the preceding Act.*

The Beach House is a small shack on the edge of the sea at Paiana Bay on the north-east coast of the island. In order to reach it from Pendarla, the capital, it is necessary to drive over the mountains and through Lailanu Pass, one of the most famous beauty spots of the island, and descend through sugar-cane and banana plantations to the sea.

The shack is comfortably furnished with beach furniture imported from America. This has been embellished by a few Samolan ideas. There are, for instance, two native war drums in one corner, a carved wooden screen painted in bizarre colours, a curtain made of scarlet native beads hanging over the door on the left which leads to the kitchenette, the shower and changing room. There is also, prominently displayed, a shining and hideous cocktail cabinet. Along the back wall are shuttered windows opening on to the verandah and the beach. The main door is on the right.

When the curtain rises, moonlight is shining strongly through the shutters and there is the muffled roar of the surf pounding on the reef a half a mile away. There is the sound of a car drawing up outside, then, after a moment or two HALI comes in and switches on the lights. SANDRA follows him. He takes her cloak and lays it on the divan. He then flings open the shutters of one of the windows.

SANDRA: Do you always drive as fast as that?

HALI: Only when I am gay and happy.

SANDRA: I must try to think of something to depress you on the way back.

HALI: You are not still angry with me?

SANDRA: I think I'm too sleepy to be angry—I'm just resigned.

HALI: We will have the little drink and then you will be no more sleepy.

SANDRA: No, thank you, Hali.

HALI: It is with such pride and pleasure that I bring you here—it is so beautiful and peaceful and there is always the sound of the sea—it is cool too, on this side of the island at night.

SANDRA: I suspect that it will be even cooler in Government House in the morning.

HALI: Nobody need ever know that we make this little adventure. It will be the quiet secret between you and me.

SANDRA: Nonsense, Hali—it will be no such thing—I detest having quiet secrets with anybody—it makes me nervous.

HALI: The whole evening has taken the nosedive.

SANDRA: It certainly has.

HALI: I have offended you by doing the quick impulsive thing when I should have carefully thought. I would not offend you for all the tea in China.

SANDRA: Rice.

HALI: It is optional.

SANDRA: Anyhow, you haven't offended me—you've merely made me feel rather silly. I know it was all my own fault in the first place but that doesn't make it any better—and as for that ass Cuckoo—I'd like to throttle her.

HALI: Was it because of her that you had the swift idea about going to the party?

SANDRA: Yes—it was.

HALI: Because she saw that we danced—and you are the Governor's lady and I am the wrong colour?

SANDRA: Let's go back now, please, Hali—it's been great fun—but the fun's over.

HALI: One small drink?

SANDRA: No, thank you.

HALI: Please, Lady Sandra—to show that you are forgiving me.

SANDRA: I've quite forgiven you—except for driving like a maniac—as I said before, it's all been my own fault—and if I hadn't been half-asleep after that idiotic party of Mitzi's, I should have noticed where we were going before we got nearly to the top of the mountains.

HALI: You did not enjoy driving through Lailanu Pass and looking at the great peaks like black fingers in the sky, and the moon shining far away on the sea?

SANDRA: Of course I did—it was lovely.

HALI: To come here was so little further—I wanted so much for you to see it——

SANDRA: I know, Hali—but you must realise——

HALI: I realise that I make the bitter mistake—I am most, most sorry.

SANDRA: There's no reason to be so utterly miserable, Hali—it doesn't matter all that much.

HALI: Please, one drink before we go?

SANDRA (*giving in*): All right—just one, then—and a very small one at that.

HALI (*delighted*): That is good—my heart begins to rise up. I will mix you the kala-kala as it should be right and proper—I have the special mellowed bottles here—most ancient—my father gave them to me.

SANDRA: A very nice paternal thought.

HALI (*at the drink cabinet*): In the old days they drink it with ground kri-kri nuts and most hot peppers, but the custom died out.

SANDRA: I'm so glad.

HALI: The missionaries said it was wicked because it made too much excitement and people forgot the new Lord God and went back to Old Tikki and Fumfumbolo.

SANDRA: What are they?

HALI: Volcanoes.

SANDRA: Most appropriate.

HALI: I will get the ice from the frig—I will be two shakes.

SANDRA: The G is soft, Hali.

HALI: You would see the kitchen? It is the last word in daring modern innovations.

SANDRA: By all means.

They both go off left.

HALI (*off*): One moment, I have forgotten the little pail.

He comes in again—goes to the drink cabinet, pours himself out a

> *tumbler of neat kala-kala, drinks it at one gulp, sighs with*
> *satisfaction, picks up the ice pail and goes off again.*

(*Off.*) Hey presto—under the tap she goes.

> *There is the sound of an ice tray clanking into the sink.*

(*Off.*) You would like to scramble the eggs, perhaps?

SANDRA: No, thank you—I gave that up in the late 'thirties.

HALI: One moment—I will put back the tray.

SANDRA: No—you take the bucket—I'll put the tray back.

HALI: It came all the way from Detroit, Michigan.

SANDRA: What did?

HALI: The frig.

> *He comes in with the ice bucket, goes to the drinks cabinet, quickly*
> *pours himself out another kala-kala, gulps it down, and is busy*
> *mixing the drinks when* SANDRA *returns.*

HALI: You like this shining cabinet for the drink?

SANDRA (*evasively*): I'm sure it's very useful.

HALI: That came all the way from Detroit, Michigan, too.

SANDRA: Obviously a very up-and-coming little town.

HALI: There—(*He hands her a glass.*)—now we drink—but we
must make the Toast——

SANDRA: Must we?

HALI: I will say to you in Samolan words—"Welcome to my
house—to my father's house, to the house of my father's
father"—"Lanialu i kin awa-lali a um koka a um koka um
koka."

SANDRA: Thank you, Hali—that sounded very gracious. (*She
drinks and gasps.*) My God! It's dynamite!

HALI (*drinking his at one go*): You should not sip, Lady Sandra—it
should be drinking—boum—like so!

SANDRA: No, thank you—I've been caught like that before.

HALI: You would like to swim?

SANDRA (*startled*): Swim!

HALI: At night the water is warm and smooth to the hot body—
it is ripping.

SANDRA: I'm sure it is—but I would really rather go home now,
if you don't mind.

HALI: You would like me to play the drums?

SANDRA: Another time I would simply adore it—but as it is getting late, I think——

HALI: They are war drums—King Kefumalani gave them to my father's great father.

SANDRA: How very sweet of him.

HALI: King Kefumalani was the last King of Samolo. He was assassinated because he made curious practices. (*He pours himself another drink.*)

SANDRA: Please don't have any more, Hali—you have to drive.

HALI (*laughing gaily*): You will have one more, too.

SANDRA: I most certainly will not.

HALI: Then I will not either. (*He puts down the glass.*) There.

SANDRA: Good—that's very considerate of you.

HALI: But I will play the drums—just once.

SANDRA (*sighing hopelessly and sitting down*): Very well.

HALI: They were not only used for war—they were used for great high jinks also. Which would you like me to play?

SANDRA: Frankly, Hali—whichever is the quickest.

HALI: When the drums start there is no time any more—you will see——

SANDRA (*glancing at her wrist-watch*): Three minutes' drum playing and then home—that is my final word.

HALI (*gleefully*): We shall see— Oh, we shall very much see! (*He drinks his drink at one gulp and goes over to the drums.*)

SANDRA (*protesting*): Hali! You said you wouldn't——

HALI (*at the drums*): Listen—listen——

> *He begins to play the drums, quite softly at first with his fingers, then more quickly and more loudly, until he is thumping with all the force of his hands.* SANDRA *watches him in dismay. It is obvious that he is becoming more and more excitable. He begins to sway his body to the rhythm and give little grunts. Finally she gets up and goes over to him.*

SANDRA: Hali—stop it——

> *He pays no attention.*

Stop it at once, do you hear me!

> *He continues to beat the drums louder and louder. She tries once more vainly to make him stop, then she pulls his arms away and kicks one of the drums over. He stands still quivering for a moment and then*

suddenly seizes her in his arms and kisses her passionately. She slaps
his face, wrenches herself free, and runs to the other side of the room.

(*Furiously.*) How dare you behave like this—you must be out of
your mind.

HALI: We will have one more beautiful little drink and you will
forgive me.

SANDRA (*firmly*): I will never forgive you, Hali, unless you drive
me home at once and stop all this idiotic nonsense.

HALI (*at the drink cabinet*): You have been very rude, Lady
Sandra—very rude indeed.

SANDRA: Now, look here, Hali——

HALI (*pouring himself a stiff drink*): You have pushed over the
drum that King Kefumalani gave to my father's great father.
That was most vulgar.

SANDRA (*trying to control the situation*): Will you please sit down
for a moment, Hali—quite quietly—I want you to listen to
what I have to say—it is very important.

HALI: I will not sit down.

SANDRA: All right—stand up then.

HALI: I will sit down. (*He sits rather suddenly on a chair.*)

SANDRA: Now then.

HALI: King Kefumalani was a wonderful man—he had great
splendid teeth and——

SANDRA: Never mind about King Thingummyjig's teeth for the
moment——

HALI: He loved my father's great father—that is why he gave
him the drum—and you, a high lady from England, come all
the way to Samolo and kick it over—that is bad, bad, bad.

SANDRA: All right, I'll pick up the damned drum—there. (*She
does so.*) Now are you satisfied?

HALI (*hopefully*): You would like me to play a little more?

SANDRA: No, I wouldn't. I want you to be quiet for a minute and
listen.

HALI: If I am quiet and listen, I hear the sea, and if I hear the sea
when my heart is low and unhappy, I cry, and if I cry I go on
and on and on and it is most ghastly.

SANDRA: Well, just forget about the sea, there's a dear, and listen
to me—I want you to give me the key of the car so that I can

drive home. If you wish to come with me, please do. If, on the other hand, you would prefer to stay here and really enjoy yourself with the drums I will send somebody back with the car for you.

HALI: It is a very beautiful car—it came all the way from Detroit, Michigan.

SANDRA: They ought to give you the Freedom of the City.

HALI (*dreamily*): All the long weary way across the sea it came—from——

SANDRA: I'm not interested for the moment in where it came from, Hali, but where it's going to—and it's going back to Government House with me in it—and at once. Please give me the key.

HALI: Umpa tishi twazi makebolo.

SANDRA (*irritably*): What does that mean?

HALI: They are very disgusting words—I would rather not say.

SANDRA: Give me the key of the car please, Hali.

HALI: That is most pretty.

SANDRA: What is?

HALI (*pointing to her sapphire and diamond clip*): That—what does it mean, please?

SANDRA: It doesn't mean anything—it's just a clip.

HALI: I will give you a ruby that will mean much—I have many jewels.

SANDRA: I would rather have the key of the car.

HALI: You are not making enjoyment here?

SANDRA (*patiently and slowly*): No, Hali—it is very late—and I want to go home.

HALI: We will have one more sweet little drink——

SANDRA (*losing her temper*): I've had enough of this, Hali. I was willing to overlook your embarrassing behaviour of a few minutes ago because you were obviously working yourself into a frenzy with those idiotic drums and didn't know what you were doing. You are also very drunk indeed, and making an abject fool of yourself, and unless you give me the key of the car immediately and let me go away—I shall never speak to you again as long as I live.

HALI: You are angry now—that is bad news.

SANDRA: I am worse than angry. I'm bitterly disappointed in you and ashamed of myself.

HALI (*cheerfully*): Then we will dance. There is no music but I will make the rhythm with my feet. (*He advances towards her.*)

SANDRA (*backing*): Please don't come near me.

HALI: But we cannot possibly dance one at each side of the room—it would look sickening.

SANDRA (*almost shrieking*): I don't want to dance!

HALI: Then we will drink.

SANDRA (*having an idea*): All right—we'll drink—where's your glass.

HALI (*delighted*): That is good—that is magnificent—that is a knock-out! You are a true blue sport.

SANDRA (*at the drink cabinet, pouring him a full tumbler*): Here.

HALI (*taking it*): You too, please.

SANDRA: No—I've had enough.

HALI: Then I will not—it is no fun.

SANDRA: Very well—to hell with it! (*She pours herself a drink and drinks it at one go.*) There——

HALI (*drinking his*): Wonderful—wonderful! This is the cat's whiskers!

SANDRA (*clutching her throat*): Oh, dear!

HALI: Do not mind—the sharp feeling will pass in a moment and the glow will begin.

SANDRA (*in a strangled voice*): That was very, very silly of me.

HALI: Wait a little—you will see how jolly you will be—you will be dancing and singing about the room and making wise-cracks.

SANDRA: I shall be doing nothing of the sort.

HALI: You do not know the real kala-kala—it makes strange magic inside.

SANDRA: That's what I'm afraid of.

HALI: You must be brave. You must burn the boats.

SANDRA: I've already singed my digestive tract.

HALI: In the old days at the big wedding ceremonials they would drink kala-kala for three days and nights.

SANDRA: That must have made the honeymoon fairly unnecessary.

HALI: But the missionaries stopped that too.

SANDRA: Spoilsports! (*She laughs.*)

HALI (*triumphantly*): There—now it begins.

SANDRA: What begins?

HALI: You start to feel larky.

SANDRA: Oh, Hali, you do say the most idiotic things.

HALI: Please to sit down.

SANDRA (*sitting*): Certainly. (*She hiccups.*) There now!

HALI: That is very lucky.

SANDRA: Who for?

HALI: You must have some more—swiftly.

SANDRA: No, I mustn't. (*She hiccups again.*) Damn.

HALI (*pouring her another drink*): Here—do not this time drink at one swallow—sip gently——

SANDRA: I don't want it, I tell you.

HALI: It is the sure cure—you must.

SANDRA (*taking the glass*): "A little learning is a dang'rous thing; Drink deep, or taste not the Pierian spring;—There shallow draughts intoxicate the brain,—And drinking largely sobers us again." Pope. (*She empties her glass at one gulp again.*) Oh dear, I forgot to sip.

HALI: Pope?

SANDRA: Yes—I learnt it when I was a tiny little girl.

HALI: You are a Catholic?

SANDRA (*giggling*): No, no, no—not the Pope—just Pope.

HALI: I do not understand.

SANDRA: He was a poet and he wrote a lot of lovely things— "And mistress of herself though China fall"—How extraordinary that I should remember that. Alexander Pope—Born 1688—Died 1744. There now.

HALI (*patiently*): Please explain.

SANDRA: Then there was "Little Lamb who made thee?" but I think that was Blake.

HALI: I will have more drink.

SANDRA: Why not? Why not indeed? "The dew was falling fast, the stars begin to blink; I heard a voice; it said 'Drink, pretty creature, drink.'"

HALI (*at the drink cabinet*): I beg your pardon—I do not quite catch——

SANDRA: William Wordsworth—Born 1770—Died 1850. I won a prize for reciting poetry at Roedean, you know.

HALI: What is Roedean?

SANDRA: It's a girl's school in Sussex. The air is tremendously bracing.

HALI: Is that a good thing?

SANDRA: Now I come to look back on it I'm not quite sure. I was also captain of the cricket team for seven months. I can't think how I could have been so versatile.

HALI: I fear I find myself at the sea again.

SANDRA: Would you like me to sing you the school song? It's very inspiring.

HALI (*delighted*): You will really sing to me?

SANDRA: Why not? We must all pull our weight in the boat.

HALI: That will be more than delightful. I am excessively musical.

SANDRA (*getting up a trifle unsteadily and raising her glass*): Wait a minute—I can't remember the first line—oh yes—— (*She sings.*)

> Oh, the cricket First Eleven
> Is the best in all the land
> It's the one above all others
> We admire on every hand.
> May your scores be never failing
> And your bowling ever true,
> O Noble First Eleven
> Here's our best of healths to you.

HALI (*confused but appreciative*): That was most catchy.

SANDRA: They've gone.

HALI: Who?

SANDRA: My hiccups. Please count ten slowly, will you.

HALI: One, two, three, four, five, six, seven, eight, nine, ten.

SANDRA: Once more, please.

HALI: One, two, three, four, six, seven, eight, nine, ten.

SANDRA: You missed out five. You *are* silly. (*She laughs inordinately.*)

HALI (*pleased*): You are happy again now?

SANDRA: Happy as a bee—busy as a sandboy.

HALI: I do not understand.

SANDRA: Which pocket do you keep the key of the car in?

HALI (*tapping his right-hand trouser pocket*): This one. But we will not talk about the car any more—It is not cheerful—we will swim.

SANDRA (*meditatively*): Swim like a fish—drink like a fish—"And under that Almighty fin—the littlest fish shall enter in"— Rupert Brooke.

HALI: You are perhaps a little drunk? That is very gay and most funny.

SANDRA: Tight as a tick—tight as a drum—— (*She looks puzzled.*)

HALI (*eagerly*): You would like me to play the drum?

SANDRA: Please do—it would be delightful.

HALI (*surprised*): You would really like?

SANDRA: But certainly—I adore drums—all sorts of drums—big drums—little drums—kettle drums—oil drums—ear drums— ——

HALI (*pleased*): You see—you are beginning to make the jokes.

SANDRA: I can do better than that—just give me time.

HALI: You would like another drink?

SANDRA (*taking out her compact*): Yes, please.

HALI (*gratified*): You really would?

SANDRA (*shaking out her powder puff*): Immensely—I would like to drink a toast to Cuckoo.

HALI (*at the drink cabinet*): She is a stupid cow.

SANDRA: Her motives are pure and she speaks straight from the shoulder. She has told everybody on the island that I have had my face lifted. (*She looks at herself in the glass.*) I wish to God I had!

HALI: Your face is most glorious.

SANDRA: That's going a little far, but thank you all the same.

HALI (*bringing her her drink*): Here is the drink.

SANDRA: Put it down on that dear little table—I will sip it rhythmically while you are playing the drums.

HALI: That will be good.

SANDRA (*sweetly*): You are still quite determined not to give me the key of the car—before you start, I mean?

HALI (*petulantly*): Oh, no, no, no—please to not start the argument again.

SANDRA: All right—all right—be it on your own head—Fire away.

HALI (*enchanted*): Haha—the evening is once more the smasheroo!

> *He goes to the drums and begins to thump them again, softly at first, then more loudly.* SANDRA *gets up, a trifle unsteadily and watches him. Then she begins to dance very slightly to the rhythm he is beating. He sees her and gives a loud crow of delight.*

HALI (*chanting*): Aouna lu trebi—Aouna lu karoma—E slunga klabonga!

SANDRA (*still dancing but shouting to make herself heard*): What does that mean?

HALI (*also shouting gleefully*): I will tell you later—when we swim in the warm sea——

> *He bangs louder and louder and begins to grunt again.* SANDRA *dances round him twice in a widening circle. On her second time round she picks up a bottle from the drink cabinet and cracks him on the back of the head with it. He gives a slight groan and staggers back against her—he seizes her in his arms and falls to the ground, dragging her with him. After a while she wriggles free from him and gets up. She stands looking at him anxiously for a moment, then kneels down and feels his heart—she gives a sigh of relief—then plunges her hand into his trouser pocket—finds the key of the car and scrutinises it carefully.*

SANDRA: "Do not lift him from the bracken—leave him lying where he fell"—William Edmondstone Aytoun. Born 1813. Died 1865.

> *She snatches up her cloak and bag and runs out of the room.*

THE LIGHTS FADE

ACT III: Scene I

The scene is the verandah. The time is about eight o'clock in the morning.

There is a breakfast table centre. There is also a side table upon which are covered dishes, coffee and tea, etc.

When the curtain rises GEORGE *is just finishing his breakfast and reading, desultorily, the Samolan* Daily Reaper. CHRISTOPHER *comes in. He is wearing jodhpurs and an open shirt.*

GEORGE: Good morning, Chris.

CHRISTOPHER: Good morning, sir.

GEORGE: Been riding?

CHRISTOPHER: Yes—just to shake up the liver a bit after Mitzi's champagne.

GEORGE: Was it a good party?

CHRISTOPHER: It turned into a bit of a rout before the end.

GEORGE: Did you bring Lady A. back?

CHRISTOPHER: No, she left with Hali Alani. She arrived with him too. It caused quite a sensation.

GEORGE: Why the devil should it?

CHRISTOPHER: Oh, I don't know. It was a sort of a surprise, that's all. I don't think Mitzi quite expected her.

GEORGE: Well, she invited her—she invited us both.

CHRISTOPHER: Oh, had she? I didn't know.

GEORGE: You should have driven her home.

CHRISTOPHER: I offered to, but she said no. You see, I was a bit involved myself.

GEORGE: Oh, you were, were you?

CHRISTOPHER: You know how it is, sir.

GEORGE: Not being blessed with the gift of second sight, I do not.

CHRISTOPHER: Well, you see, I'd had a bit of a row with Sylvia last week at the tennis dance—and—well—we were making it up.

GEORGE: More's the pity.

CHRISTOPHER: I thought you liked Sylvia, sir.

GEORGE (*irritably*): It isn't a question of whether I like Sylvia, and I'm not particularly interested in whom you quarrel with, but you ought to have had enough sense to drive Lady A. home from the party.

CHRISTOPHER: But, sir . . .

GEORGE: You say it caused a sensation when she arrived with Hali. You might have known it would cause still more of a sensation if she left with him. Why didn't you use your head?

CHRISTOPHER: As I told you, sir, I did offer to, but you see . . .

GEORGE: She ought never to have gone. Now we shall have the whole island gossiping.

> BOFFIN *comes in.*

BOFFIN: Good morning, George.

GEORGE: Good morning. Did you sleep well?

BOFFIN: Beautifully. I feel ready for anything. Good morning, Captain Mortlock—how was the party?

CHRISTOPHER (*glumly*): Oh, it was all right.

BOFFIN: Did your hostess oblige with any of her side-splitting impersonations?

GEORGE: He was too busy giving an impersonation himself to notice. A very good impersonation of a damned bad A.D.C.

CHRISTOPHER: Oh, sir!

GEORGE: Go on. Cut along and do a job of work, if you're capable of it. You get on my nerves.

CHRISTOPHER (*hurt*): Yes, sir.

> *He goes.*

BOFFIN: Poor boy. You seem rather testy this morning. Is anything wrong?

GEORGE: I was ticking him off for not bringing Sandra home from the party.

BOFFIN: Perhaps she didn't want him to.

GEORGE: That's not the point. He should have done it whether she wanted him to or not.

BOFFIN: It might have caused a mild scandal if he had carried her off by force.

GEORGE: I've been kicking myself all night long.

BOFFIN: You must be exhausted.

GEORGE: I should never have let her go off alone with Hali in the first place.

BOFFIN: It didn't seem to me that you had much choice. Anyhow you started the whole thing yourself.

GEORGE: I know I did. But I didn't mean her to go cavorting about all over the island with him. You should have seen Cuckoo's face when they went off together!

BOFFIN: I did. It's not a face I care for.

GEORGE: She's probably been on the telephone to half the Colony by now.

> SANDRA *comes in. She is looking fresh and radiant but she is feeling dreadful. However she is making a valiant effort to over-ride it.*

SANDRA (*kissing* GEORGE): Good morning, darling. Good morning, Boffin—I do hope that you slept like a top. You really were an angel last night to play that hellish piano so beautifully. It absolutely saved the situation. I really must apologise for this barbarous idea of George's of having communal breakfast. I've tried to reason with him but he insists. He saw a country-house comedy once in which everyone was frightfully witty all through the last act and kept on helping themselves to kedgeree.

GEORGE: You're very bright this morning.

SANDRA: Why shouldn't I be? I was up with the lark and sitting on my verandah sipping my early tea and watching the sunrise.

GEORGE: As your room faces due west, you must have had a periscope.

SANDRA: Don't be so crotchety, dear. I mean I was watching the *effect* of the sunrise. It was spectacular. First the mountains turned to pink, and then to mauve and blue, and all the palms and things looked emerald green and . . .

BOFFIN: Like between programmes at the Odeon.

SANDRA (*going over to the side-table*): Isn't anybody going to have anything to eat? (*She lifts the lid of one of the dishes.*) My God, there really *is* kedgeree!

GEORGE: What time did you get home?

SANDRA: Oh, not very late. We didn't stay long.

GEORGE: You should have let Chris drive you back.

SANDRA (*helping herself sparingly to food*): Why?

GEORGE: It would have looked better.

SANDRA: What nonsense.

GEORGE: It isn't nonsense. You know how people talk.

SANDRA: Hali would have been bitterly hurt if I had suddenly abandoned him and gone home with Chris.

GEORGE: You oughtn't to have gone to the party alone with him in the first place.

SANDRA: If you didn't want me to, why didn't you say so?

GEORGE: You know perfectly well I couldn't, straight out in front of everyone.

SANDRA (*coming to the table with her plate*): Don't you think, darling, that you're being just the tiniest bit unreasonable? First, you ask me to use my "woman's wiles" to fascinate Hali and induce him to modify his political opinions—which incidentally he hasn't the faintest intention of doing—then, when I suggested that he should take me to Mitzi's because you were too lazy to go—you were so enthusiastic that you practically tucked us into the car.

GEORGE: I was not enthusiastic. I tried to get Boffin to go with you.

SANDRA: Boffin had a splitting headache, didn't you, dear?

BOFFIN: Yes. I had wind under the heart as well and a touch of athlete's foot.

SANDRA (*to* GEORGE): And now you turn on me because I didn't leave poor Hali flat and come home in a haze of official sanctity with the A.D.C. Poor Chris was off duty anyhow, and making heavy weather with that girl with the vast bust— Sylvia something or other.

BOFFIN: "Who is Sylvia? What is she, that all our swains commend her?"

SANDRA (*automatically*): William Shakespeare. Born 1564. Died 1616.

CHRISTOPHER *comes back.*

CHRISTOPHER: The Chief of Police wants to see you, sir. He says it's urgent.

SANDRA (*involuntarily*): Oh! (*She gives a hiccup.*) There now!

GEORGE: What's the matter?

SANDRA: I've got hiccups again.

BOFFIN: Again?

SANDRA: I had them in the night.

GEORGE (*to* CHRISTOPHER): Tell Bob Frome to come out here.

CHRISTOPHER: Yes, sir. (*He goes.*)

GEORGE: I wonder what the blazes is wrong now!

BOFFIN: Water off a steel knife.

GEORGE: What are you talking about?

BOFFIN: Sandra's hiccups.

SANDRA: Give me some kala-kala.

GEORGE: You can't drink that stuff at eight o'clock in the morning.

SANDRA: Why not? What's the time of day got to do with it? (*She hiccups.*) Damn!

BOFFIN (*bringing her a glass of water and a knife from the side table*): Here—try the water cure first.

SANDRA (*gloomily*): It won't do any good.

BOFFIN: Don't take up a defeatist attitude at the outset. Try to have faith.

SANDRA: Kala-kala's stronger than any faith. That's why the missionaries took such a dim view of it.

BOFFIN: Missionaries?

SANDRA: I never really cared much for missionaries but I must admit that every once in a while they had very sound ideas.

BOFFIN (*pouring the water out of one glass into another over a knife*): Now—drink it slowly.

SANDRA: White Man's magic. (*She hiccups.*) Oh dear.

ROBERT FROME *comes in, followed by* CHRISTOPHER, *who stands near the rail.*

GEORGE: Good morning, Bob. What's wrong?

BOB: Quite a lot, I'm afraid, sir. (*He looks round at everyone.*)

GEORGE: Would you rather talk to me alone?

BOB: Well—as a matter of fact——

SANDRA: I must know what's happened. Boffin and I are perfectly trustworthy. We won't say a word if it's all that secret.

BOB: I'm afraid it won't be a secret long, anyhow.

SANDRA: They've gone.

BOB: I beg your pardon?

SANDRA: Never mind. Go on.

BOB: Actually I'm glad you're here, Lady A. I want to see you rather particularly.

GEORGE: Don't be so damned mysterious, Bob. Let's have it. What's happened?

BOB: It's Hali Alani. He's had his head bashed in.

SANDRA: Bashed *in*? Oh, surely not!

BOB: He's in the hospital now, with concussion.

GEORGE: This is serious. When did it happen?

BOB: Some time in the early hours of the morning. He was found in his beach house at Paiana Bay—unconscious.

GEORGE: Who found him?

BOB: The local policeman there. He noticed the lights were on in the bungalow, so he thought he'd better check up. He knocked and got no answer, and so he went in and found Hali lying on the floor. Apparently someone had crept up behind him and hit him on the head with a bottle.

SANDRA: How sordid!

GEORGE: Any finger-prints?

BOB: My chaps are working on that now.

SANDRA: Are they, really?

BOB: Yes—I sent them out there an hour ago.

SANDRA: Very efficient.

BOB: I understand that you accompanied Hali Alani to Mrs. Radlett's party at the Opula Club, Lady A.?

SANDRA: Yes, I did.

BOB: Can you remember at what time you left the party?

SANDRA: No—not exactly. Chris was there. He saw us go. What time would you say it was, Chris?

CHRISTOPHER: Oh—round about twelve-thirty, I should think.

BOB (*to* SANDRA): And he drove you straight back here?

SANDRA (*lighting a cigarette*): Of course.

BOB: He drove the car himself? There was no chauffeur?

SANDRA: No, I only wish there had been. Hali drives terribly fast. I can't bear being driven terribly fast, can you, Boffin?

BOFFIN: It *can* be fun if you stick to the wrong side of the road.

SANDRA (*with vivacity*): It makes me quite frantic. My foot keeps pressing down on an imaginary brake or an imaginary clutch. I suppose if one didn't drive oneself it wouldn't be so bad. It's like professional pilots flying on commercial airlines as passengers. They go through absolute tortures on account of *knowing* that something's wrong ages before anyone else does. Do you remember, George, last year when Bogey Watling told us about his plane having to make a forced landing in a frightening swamp somewhere or other? He said that . . .

GEORGE: Never mind about Bogey Watling now, my love. Go on, Bob.

BOB: Whoever committed the crime must have pinched the car too.

GEORGE: Pinched the car?

BOB: Yes. It was found smashed up in a ditch about a mile away from here.

SANDRA: How extraordinary!

BOB (*to* SANDRA): You say that Hali dropped you here at approximately twelve-forty-five?

SANDRA: Yes. I suppose it would be about that time if we left the club at twelve-thirty.

BOB: That means he would have got to the beach house at Paiana at approximately one-forty-five if he dropped you here at twelve-forty-five. It isn't very far to Paiana as the crow flies but that road over the pass is so twisty that even Hali couldn't drive very fast on it.

SANDRA: Oh, yes he could. (*She recovers herself.*) I mean—judging by the way we shot up here—I mean he's quite capable of hurtling up and down the mountains like a bullet out of a gun.

BOFFIN: A confused metaphor.

BOB: Well, thank you very much, Lady A. I won't bother you any more for the moment.

SANDRA: But you're not bothering me in the least, Bob. I'm only too delighted to help in any way I can. Poor Hali. What could he have been up to in a sinister little beach house all alone?

GEORGE: Perhaps he wasn't all alone.

BOB: He certainly wasn't. We have every proof of that.

SANDRA: What kind of proof?

BOB: Well, there were signs that a fairly drunken orgy had taken place.

SANDRA: Disgusting!

BOFFIN: What sort of signs?

BOB: Oh, you know—the usual thing—cigarette-ends, empty bottles, broken glasses, furniture all over the place.

SANDRA: It sounds like poor Alice's flat in Curzon Street.

GEORGE: We don't want to hear about poor Alice at the moment, my dear.

SANDRA: I know you never liked her, but she had a certain frowsy charm, hadn't she, Boffin?

BOFFIN: Frowsy is the operative word.

GEORGE: We'd better go into my office, Bob. We shan't be interrupted there.

SANDRA: You can't. It's being "done". I saw seven maids with seven mops ambling towards it a little while ago.

GEORGE (to BOB): You say Hali had someone else there with him, and that he'd been drinking?

BOB: Yes, sir.

SANDRA: But I always thought Hali was virtually a teetotaller.

BOB: He kicks over the traces sometimes. Once, at a party in the hills, he cracked two people's skulls together.

SANDRA: Perhaps it was one of them who cracked his last night. After all, fair's fair.

GEORGE: This is no moment for flippancy, Sandra. It's damned serious.

SANDRA: I'm so surprised at Hali turning out to be a dipso! Why, we had literally to force him to have even one cocktail here last night, didn't we? You were here yourself, Bob. You saw.

BOB: He was on his best behaviour here, naturally.

SANDRA: I don't know why you say naturally. Cuckoo certainly wasn't on *her* best behaviour.

GEORGE: What's Cuckoo got to do with it?

SANDRA: A great deal. Cuckoo is responsible for more than you
realise, George. She's a pompous, self-righteous, meddling ass.

BOFFIN: Hear, hear!

SANDRA: And the next time she brings her half-witted, adenoidal
children here I'll kick them into the gold-fish pond.

BOB: I think I'd better be getting along now, sir.

GEORGE: Yes. I think perhaps you had.

BOB: Do you think I could do some telephoning from the
A.D.C.'s room? It would save time.

GEORGE: Of course. Take him, Chris.

CHRISTOPHER: Yes, sir.

BOB: Thank you again, Lady A. (*To* GEORGE.) I'll keep you
posted, sir, as to what happens.

GEORGE: Good. Thanks.

BOB *and* CHRISTOPHER *go out.*

SANDRA: Well! What an excitement!

GEORGE: I don't like this. I don't like this at all.

SANDRA: Give me some more coffee, will you, Boffin?

BOFFIN (*taking her cup and going to the side-table*): Black or white?

SANDRA: Jet-black, please, dear.

GEORGE: I wonder who the devil did it?

SANDRA (*absently*): Did what?

GEORGE: Tried to murder Hali, of course.

SANDRA: Murder! Really, George, aren't you being a little
melodramatic?

GEORGE: Well, he had his head bashed in with a bottle.

SANDRA: Probably only in fun.

GEORGE: Was he drunk at Mitzi's party?

SANDRA: Of course he wasn't. He behaved exquisitely. There's a
certain old-world courtesy about Hali that I find most
engaging. Didn't you notice it at dinner, Boffin?

BOFFIN: I was too riveted by Admiral Turling's conversation to
notice anything else. I had no idea sailors' lives were so
monotonous. As far as I could gather he had Mrs. Turling in
every port.

GEORGE: I don't altogether trust that old-world courtesy. I
suspect that underneath it he is a horse of quite a different
colour.

SANDRA: Do you mean a dark-coloured horse or a coloured dark horse?

GEORGE: It's nothing to joke about. This business might lead to a lot of trouble—bad trouble.

SANDRA: I don't see any reason to make such a terrible issue of it. It's all quite obvious to me.

GEORGE: Oh, it is, is it?

SANDRA: Of course.

GEORGE: Perhaps you'll explain then, if you know so much about it.

SANDRA: I don't *know* anything. But I can make a pretty shrewd guess.

BOFFIN: So can I.

SANDRA (*shooting him a quick look*): What do you mean by that?

BOFFIN: Exactly what you mean, dear, I suspect.

GEORGE: If you either of you have any ideas that might shed a little light on the situation I should be very pleased to hear them.

SANDRA: Well, my theory is that he had a woman out there with him in the beach house and that they had a row, and she fetched him a nice wallop with the bottle and took his car and drove home.

GEORGE: Why was the car abandoned in a ditch?

BOFFIN (*looking at* SANDRA): Perhaps she didn't drive very well. Or perhaps she was drunk—what do you think, Sandra?

SANDRA: I couldn't agree with you more. I can visualise the whole thing. She was probably one of those almond-eyed half-caste women, very sinuous and clattering with cheap jewellery.

GEORGE: How did she get there? It's a long way away and quite isolated.

SANDRA: I expect he'd sent her over earlier in the day and she was waiting for him there, crouching in the shadows with her eyes gleaming like half-moons.

BOFFIN: Half-caste half-moons.

SANDRA: Perhaps it was a sort of show-down. She might have had a child by him, and . . .

GEORGE: One of those strong swimmers, no doubt.

SANDRA: It's all very fine for you to jeer, but I bet I'm right.

GEORGE: You say Hali dropped you off here at approximately twelve-forty-five?

SANDRA: No, it was Bob who said that. Don't you remember he kept adding up all the times——

GEORGE: Be that as it may, Hali did drop you here after the party, didn't he?

SANDRA: Of course. I couldn't very well have walked, could I? It's miles.

GEORGE: You'd be willing to swear to that in a court of law?

SANDRA: You always have to swear to everything in a court of law on account of them rushing at you with that little Bible.

GEORGE: Do you remember which sentry was on duty at the door last night?

SANDRA (*after an imperceptible pause*): Distinctly. The very tall thin one with the enormous Adam's apple.

GEORGE: Did you say good-night to him?

SANDRA: No. I didn't want to wake him.

GEORGE: Wake him! You mean he was asleep?

SANDRA: Fast asleep. And I for one don't blame him. Having to stand there hour after hour with nothing to look at but that awful old banyan tree. It's enough to give one the creeps.

GEORGE: You are telling me that the sentry on duty outside Government House was fast asleep?

SANDRA: If you say anything about it I shall never forgive you. I should hate to get the poor boy into trouble.

GEORGE: You are telling me the truth, Sandra, aren't you?

SANDRA: George, whatever is the matter with you? You're behaving exactly like one of those Agatha Christie detective inspectors with pin-stripe suits and bowler hats.

GEORGE: Are you or are you not telling me the truth?

SANDRA: Of course I am. Why on earth shouldn't I?

GEORGE: You left the party with Hali. He drove you back here . . .

SANDRA: Far too fast. We nearly killed two chickens and we missed the lamp standard at the cross-roads by inches.

GEORGE: And he wasn't drunk?

SANDRA: No. He just likes driving like a maniac.

GEORGE: He dropped you here and went on by himself?

SANDRA: He flashed off down the drive like a streak with the exhaust full out. I wonder you didn't hear it, it was enough to wake the dead.

GEORGE: But it didn't wake the sentry?

SANDRA (*after a slight pause*): No. He just gave a little grunt and turned over.

GEORGE: Was he lying down?

SANDRA: No—just sort of leaning, and he didn't exactly turn over, he just changed his position.

GEORGE: You did not go with Hali?

SANDRA (*shocked*): George!

GEORGE: It was not you who were with him at the beach house?

BOFFIN: Clattering with cheap jewllery?

GEORGE: Shut up, Boffin.

SANDRA (*with dignity*): I think, George, that this inquisition has gone far enough.

GEORGE: You haven't answered my question.

SANDRA: It didn't deserve an answer. No man with the faintest sensitivity of perception would have asked it.

GEORGE: Now look here, Sandra——

SANDRA (*mowing him down*): I am willing to forgive you for being a little crotchety and difficult in the mornings. That is only to be expected, because you eat far too much and take no exercise whatever. I should like to remind you that this is a very hot and livery climate, far, far removed from the bracing, invigorating breezes of Huddersfield.

GEORGE: I haven't set foot in Huddersfield for fifteen years.

SANDRA: That in itself is a shameful admission and only proves how dismally ambition and the lust for power has corrupted you. A man who will ruthlessly abandon his own birthplace and cold-shoulder his childhood playmates merely for political advancement—the man who would do these things—the man who would so complacently betray his ideals, is most certainly not the man I married. Where—I ask you—is the man I married?

GEORGE: Standing directly in front of you, my love, and stop talking nonsense.

SANDRA: I am willing to forgive you for your curious behaviour this morning because it is my considered opinion that you are far from well.

GEORGE: Sandra . . .

SANDRA: Doctor Crosbie said only the other day when you were gorging those Bombay mangoes at lunch, that you were insulting your metabolism.

GEORGE: My metabolism, Sandra, has nothing whatever to do with the subject under discussion.

SANDRA: Of course if you wish to insult your metabolism from morning till night, that is entirely your own affair. But for you to insult me with your base insinuations and lascivious innuendoes in front of poor Boffin, who has come all the way out here to relax and bask in this glorious climate——

GEORGE: You said just now that it was hot and livery.

SANDRA: I am going to my room. I have a great deal to do this morning, so I shall not see you again until luncheon, by which time I hope that you will have recovered your manners.

GEORGE (*firmly*): Once and for all, Sandra, did you or did you not go with Hali Alani to his beach house last night and bash him over the head with a bottle?

SANDRA: Certainly I did. And if you don't stop bellowing at me I'll do the same to you. Come, Boffin——

She sweeps out, followed by BOFFIN.

THE LIGHTS FADE

Scene II

The verandah. About four hours later.

As the curtain rises, SANYAMO *comes in, followed by* PUNALO ALANI.

SANYAMO: Excellency ha-anu watu dua moa.

PUNALO: Luka, Sanyamo.

SANYAMO: Punalo Alani koka kan gula?

PUNALO: O-o luka, Sanyamo. In this particular place it is more fitting that we speak English.

SANYAMO: Yes, sir, Punalo Alani. You will please to sit?

PUNALO (*seating himself*): Thank you.

SANYAMO: Cigarette?

PUNALO: No, thank you. Not for the moment.

SANYAMO: Your son Hali Alani was here last night.

PUNALO: Yes, I know.

SANYAMO: He is a strong, beautiful man. He walk long long time in garden with Lady Excellency and she give him white flower.

PUNALO: Did she indeed?

SANYAMO: Then they sit together on verandah quite close and talk and talk, and visiting gentleman play piano inside.

PUNALO: Thank you, Sanyamo.

SANYAMO: Then away they go—piff-paff in the motor-car—quick like light.

PUNALO: At what time did Lady Excellency return?

SANYAMO: Twenty-five minutes past four. I check with sentry.

PUNALO: Good.

SANYAMO: She not come back through main gate. She climb through hibiscus hedge and creep softly up drive like mouse.

PUNALO: Did sentry see her?

SANYAMO: Yes. But he pretended look other way. He is very devoted to Lady Excellency. She give him Jacqmar scarf for his girl and rattle with small bell for baby.

PUNALO: I see.

SANYAMO: Naleena spend two hours trying to fix Lady Excellency's evening shoes, but no use. They've had it.

PUNALO: Thank you, Sanyamo. You have told his Excellency that I am here?

SANYAMO: Yes. He come now.

> GEORGE *comes in.* SANYAMO *bows and goes out.* PUNALO ALANI *rises.*

GEORGE (*shaking hands*): Good morning, Punalo Alani.

PUNALO: Your Excellency does me great honour.

GEORGE (*with slight brusqueness*): I got your message saying that you wanted to see me and that it was urgent.

PUNALO: That is so, Excellency.

GEORGE: Then sit down and tell me what's on your mind.

PUNALO: Very well. (*He sits.*) I presume that you are aware that my son Hali has met with a slight accident?

GEORGE: Yes. I believe I did hear something about it. He got beaten up, didn't he?

PUNALO: Beaten down I think would be a more accurate description.

GEORGE (*with rather overdone airiness*): Have it your own way.

PUNALO: The incident occurred at his beach house at Paiana Bay during the early hours of this morning.

GEORGE (*comfortingly*): I shouldn't attach too much importance to it if I were you. He was probably having a bit of a party with a few friends and someone spoke out of turn. Boys will be boys, you know.

PUNALO: My son has four wives, your Excellency. I think we may safely assume that he has passed the age of puberty.

GEORGE: Oh! He has four wives, has he? Nobody ever told me that before.

PUNALO: Only one is official according to the rites of the Christian faith. The other three are what you might call supplementary auxiliaries.

GEORGE: I might, but I doubt if I should.

PUNALO: The customs of a country when deeply embedded in centuries of tradition are difficult to uproot. That is the rock upon which many so-called progressive policies are apt to founder.

GEORGE: Possibly. But I gather that you didn't come all the way up here to discuss progressive policies or your son's domestic problems.

PUNALO: No, Your Excellency, I came to discuss yours.

GEORGE: Mine?

PUNALO: Yes. It seems to me, in view of the present unfortunate situation, that they might become considerably embarrassing.

GEORGE: What unfortunate situation? What are you talking about?

PUNALO: My son, as you are aware, is in a position of great political importance.

GEORGE: In that case perhaps it would be better if he were a teetotaller.

PUNALO: Sir Winston Churchill isn't.

GEORGE: Be that as it may, it seems to have little bearing on the present discussion.

PUNALO: I am willing to admit that my son occasionally disregards the responsibilities of his high office and behaves, shall we say, a trifle impetuously.

GEORGE: I wish you would come to the point, Punalo Alani.

PUNALO: Your wife—Lady Alexandra——

GEORGE: I think perhaps it would be as well if we left my wife's name out of this conversation.

PUNALO: That, I fear, is impossible, as she is the crux of the whole affair.

GEORGE (*his temper fraying*): What the devil do you mean?

PUNALO: You know perfectly well what took place last night at my son's beach house, don't you, Your Excellency?

GEORGE: What I know or do not know is beside the point. Please say what you have to say, as briefly as possible.

PUNALO: I agree. Time is infinitely precious to us. Unless we work swiftly and in the closest co-operation we shall be unable to avert a grave public scandal.

GEORGE: What on earth are you talking about?

PUNALO (*inexorably*): A scandal that will not only do irreparable damage to your wife's reputation, but that might possibly result in your being forced to resign your position as Governor of this island. That would be a fatal blow to your career and a grievous deprivation for my people, who love and honour you both.

GEORGE: Skip the flowery compliments for the moment, Punalo. Whatever you think you know and whatever you may think I know, you haven't got one shred of proof that my wife went to the beach house with Hali last night.

PUNALO: As a matter of fact, I have. Irrefutable proof.

GEORGE: What is it?

PUNALO: A sapphire and diamond clip inscribed, with some austerity, on the gold underpart "Sandra from George".

GEORGE: Give it to me at once!

PUNALO: That I cannot do. It is in my safe at home.

GEORGE: Who found it?

PUNALO: The night watchman. But do not be alarmed, he cannot read.

GEORGE: Why didn't you bring it with you?

PUNALO: It is better where it is for the moment.

GEORGE: I can hardly bring myself to believe that a man of your eminence would sink so low as this, Punalo Alani. How much do you want?

PUNALO: If you are suspecting me of blackmailing you for money, Your Excellency, you are very foolish. I am a considerably richer man than you are ever likely to be.

GEORGE: I have no idea what devious motive you have in all this, but whatever it is I'll have no part of it. Is that clear?

PUNALO: No, Your Excellency. That won't do, that won't do at all. For Heaven's sake put aside your pride and anger and reflect calmly for a moment. The situation is too serious to be dismissed with a few bitter words.

GEORGE: I have no intention of being blackmailed by you or anybody else.

PUNALO (*suddenly raising his voice authoritatively*): Stop blustering, Your Excellency. You are in an extremely delicate position. We live in an age of publicity. If any mention of last night's regrettable incident gets into the local newspapers it will be only a matter of hours before it is headlined across the world.

GEORGE: Why should it get into the local newspapers?

PUNALO: The fact that my son was attacked is already known. Reporters and photographers have been besieging the hospital since early this morning. So far no statement has been made. But a statement must be made within the next few hours. A suitable culprit must be procured to confess to the attempted murder of my son.

GEORGE: Attempted murder! Damned nonsense!

PUNALO: It is also known that Lady Alexandra left Mrs. Radlett's party at the Opula Club alone with my son. Unless we can establish a water-tight alibi for her, nothing can save her from being hopelessly compromised.

GEORGE: Hali brought my wife back to this house last night at twelve-forty-five precisely.

PUNALO: To quote your own words at a recent meeting of the Executive Committee, "Do not let us build the structure of our policy upon the shifting sands of illusion."

GEORGE (*after a slight pause*): What did you mean just now when you said that a suitable culprit must be procured?

PUNALO (*with a faint smile*): Exactly what I said. Fortunately I have a few "possibles" lined up already.

GEORGE: You mean that a man will be bribed to confess to a crime of which he is completely innocent?

PUNALO: Certainly. He will be tried and sentenced to a term of imprisonment. After a few days he will escape to one of the other islands. It is quite easy to arrange.

GEORGE (*exploding*): Of all the immoral, corrupt . . .

PUNALO: Try to be realistic, Your Excellency.

GEORGE: Do you seriously imagine that even in order to shield my wife I would allow a man to be convicted of a crime he didn't commit?

PUNALO: The choice lies between that and allowing your wife to be convicted in the eyes of the world of a crime she did commit.

GEORGE: Crime! She was defending her honour from the disgusting advances of your inebriated son.

PUNALO: Your wife is a very attractive and charming woman. And as you said yourself a little while ago, "Boys will be boys."

GEORGE: What is your object in all this, Punalo Alani?

PUNALO: I wish to save Lady Alexandra from the degradation of a public scandal. I am devoted to her. We all are. I should hate to see her subjected to the vulgarities of modern journalism. I can visualise only too clearly the inevitable headlines: "Governor's Wife in Beach House Brawl"—"Governor's Lady Bashes Boy-Friend with Bottle in Luxury Bungalow".

GEORGE: What do you want? What are you after?

PUNALO: I have already told you. To avoid a scandal and save the reputation of a gracious and charming lady.

GEORGE: Then why not give the clip back and say nothing about it?

PUNALO: The clip, as I have already said, is of no importance in itself. It only might be considered of value if it could be used as a lever.

GEORGE: Lever?

PUNALO: To prise loose perhaps a little of Your Excellency's political dogmatism.

GEORGE: Are you presuming to dictate to me, Punalo Alani?

PUNALO: Frankly, yes, and I am sure that when your immediate irritation subsides, you will be the first to see that I am in an admirable position to do so.

GEORGE: Now see here, Punalo Alani——

PUNALO (*disregarding him*): I will even go so far as to deliver an ultimatum.

GEORGE: You can deliver ultimatums until you are blue in the face, Punalo Alani, but I suggest that you deliver them by letter as I have no intention of tolerating this discussion for a moment longer.

PUNALO (*inexorably*): My ultimatum is this. Unless you give me your solemn promise as a man of honour that you will veto the Public Conveniences Bill, and in addition to that, withdraw your allegiance to the Samolan Socialist National Party at the forthcoming elections, I will show your wife's clip to the Press and, to coin a phrase, bust the works wide open.

GEORGE: I'll see you in Hell first!

At this moment SANDRA *comes in with* BOFFIN.

SANDRA (*with quiet defiance*): I have been for a drive, George, with Boffin. He has a stop-watch and we have kept a time chart in case there should be any misunderstandings afterwards. We left here in the Vauxhall at eleven-five exactly. You can check that with the sentry, he was wide awake. We stopped at Caldwell's at eleven-thirty-two because Boffin wanted to buy a rubber sponge and some Eno's Fruit Salts. We left there at eleven-forty-two and arrived at the Royal Turtle Hotel at twelve-seven by the hotel clock and twelve-three by Boffin's watch. We had a very nasty rum punch each and left there at twelve-twenty-six, and here we are. Time please, Boffin.

BOFFIN (*looking at his watch*): One-ten.

SANDRA: Good morning, Punalo Alani. What a surprise to find you here. How is your son?

PUNALO: He regained consciousness at nine-five and was sick at nine-twenty-two.

GEORGE: Punalo and I are having a private conversation, Sandra.

SANDRA: In that case you should be in your office. This is a communal verandah. We can't sit in the hall, the drawing-room's covered in dust sheets, and the garden's too hot.

GEORGE: Sandra . . .

SANDRA (*ignoring him*): Ring for Sanyamo to bring the drinks, will you, Boffin? The bell's by the door.

BOFFIN: With all the pleasure in the world. I can still taste that beastly rum.

SANDRA: Have you asked Punalo Alani to stay to lunch, George?

GEORGE: No. I most certainly have not.

SANDRA: Then all I can say is that it's most inhospitable of you.

GEORGE: Punalo Alani came here to discuss business, Sandra. (*He looks at* PUNALO.) Very unpleasant business.

SANDRA: Well, there's a time and a place for everything, even unpleasantness, and this isn't either. (*To* PUNALO.) You will stay, won't you?

PUNALO: You are very gracious, Lady Alexandra.

SANDRA: There's only curry, but there's masses of it.

PUNALO: I really think that perhaps I——

SANDRA: Of course if you don't like curry we could have an egg dish whipped up for you in a flash——

PUNALO: It is not because of the curry that I hesitated, Lady Alexandra, as a matter of fact I am exceedingly fond of it.

SANDRA: That's settled them. (*To* BOFFIN.) You've no idea how marvellously they do it here. It's the trimmings that make the whole difference. Chopped mangoes, grated coconut, sliced papaya, fried banana and little bits of bacon and kri-kri nuts—and you mash the whole caboodle into a sort of ambrosial dog's dinner and it's hot as hell and blows your head right off.

BOFFIN: I've always longed to have my head blown right off.

GEORGE: Come to my office, will you please, Punalo?

SANDRA (*firmly*): No, George—I really can't allow that. Once you get into that office there's no getting you out again. Lunch is practically ready now, and I don't want it ruined.

SANYAMO *comes in with the drink tray.*

BOFFIN (*going to it*): Thank God!

SANDRA: I hope there's a "Westward Ho" in the shaker, Sanyamo?

SANYAMO: Yes, my lady.

SANDRA: Good. You can leave it, then. We'll help ourselves.

SANYAMO: Very good, my lady.

SANDRA (*to* PUNALO): "Westward Ho" is our own kala-kala speciality. I love kala-kala. It makes one so cheerful and uninhibited.

BOFFIN: The hair of the dog.

PUNALO: I have some of the old much-mellowed kala-kala in my cellars, Lady Alexandra. I would be delighted to send you a case if you would accept it. But I must warn you that it is very, very strong.

SANDRA: I had a feeling that it might be. Thank you, Punalo Alani. There is nothing I should like more.

CHRISTOPHER *comes in.*

CHRISTOPHER: Hali Alani is here, Lady A. He says he wants to speak to you privately and that it's very important.

SANDRA (*to* SANYAMO, *who is leaving*): Two extra for lunch, Sanyamo.

SANYAMO: Very good, my lady. (*He goes.*)

GEORGE: Well, I'll be damned!

SANDRA: You really must try to cultivate a little more social poise, George—World Revolution or no World Revolution. Bring Hali in, Chris. Tell him we can talk privately after lunch but certainly not before. I'm famished. (*To* GEORGE, *gaily.*) I might take him for a little walk in the garden—if he can stand up after last night!

CHRISTOPHER: All right, Lady A.

He goes.

BOFFIN (*handing round cocktails*): Cocktail, Mr. Alani?

PUNALO (*taking one*): Thank you.

BOFFIN: We haven't been officially introduced. My name is Blair-Kennedy.

PUNALO: I knew your father well, Mr. Kennedy. I was his fag at Eton.

BOFFIN: I do hope he was nice to you. He was horrid to me. (*Offering a cocktail to* GEORGE.) George?

GEORGE: No, thanks. I don't approve of drinking in the middle of the day, and I don't approve of kala-kala at any time.

SANDRA: Don't say that, dear, when Punalo Alani is just embarking on it. You'll give him a guilt complex.

GEORGE: I should think his own conscience would do that.

SANDRA: Do relax, George! You can be as cross as you like again after lunch, but do stop snarling now, there's a dear. (*She pats his arm affectionately.*) Oh, by the way, I forgot to tell you, I met that scruffy little reporter from the *Daily Reaper* in the town. Just as we were coming out of Caldwell's.

GEORGE (*sharply*): What did you say to him?

SANDRA: Nothing much. He begged me with tears in his eyes to give him an exclusive interview.

GEORGE: What about?

SANDRA: Oh, I don't know. The Women's Federation, I expect, or the Hospital Fund, or some of my other island activities.

BOFFIN: They'd certainly make fascinating reading.

SANDRA: Be quiet, Boffin dear. (*To* GEORGE.) There's no need to look so stricken, George. I told him I never gave Press interviews and that he'd better talk to you. He's coming at four-thirty.

GEORGE: Then he can go away again.

SANDRA: It would be churlish to refuse to see him. Just fob him off with a few little anecdotes about your early struggles.

GEORGE: It's not my early struggles he wants to hear about Sandra. It's your recent ones.

SANDRA (*sweetly*): Hush, George, I can see in your eye that you are on the verge of being indiscreet.

> HALI *comes in. He looks far from well, and his head is bandaged.* CHRISTOPHER *follows him.*

(*Advancing to meet him.*) How nice of you to come, Hali. Your father's already here. It's quite a family party, isn't it?

HALI (*bowing as he shakes hands*): I knew that my father would be here. That is one of the reasons that I came.

SANDRA (*looking at his bandage*): Poor Hali. You *did* get a wallop, didn't you?

HALI: There is much that I would say, but I cannot find words.

GEORGE: Of all the barefaced impertinence . . .

HALI: I appreciate the conflict that churns your breast, Your Excellency. I apologise with much humbleness. For my father I apologise also.

PUNALO (*angrily*): You are behaving like a fool, Hali. Please go home at once.

HALI (*also angrily*): E imbalaaki lu Koka!

PUNALO: Hola awa-lali an kin moa. Lu sumpaali twaddidi.

HALI: Lu dabaani kokalo e bero liaki. Gonbaana Gonbaana!

PUNALO (*violently*): Somba Kola um Doka! Somba Gulana koob!

SANDRA: Do speak in English, both of you. You sound like a Yugoslavian Drama Festival.

HALI: I apologise again, Lady Sandra. This time for the filthy manners both of my shameful father and myself.

SANDRA: It doesn't matter all that much, Hali. It's just that it's tantalising for us not to know what you're saying to each other.

BOFFIN: I can give a rough guess.

HALI: Another reason I came, Lady Sandra, was to bring you back your most pretty diamond and sapphire clip.

PUNALO (*involuntarily*): Hali!

HALI (*ignoring him*): It was found in my car early this morning. (*He takes the clip from his pocket and hands it to* SANDRA.)

SANDRA (*taking it*): How thoughtful of you, Hali! I can't thank you enough. I knew I must have dropped it somewhere. I'm always doing things like that. I once lost a pearl necklace in a street fight. Of course they weren't real pearls and it wasn't a real street fight—just a film première.

BOFFIN: It's the sentimental value that counts.

HALI: It is most dismal to lose something of sentimental value.

BOFFIN: Yes. Like India.

SANDRA (*holding up the clip to* GEORGE): Well, this is crammed with sentiment for me. Do you remember it, darling?

GEORGE (*grimly*): Only too well.

BOFFIN (*to* HALI): Would you like a cocktail?

HALI (*repressing a shudder*): No, thank you. I am upon the wagon.

PUNALO: That is good news, my son!

GEORGE: Better late than never.

SANDRA: George!

HALI (*looking fixedly at his father*): I have more good news also for my father. It will exhilarate him tip-top.

PUNALO: What is it, Hali?

HALI: The man who made the sharp violent attack on me and stole away my sweet car, has given himself up to the police.

PUNALO (*unmoved*): Which on the list? Number two or number three?

HALI: Number three. Unfortunately number two is in Honolulu.

PUNALO (*smiling at* GEORGE): Good. We have used him before. He is quite reliable.

BOFFIN: Imagine our excitement if only we knew what the hell they were talking about?

HALI: I do not like the dirty games, Father. You must please to explain to His Excellency that he has not the obligations of any sort.

PUNALO (*resigned*): That is understood, my son.

HALI: You will also make the lowest apology to His Excellency for your most naughty waste of his time.

PUNALO: That too is understood, my son.

GEORGE: Just a minute— (*To* HALI.) Who is this man you say has given himself up?

PUNALO: He is a fanatic. He has already made several attempts to injure my son. Each time he has been imprisoned, and each time—strange enough—he has managed to make his escape. It is very disquieting.

SANDRA: I am grateful to you, Hali. For all the trouble you have taken.

HALI: I would make the most untold efforts to return myself into your best graces.

GEORGE: Does the Chief of Police know about this?

HALI: Yes. It was to him that the poor foolish fellow abandoned himself.

SANDRA: You put things so graphically, Hali. You will stay to lunch, won't you?

HALI (*looking at* GEORGE): Perhaps His Excellency . . .

SANDRA: I am sure His Excellency will be enchanted. I wonder if curry is good for concussion?

HALI: I have taken the liberty of bringing you a small gift, Lady Sandra. In the event that you would pardon my foolishness and no longer frown on me with displeasure. It is outside in the hall.

SANDRA: How very sweet of you, Hali. What is it?

HALI: It is an ancient native drum that was given to my father's great father by King Kefumalani.

SANDRA: How exciting! George, you must learn to play it after lunch. It will sort of release you.

HALI (*sincerely*): You have then really forgiven me?

SANDRA: Of course I forgive you, Hali. I hope too that you will forgive me.

BOFFIN: I'm still confused, but this is obviously a beautiful moment.

HALI: But, Your Excellency, you still have the black look.

SANDRA: He can't help that. He comes from the Black Country.

GEORGE (*relenting*): Thank you, Hali. You have behaved exceedingly well. Which is more than I can say for your father.

PUNALO: "To err is human—to forgive, divine."

SANDRA: Pope again.

HALI: Born 1688. Died 1744.

SANYAMO (*entering*): Luncheon is served, Your Excellencies!

THE CURTAIN FALLS

NUDE WITH VIOLIN

A light comedy in three Acts

For

JOHN GIELGUD

*with admiration
and affection*

Nude With Violin was first produced in London at the Globe Theatre, Shaftesbury Avenue, on 7 November 1956. It was presented by H. M. Tennent Ltd, with the following cast:

SEBASTIEN	John Gielgud
MARIE-CELESTE	Gillian Webb
CLINTON PREMINGER, Junior	John Sterland
ISOBEL SORODIN	Joyce Carey
JANE	Anne Castle
COLIN	Basil Henson
PAMELA	Patricia Raine
JACOB FRIEDLAND	David Horne
ANYA PAVLIKOV	Patience Collier
CHERRY-MAY WATERSON	Kathleen Harrison
FABRICE	Douglas Robinson
OBADIAH LEWELLYN	Thomas Baptiste
GEORGE	Keith Green
LAUDERDALE	Nicky Edmett

Directed by JOHN GIELGUD and THE AUTHOR
Setting by PAUL ANSTEE

———

The action of the play takes place in Paul Sorodin's studio in Paris.

ACT I
Afternoon.

ACT II
Scene I. *A few hours later.*
Scene II. *The following afternoon.*

ACT III
Scene I. *A few hours later.*
Scene II. *The following morning.*

ACT I

The scene is Paul Sorodin's studio in Paris. It is large and luxuriously furnished. There are some fine paintings and sculptures but no evidence of Sorodin's own work.

In the centre there are two double doors which open into a hall and thence to the front door. Down right a small door leads to the library. Above this is a solid writing-desk. The left wall is taken up by a vast window through which can be seen trees and the roofs of houses in the distance. A couple of modern armchairs and a sofa are placed at the director's discretion. There is a refectory table under the window set with cakes and sandwiches and a magnum of champagne ornamented with a large black bow.

When the curtain rises it is about four o'clock on a summer afternoon in the year 1954.

After a moment or two, SEBASTIEN LACREOLE *enters, bearing two plates of patisserie. He is a dark, rather swarthy man and might be any age between forty and fifty-five. He is impeccably dressed in black trousers and a white coat on the left sleeve of which there is a wide mourning band of black silk. As he puts the plates on the table the telephone rings. He goes to it.*

SEBASTIEN (*at telephone*): Allô—J'écoute—ici Invalides 26–45—Oui, monsieur—Non, monsieur—Oui, monsieur, je suis complètement d'accord: pour nous c'est une tragédie mais, pour le monde une catastrophe. Merci, monsieur—Monsieur est trop aimable—Sans faute, monsieur—Au revoir, monsieur.

He hangs up the receiver and is about to return to the table when the front door bell rings. He crosses and opens the shutters. MARIE-CELESTE, *a middle-aged "Bonne", enters.*

MARIE-CELESTE: Il y a un monsieur à la porte.
SEBASTIEN: Quelle espèce de monsieur?

MARIE-CELESTE: Je ne sais pas, je ne suis pas clairvoyante moi, je crois qu'il est Anglais ou peut-être Américain.

SEBASTIEN: Journaliste?

MARIE-CELESTE (*to left of armchair*): Écoutes, mon coco, comment est-ce que je peux te dire? Je lui ai dit rien que Bonjour.

SEBASTIEN: Merde!

MARIE-CELESTE: D'accord. Je m'en fou de tout ce bruit.

> At this moment CLINTON PREMINGER, *junior, comes tentatively into the room. He is an earnest-looking young American in the late twenties or early thirties.*

CLINTON (*laboriously*): Excusez-moi.

SEBASTIEN: Monsieur?

CLINTON: Parlez-vous anglais?

SEBASTIEN: Yes, monsieur.

CLINTON: Thank God.

> MARIE-CELESTE *exits.*

SEBASTIEN: This is a house of mourning, monsieur.

CLINTON: I know. That's why I'm here—I mean I have to see Madame Sorodin, it's business—urgent business.

SEBASTIEN: Madame Sorodin has not yet returned from the funeral and when she does I feel that she will be in no mood to discuss business, however urgent.

CLINTON: I guess you're Sébastien.

SEBASTIEN: Your guess is correct, monsieur.

CLINTON: I have some notes on you.

SEBASTIEN: Have you indeed?

CLINTON: I represent *Life* Magazine.

SEBASTIEN: It is in questionable taste to force *Life* Magazine into a house of death, monsieur.

CLINTON: My name is Clinton Preminger, junior.

SEBASTIEN: It would be all the same if you were Clinton Preminger, senior.

CLINTON: Now see here, I'm not an ordinary Press reporter out for scoop headlines, I'm a serious writer.

SEBASTIEN: I am delighted to hear it.

CLINTON: For over two years I've been assembling material for a comprehensive study of Sorodin and his paintings. It's to be called "Triton among the Minnows".

SEBASTIEN: Most appropriate.

CLINTON: I came by sea to give myself time to get all my notes in order and when I landed at Cherbourg I found that he had died. You can imagine the shock!

SEBASTIEN: It was a shock to the whole world, monsieur.

MARIE-CELESTE (*entering from service door with a jar of pâté*): Il est beau gars, qu'est-ce qu'il dit?

SEBASTIEN (*crossing to* MARIE-CELESTE *and taking the pâté*): Rien d'importance . . . sauve toi!

MARIE-CELESTE: Bon. Je me sauve.

    She goes out.

SEBASTIEN: You say you have some notes on me? What sort of notes?

CLINTON: Merely factual. I have them here in my file—just a moment. (*Looks in file.*) S-S-Sebastien.

SEBASTIEN: I sound like an Atlantic liner.

CLINTON: Sébastien Lacreeole. Is that right?

SEBASTIEN: Not quite. There should be an accent on the first E in the Lacréole.

CLINTON: My French isn't too good.

SEBASTIEN: You must persevere.

CLINTON (*consulting his notes*): You entered the service of Paul Sorodin in July 1946 in the capacity of valet.

SEBASTIEN: Correct.

CLINTON: You don't talk like a valet.

SEBASTIEN: You can't have everything.

CLINTON: You are of mixed parentage.

SEBASTIEN: You have a genius for understatement, monsieur.

CLINTON: Born in Martinique, date uncertain.

SEBASTIEN: My whole life has been uncertain.

CLINTON (*still at his notes*): Deported from Syria in 1929. No offence specified.

SEBASTIEN: The Syrians are terribly vague.

CLINTON: Imprisoned in Saigon 1933. Offence specified.

SEBASTIEN (*reminiscently*): I remember it well.

CLINTON: Resident in England 1936.

SEBASTIEN: The happiest time of my life.

CLINTON: Landed in Los Angeles 1937.

SEBASTIEN: The saddest.

CLINTON: Married in Rio de Janeiro 1939. Wife living.

SEBASTIEN: With a customs officer.

CLINTON: From 1942 to 1946, proprietor of a rooming-house in Mexico City.

SEBASTIEN: Your delicacy does you credit, monsieur.

CLINTON (*closing file*): Those are all my notes on you up to date.

SEBASTIEN: Quite accurate as far as they go.

CLINTON (*earnestly*): I'd like you to understand that by reading them to you I had no intention of embarrassing you.

SEBASTIEN: Thank you. You didn't.

CLINTON: I despise moral attitudes. I believe that life is for living, don't you?

SEBASTIEN: It's difficult to know what else one could do with it.

CLINTON: Personally I have no inhibitions. I took a course of psychiatry at Yale.

SEBASTIEN: That explains everything.

CLINTON: I've studied Jung and Freud and Adler and Kinsey and all the big boys.

SEBASTIEN: Mr. Kinsey himself studied quite a number of the big boys.

CLINTON: What I mean to say is that nothing shocks me. I think that every man should do what he wants to do.

SEBASTIEN: A tolerant philosophy but apt to lead to untidiness.

CLINTON: Where did you learn to speak such good English?

SEBASTIEN: The Esplanade Hotel, Bournemouth.

CLINTON: What were you doing there?

SEBASTIEN: Looking after an elderly lady. No offence specified.

CLINTON: You liked working for Paul Sorodin?

SEBASTIEN: Very much indeed, monsieur. He was a great man.

CLINTON: Was he difficult, temperamental? I mean did he fly into violent rages?

SEBASTIEN: Frequently.

CLINTON: Did he ever strike you?

SEBASTIEN: No. He once threw a pork chop at me but it only broke the clock.

CLINTON (*scribbling a note*): Excuse me.

CLINTON: I really think, Monsieur Preminger, that as Madame

Sorodin may return from Père Lachaise at any moment, it would be tactful of you to leave now. The presence here of a stranger would be an intrusion on her grief.

CLINTON: Grief? Just a moment— (*He searches through his file, finds a paper and scans it.*) Sorodin deserted her in 1926, didn't he?

SEBASTIEN: 1925.

CLINTON: And she hasn't seen him since?

SEBASTIEN: I believe that they once met by accident in the Galeries Lafayette.

CLINTON: I shouldn't imagine she'd be suffering much grief after all those years.

SEBASTIEN (*reprovingly*): He was her husband and the father of her children.

CLINTON: Why did she never divorce him?

SEBASTIEN: She is a woman of the highest principles, and a Catholic.

CLINTON: Can you beat that?

SEBASTIEN: People have tried, monsieur, but seldom with unqualified success.

CLINTON: Tell me. Did he hate her?

SEBASTIEN: Not at all. He once painted a moustache on her photograph but only in a spirit of fun.

CLINTON (*rising*): You know, I like you, Sébastien.

SEBASTIEN: Thank you.

CLINTON: I really am crazy to meet Madame Sorodin. Can I stay until she arrives if I promise to go the moment you tip me the wink?

SEBASTIEN: It would be as much as my place is worth.

CLINTON: But your place can't be worth much now anyway, can it?

SEBASTIEN: That remains to be seen.

CLINTON: Are you taken care of in the will?

SEBASTIEN: Mr. Sorodin left no will.

CLINTON: Gosh! That means that everything will go to her, doesn't it?

SEBASTIEN: I presume so.

CLINTON: No wonder she came haring over here for the public funeral.

SEBASTIEN: Your flippancy appals me, monsieur.

CLINTON: Do you like her?

SEBASTIEN: I am in no position to say, having only just met her.

CLINTON: Does she like you?

SEBASTIEN: I doubt it, monsieur. Paul Sorodin was more than my employer, he was my friend. I travelled with him far and wide. He found me good company: we laughed together and drank together and took our pleasures lightly. Whether Madame Sorodin liked me or not I am fairly sure that she could never approve of me. Our views of life are so diametrically opposed.

CLINTON: I'll bet the hell they are.

The telephone rings.

SEBASTIEN: Excuse me. (*He goes to telephone.*) Allô—j'écoute—ici Invalides 26–45—Si, señor—Aun no, señor—Si, señor, estamos completamente de acuerdo, dara nosotros es una tragedia, pero para el mundo es una catástrofe—Muchas gracias, señor—Usted es muy amable señor—Sin falta, señor—Hasta luego, señor. (*He hangs up.*)

CLINTON: How many languages do you speak?

SEBASTIEN: Fourteen, including dialects. My Swahili is a bit rusty at the moment; there are so few opportunities of speaking it in Paris.

CLINTON: Was Sorodin a linguist?

SEBASTIEN: Only when he was drunk.

CLINTON: Was he a heavy drinker?

SEBASTIEN: In certain circumstances, yes, but sometimes he could go for hours without touching a drop.

CLINTON: Are you laughing at me by any chance?

SEBASTIEN: A little, Monsieur Preminger.

CLINTON: Why? What is there about me that's so funny?

SEBASTIEN: Your naïveté, monsieur. If, as you say, you intend to write a serious biography of Paul Sorodin I cannot help feeling that your approach should be a trifle less ingenuous.

CLINTON: My approach is logical. Facts first, analysis afterwards. You must know more about him than anybody. You could help me a lot if only you would.

SEBASTIEN: Why should I?

CLINTON: For the sake of posterity, if for no other reason.

SEBASTIEN: Sorodin will be remembered even without the aid of *Life* Magazine, Monsieur Preminger, and within a few years your biography of him will only be one among hundreds.

The front door bell rings.

Here they are. You'd better go.

CLINTON: Five minutes, just five minutes—you promised.

SEBASTIEN: I did no such thing.

CLINTON: Please. I swear I'll go the moment you give me the hint.

SEBASTIEN: What sort of hint can I possibly give you?

CLINTON: Offer me a cigarette. I shall refuse it and leave at once.

SEBASTIEN (*weakening*): It is all highly irregular.

CLINTON: Please. Be a pal. It means so much to me. (*Puts his hand in pocket for tip.* SEBASTIEN *turns from him.*) And call me at the hotel later and we can make a date for dinner.

SEBASTIEN: Which hotel?

CLINTON: The George V.

SEBASTIEN: I might have known it.

CLINTON: Okay?

SEBASTIEN (*resigned*): Okay.

> MARIE-CELESTE *flings open the double doors and stands aside to allow* ISOBEL, JANE, COLIN, PAMELA *and* JACOB FRIEDLAND *to enter. They are all, naturally, in mourning.*
>
> ISOBEL, *a woman in the early fifties, is a fairly typical example of the English upper middle-class. Her clothes are well cut but in no way remarkable.*
>
> *At the moment she looks a trifle harassed. She sits in the armchair.* COLIN, *her son, although not in uniform is quite unmistakably a major in the Army; he stands behind* ISOBEL. PAMELA, *his wife, is equally unmistakably the wife of a major in the Army. She has a forthright manner and is accustomed to speaking her mind, which limits the scope of her conversation. She comes to right of* COLIN. JANE *differs from her mother and brother in that she has a definite style of her own and a sense of humour which perhaps she has inherited from her father. She goes to desk chair.* JACOB FRIEDLAND, *an art dealer of considerable renown, is dapper, shrewd and kindly enough although his manner is inclined to be pompous and didactic on occasion.*

ISOBEL (*as she comes in*): It was all very impressive and really very moving but I am thankful that it is over.

MARIE-CELESTE: Madame a besoin de quelque chose? Un cachet Faivre peut-être?

ISOBEL: No—non merci beaucoup.

MARIE-CELESTE *retires*

JACOB (*seeing* CLINTON. *To* SEBASTIEN): Who is this?

SEBASTIEN: Monsieur Clinton Preminger, junior, monsieur. He represents *Life* Magazine.

JACOB: I thought my instructions were quite clear, Sébastien.

CLINTON: Please don't blame him, sir, it's all my fault. He tried to make me go but I wouldn't.

JACOB: I am afraid I must ask you to leave immediately. This is a moment when privacy should be respected. (*Sits right end of sofa.*)

CLINTON: Are you Mr. Jacob Friedland?

JACOB: I am.

CLINTON: I have some notes on you.

JACOB: Kindly show Mr. Preminger out, Sébastien.

CLINTON: Just a moment, please. Mrs. Sorodin, I appeal to you. I am writing a series of articles on your late husband's work. He was a great man, a giant. I know that you have lived apart from him for many years but you must be proud to bear his name, you must still feel in your heart a little tenderness for him, you who loved him when he was young, when he was on the threshold of his greatness, you who once held him in your arms——

SEBASTIEN (*offering him a silver box*): A cigarette, Monsieur Preminger?

CLINTON (*absently taking one*): Thanks.

JACOB: Mr. Preminger——

CLINTON: And you, Mr. Friedland. You who braved the ignorant scorn of his early critics and set his feet so firmly on the ladder of success, you I feel sure will not turn a deaf ear to me. Without your help and advice and friendly co-operation I can achieve nothing, nothing but a paltry journalistic shadow of the truth that was in this wonderful man——

SEBASTIEN (*with an edge to his voice*): A light, Monsieur Pre-
    minger?
CLINTON (*automatically*): Thanks.

    SEBASTIEN *shrugs his shoulders and lights his cigarette.*

Please help me, Mr. Friedland, in the same spirit that you have
helped and encouraged talent all your life—Mrs. Sorodin, I appeal
to you again——
ISOBEL (*flustered and rising*): Oh dear—this is really most awk-
    ward—I don't know what to say—Jane—Colin——
COLIN: Sit down, mother. (*She sits again.*) I'll deal with this. (*To*
    CLINTON.) Now look here, young man. I don't care what
    magazine you represent or who you are or where you come
    from, but if you don't leave this house within fifty seconds I'll
    throw you out.
JACOB: Just a moment, Colin. (*To* CLINTON.) I fully appreciate
    your position, Mr. Preminger, and I will do all I can to help
    you on condition that you leave us alone now in the private
    sorrow that has come to us.
CLINTON (*carried away*): It's not a private sorrow, it's a public
    disaster!
SEBASTIEN (*menacingly*): Another cigarette, Monsieur Preminger?
COLIN: What the devil do you keep offering him cigarettes for?
CLINTON (*stricken*): Cigarette!—My   God!—Sorry,   Sébastien.
    Good-bye.

    He goes rapidly out of the room.

PAMELA (*after a slight pause*): The man's obviously a lunatic.
SEBASTIEN: No, madame, merely an enthusiast. He took a
    course of psychiatry at Yale.
PAMELA: What's Yale?
ISOBEL: It's a university in America, dear, just like Cambridge,
    you know, only quite different.
COLIN: He'd have been better advised to take a course in
    manners.
JACOB: You had no business to let him in, Sébastien, I am very
    displeased.
COLIN: I suppose he bribed you.
JANE (*frowning*): Really, Colin.
SEBASTIEN: I am not in the habit of accepting bribes, sir.

JANE: I'm sure you're not, Sébastien.

SEBASTIEN: Thank you, miss.

JANE: Where did you learn to speak such perfect English?

SEBASTIEN: In Bournemouth, miss. I was in service there some years ago.

PAMELA: Domestic service?

SEBASTIEN: Some of my duties were almost overwhelmingly domestic. May I offer mesdames, messieurs some refreshment?

JANE: I must say I should love a drink, it's been a very tiring day.

SEBASTIEN: Champagne, miss?

JANE: Yes please, that would be lovely.

COLIN: Good Lord! A Magnum! Where did that come from?

SEBASTIEN: I was given me for a Christmas present by Mr. Sorodin. I wished to contribute in my own humble way to this melancholy but historic occasion. (*To* ISOBEL.) I hope madame will accept it in the spirit in which it is offered?

ISOBEL: Really—I hardly know what to say—thank you, Sébastien—hand me my bag, Pamela dear, if I am going to have champagne I must take off my hat.

SEBASTIEN (*opens bottle and fills glasses*): I would like to repudiate the black bow. It was Marie-Céleste's idea. She has an exaggerated sense of the fantastic.

> ISOBEL *takes off her hat and pats her hair into place with the aid of her hand mirror.*

JANE: (*handing* ISOBEL *a glass of wine*): Here, mother, it will do you good. (*The champagne is handed round.*)

ISOBEL: I doubt that, Jane. Champagne really doesn't agree with me, the last time I had any was at poor Ettie's wedding—you remember, Colin—I was ill for days.

JACOB: Perhaps it was a bad year.

ISOBEL: Oh indeed it was, everything went wrong.

JANE: You must drink, too, Sébastien.

SEBASTIEN: Thank you, miss, I will be honoured.

JACOB: By all means. Fill a glass for him, Colin.

> COLIN *fills a wine glass.*

SEBASTIEN: May I be permitted to propose a toast?

COLIN: Oh God! (*Handing glass to* SEBASTIEN.)

JANE: Shut up, Colin. Please do, Sébastien.

SEBASTIEN (*raising his glass*): I drink to the memory of my master Paul Sorodin. A man of charm and humour and courage: a man who, until death smudged out the twinkle in his eye, contrived to enjoy life to the full and at the same time remain a hero to his own valet. Madame. Ladies and Gentlemen. Paul Sorodin. (*He drains his glass in one gulp, dashes it to the ground——and goes swiftly out of the room.*)

PAMELA (*after a slight pause*): Well, really—what a funny thing to do!

ISOBEL: A little theatrical perhaps, dear, but after all he *is* a foreigner.

PAMELA: I can't stand him, it's no use I just can't stand him. He gives me the creeps.

JANE: I rather like him.

PAMELA: Really, Jane, what is there about him that you could possibly like?

JANE: He has charm, I think.

COLIN (*contemptuously*): Charm! The chap's a Dago. I wouldn't trust him an inch.

PAMELA: A strong touch of the tar brush, if you ask me.

JANE: Nobody did, Pamela.

PAMELA: There is no need to be rude.

JANE: Father was obviously devoted to him.

ISOBEL: I fear your poor father was often devoted to undesirable characters.

JANE: We have no proof that Sébastien is an undesirable character. We met him for the first time two days ago.

COLIN: You have only to look at him. I know the type. Oily.

JANE: I liked what he said about father.

ISOBEL: I know that over the years you have built up in your mind a romantic conception of your father, Jane, darling——

JANE: He was a romantic man.

ISOBEL: I also know, modern values being what they are, that you can see nothing wrong in the unprincipled life he chose to lead.

JANE: Men of genius see life in their own terms; their principles are different from those of ordinary people.

ISOBEL: I am sure I have no wish to argue with you, but I do
think you might spare a little of your loyalty to your poor
mother, rather than devote it all to the man who betrayed her
and made her life a hell upon earth.

COLIN: Hear, hear. (*Sitting on stool.*)

JANE (*smiling*): Darling mother, what absolute nonsense! You
lived with father for exactly six years. Admittedly your life may
have been a bit difficult for that very brief period, but since
then it has been extremely comfortable.

ISOBEL: I have no intention of pursuing this discussion any
further, Jane, it is really most unsuitable, considering why we
are here and everything.

JANE: Did you love my father, Jacob?

JACOB: His impact on my world, the world of Art, was
stupendous; his influence far-reaching and incalculable.

JANE: But you were fond of him—as a man I mean? Did you
look forward to seeing him, to dining with him? Was he gay
and attractive and good company?

JACOB: He could be all those things when he chose.

PAMELA: But his paintings! I know I'm ignorant and don't know
anything about art really, but what do they *mean*? I've never
been able to understand.

JACOB (*portentously*): Go into the Tate Gallery, my dear, and look
at Sorodin's "Portrait of Marjorie". Stand before it quietly,
receptively. Stand for an hour, two hours, three hours if need
be, then go away.

PAMELA: Three hours is an awfully long time.

JACOB: It takes a lifetime to appreciate a masterpiece.

COLIN: Is "Portrait of Marjorie" the one with all those rings and
dots?

JACOB: It is the apotheosis of his "Circular" period. One of the
few great modern paintings in the world.

COLIN: But why is it called "Portrait of Marjorie"? It isn't a
portrait at all. I mean it isn't like anyone or anything.

JACOB (*patiently*): It is Sorodin's abstract conception of a woman
called Marjorie.

PAMELA: Marjorie who?

JANE: Does it matter?

JACOB (*giving up*): The fact remains that the Tate bought "Portrait of Marjorie" for three thousand pounds in 1936. It would be worth treble the amount to-day.

COLIN: Well, it's beyond me, that's all I can say, I can't make head or tail of it.

JACOB: Sorodin's creative genius was concentrated into three great periods. The first, what is now described as his "Farouche" period, lasted from 1927 until the early thirties. His first exhibition caused an uproar. There were jeers and catcalls. One elderly art critic struck at one of the canvases with his umbrella. A lady from Des Moines, Iowa, fainted dead away and had to be taken to the American hospital.

ISOBEL: Poor thing. That's where they took poor Edith Carrington when she had that dreadful rash.

JACOB: The "Circular" period was an evolution and a reaction at the same time. Through the dark years of the war I had no message from him. Indeed I imagined he must be dead. It was not until he returned to Paris in 1946 that I realised the full significance of the private war he had been waging with his own genius, a struggle that resulted in the greatest victory of his career. The "Jamaican" period.

COLIN: All those fat negresses?

JACOB (*sharply*): Yes, all those fat negresses, all that primitive simplicity and glorious colour as well. The first painting he showed me on that fabulous day is now in the Louvre.

JANE: "Girl with Breadfruit"?

JACOB: No. "Boy with Plantain". "Girl with Breadfruit" is in Prague.

ISOBEL: That was the one we used for our Christmas cards the year before last, you remember, Colin? Your Aunt Freda wrote "Indecent" on it in red ink and sent it back.

COLIN: More champagne, mother?

ISOBEL: No thank you, dear.

JANE (*rising*): I'd like some more and I'm sure Jacob would. He's had a horrid week dealing with everything. (*She goes to the table.*)

ISOBEL: You've been most considerate, Jacob, to make all the arrangements and support me through to-day's ordeal. I could never have endured it without you.

JANE: You really shouldn't have come, mother.

ISOBEL: Nonsense dear, it was my duty.

JANE: Personally I think it was unnecessary. Nobody was deceived.

ISOBEL: What a disagreeable thing to say, Jane. I'm sure I had no wish to deceive anyone.

COLIN: Jane's been in a bad mood all day, argumentative and thoroughly tiresome. (*To* JANE.) Why don't you snap out of it?

JANE: I haven't been anything of the sort, but I hated us being here, I hated the whole business, all those crowds and press cameras and professional mourners. I felt ashamed.

JACOB: It was most important from every point of view for Paul Sorodin's widow and children to be present at his funeral.

JANE: Every point of view but father's.

ISOBEL: Really, Jane.

JANE: He'd have thought we were hypocrites, as indeed we were.

ISOBEL: I resent your attitude, Jane. Your father was my husband——

JANE: He wouldn't have been if only you had divorced him when he wanted you to, years ago.

PAMELA: I must say this is hardly the moment to go into all that.

ISOBEL: Pamela is quite right. This is indeed no moment to go into that. You should be ashamed of yourself.

JANE: I am, I've already said so, I'm ashamed of us all. Allowing ourselves to be photographed all ends up looking like a lot of black crows.

COLIN: Why don't you stop upsetting mother? She has enough to put up with, God knows.

JANE: She has nothing whatever to put up with. I don't blame her for hating father, we all know he behaved badly to her in the past and deserted her and made her miserable, but all that was years and years ago.

COLIN: What's the point of raking it all up now, then?

JANE: What I do blame her for is not setting him free when he

wanted to be set free and on top of that making us all come
traipsing over here to cash in on his death.

ISOBEL: Once and for all, Jane, I forbid you to talk like that. You
are perfectly well aware that even if I had been willing to
divorce your father, to have done so would directly have
contravened the canons of my Faith. I know you have grown
apart from us during the last few years, I expect it is my fault,
everything is always my fault. But I must say I have been
deeply grieved by your attitude to me throughout all this
trying ordeal. I feel utterly exhausted. Colin, will you and
Pamela take me back to the hotel. I have no more to say.

JANE (going to her): I'm sorry, mother. I didn't mean to grieve
you, but I do wish you could see my point just a little.

ISOBEL: You should never have taken that Journalism course at
the Polytechnic, it's ruined your character.

JANE: Oh, mother, you are funny, really you are.

ISOBEL: I'm sure I don't see anything to laugh at.

JANE: Are you really cross or only pretending to be?

ISOBEL: I don't know what you mean.

JANE: Well, you've been pretending to be sad all day, I see no
reason why you shouldn't be pretending to be upset now.

ISOBEL (rising): Come, Colin. (COLIN rises.)

JANE (sitting ISOBEL down again): You can't possibly go away
before we've decided what's to be done about Sébastien.

COLIN: Sébastien? What are you talking about? Why should
anything be done about him?

JANE: Father left no will. Sébastien served him faithfully during
his last years. Something will have to be done about him.

PAMELA: I expect he has taken good care to feather his own nest.

JANE: Jacob. Do you agree with me?

JACOB: There is certainly something in what you say.

COLIN: Pay him a month's wages and good riddance.

JANE: That's not enough. We're leaving first thing in the
morning. It must be settled before we go.

PAMELA: I agree with Colin. Give him a month's wages and send
him away with a flea in his ear.

JANE: He must have a pension.

COLIN: Pension! You must be out of your mind.

JANE: It's a question of common decency. Mother, you as father's widow cannot afford to appear mean in the eyes of the world. You can't repay his years of devotion to father with a month's wages. What do you think, Jacob?

JACOB: In the circumstances I think Jane is right.

COLIN: Well, I'm damned if I do.

PAMELA: Neither do I.

ISOBEL: Is that your considered opinion, Jacob?

JACOB: Yes. I think he should be given the choice of a pension or a lump sum, whichever he prefers.

ISOBEL: Oh dear. Well, if you really feel it's necessary, I suppose we must agree. Will you interview him?

JACOB: Willingly. But I think it would be more tactful if you told him yourself.

ISOBEL: I have already told you I'm tired, Jacob. I want to go back to the hotel and lie down.

JACOB: He is a very articulate man, Isobel. There is nothing to prevent him giving all sorts of interviews to the Press. A gesture from you at this particular moment would, I am sure, be a wise move.

ISOBEL (*resigned*): Very well. Ring for him.

COLIN *presses the bell near the service door.* COLIN *and* PAMELA *stand behind her like sentries.*

COLIN: Bear up, mother. We can always rely on you to say the right thing.

ISOBEL (*patting his hand*): Thank you, dear.

SEBASTIEN *comes into the room. He is wearing an expression of polite subservience.*

SEBASTIEN: You rang, madame?

ISOBEL (*in command*): Yes, Sébastien. I wish to speak to you for a moment.

SEBASTIEN: At your service, madame.

ISOBEL: First of all I want to thank you for the—er—loyal service you gave my late husband. I would like to say that I find your obvious devotion to him touching, really most touching.

SEBASTIEN: Thank you, madame.

ISOBEL: As you are no doubt aware, Mr. Sorodin left no will.

SEBASTIEN: Yes, madame. I am aware of that.

ISOBEL: And—er—realising that his sudden death might have left you in an embarrassing situation——

SEBASTIEN: In what way, madame?

ISOBEL (*with an effort*): Financially.

SEBASTIEN: The financial aspect has not yet occurred to me. Doubtless it will later.

ISOBEL (*flummoxed*): Oh.

SEBASTIEN: I have frequently been embarrassed in my life, madame, but more often by lack of taste than by lack of money.

 The telephone rings.

Excuse me. (*He goes to it and lifts the receiver.*) Allô: J'écoute—ici Invalides 26–45—Ja, mein Herr—Nein, mein Herr—Ja, ich bin vollkommen Ihrer Meinung—für uns ist es eine Tragödie, für die Welt, aber, ist es eine Katastrophe—Ja, mein Herr—Ich danke Ihnen—Auf Wiedersehen, mein Herr. (*He hangs up.*)

JACOB: Who was that?

SEBASTIEN: Herr Otto Grunschnabel, the director of the "Health in Art" Centre in Hamburg. It is a really remarkable organisation. All art students of both sexes between the ages of fifteen and twenty-five are taken in groups into fields twice a week to establish contact with natural phenomena and acquire physical fitness at the same time.

JANE: I didn't know there were any fields in Hamburg.

SEBASTIEN: There aren't. They go by electric train and walk back in formation, carrying their easels.

JACOB: What did he want anyhow?

SEBASTIEN: Merely a message of condolence. He was a great friend of Mr. Sorodin's. When we were in Germany he used to supply us with models.

COLIN (*contemptuously*): Models!

SEBASTIEN: A comprehensive term, sir. (*To* ISOBEL.) You were about to say, madame?——

ISOBEL: I was about to say that, in consideration of your services to my late husband, Mr. Friedland and I have decided to offer you the choice of a sum of money to be paid in the near future, or—or a small pension. Which would you prefer?

SEBASTIEN: Without wishing to be discourteous, neither, madame.

PAMELA: Well, really!

SEBASTIEN: Please believe me when I say how profoundly I appreciate your kindness and consideration. To you, Miss Jane, and you, Mr. Friedland, I must also express my gratitude. I happened to be listening outside the door just now when the matter was being discussed.

COLIN: Typical! Exactly what I should have expected.

JANE (*amused*): That was disgraceful of you, Sébastien.

SEBASTIEN: You will understand therefore how much it pains me, in the face of such spontaneous generosity—to be the bearer of what I fear will be most disturbing news.

JACOB: Disturbing news! What do you mean?

SEBASTIEN: Although Mr. Sorodin left no will, he *did* leave a letter.

JACOB: Letter?

SEBASTIEN: A personal letter addressed to me. It was written in the early hours of the morning of January the First of this year and was witnessed by Marie-Céleste and the head waiter from the "Grâce à Dieu". He had organised the catering.

COLIN: Catering?

SEBASTIEN: We had given a little party. Nothing grandiose, you understand, just a small gathering of intimate friends, quite informal.

JACOB (*obviously disturbed*): Never mind about that. What is all this leading up to?

COLIN: Blackmail. I can smell it a mile off.

JACOB: Where is this letter?

SEBASTIEN: In a strong-box in the Royal Bank of Canada. But I have a copy of it.

JACOB (*authoritatively*): Let me see it, please.

SEBASTIEN: No, monsieur. That would be a betrayal of confidence. Also it is very long and contains many irrelevancies of a personal nature. I am, however, perfectly prepared to read you any extracts that are pertinent to the present circumstances.

JACOB: What is the meaning of all this? What are you up to?

SEBASTIEN: I am not up to anything. I am merely embarrassed, for reasons that will be only too apparent later on.

JACOB: Come to the point, please. Read the letter.

SEBASTIEN (*looking at* ISOBEL): Have I madame's permission?

ISOBEL (*agitated*): I suppose so—Jacob—what am I to say?

JACOB (*to* SEBASTIEN): You have madame's permission to proceed.

COLIN: There's something fishy about this.

JANE: Shut up, Colin.

JACOB (*impatiently*): Go on.

SEBASTIEN (*with a slight shrug*): Very well. Actually I would have preferred to read it to you or to your lawyer in private, Monsieur Friedland. However, if you insist, I have no choice. Just a moment. (*In tense silence he produces a wad of papers from his inner pocket, glances through them, extracts a typewritten letter and places the rest carefully back in his pocket. He clears his throat and looks at everyone with a slight smile.*) Ready?

COLIN: For God's sake get on with it.

SEBASTIEN (*reading*): "My dear Sébastien. In case the validity of this personal letter to you should ever be questioned, I will begin it by stating that I am sane and healthy and in full possession of my faculties—" (*He looks up.*) Actually he had a slight head cold at the time.

JACOB: Never mind about that—go on.

JANE: The news in your letter must be very bad, Sébastien, you are so obviously enjoying yourself.

SEBASTIEN: Not exactly bad, Miss Jane. Shall we say—startling!

JACOB (*almost shouting*): Read it!

SEBASTIEN (*continuing to read*): "In the event of my demise, I have decided to leave no will and testament, for the simple reason that always having spent any money I earned the moment I received it and frequenty before I received it, I have nothing to leave to anyone beyond a few personal effects. In recognition of your loyal service to me since July 13th, 1946 I should have liked to have bequeathed you a handsome emolument, or at least to have repaid the two hundred and seventy thousand francs I owe you. However, you will doubtless be able to recover this paltry sum from that stingy old bastard, Jacob Friedland." (*He looks up and smiles deprecatingly.*)

JACOB (*grimly*): Continue.

SEBASTIEN: "The whole of my estate will inevitably revert to my loving wife as a just and fitting recompense for the monumental lack of understanding she has lavished on me since we first met on Armistice night 1918, when, owing to an excess of patriotism and inferior Sauterne, she consented to join her life to mine."

COLIN (*protectively*): Mother, I really think——

ISOBEL: Hush, Colin. I would like to hear the rest of the letter.

JACOB: Perhaps it would be advisable, Isobel, for you to return to the hotel with Pamela and Jane. I can deal with this.

ISOBEL: No, Jacob. My husband's insults, even from beyond the grave, are powerless to hurt me.

COLIN: Good for you, mother.

JACOB: Whatever you wish, my dear. (*To* SEBASTIEN.) Go on.

SEBASTIEN (*reading*): "I am well aware that thanks to Mr. Friedland's unscrupulous business acumen, my canvases have achieved a commercial value grossly out of proportion to their merits. In fairness to him, however, I must state that I have reaped considerable financial benefit from his quite remarkable capacity for deceiving the public. My wife and family, also thanks to him, have received over the years a fair percentage of the profits, although I consider this sop to the laws of matrimony unnecessary as my wife has always enjoyed a more than adequate income of her own"—(SEBASTIEN *looks up*.)— there now comes a rather long dissertation on the iniquities of the marriage and divorce laws. It is actually irrelevant to the present situation but quite amusing in a bawdy way. Mr. Sorodin had a rich and varied vocabulary, as you may remember. Would you like me to read it or skip to the more important part of the letter, the "clou" as we say in France?

JACOB (*tersely*): Skip it and go on.

SEBASTIEN: Very well. (*He reads in a barely distinguishable undertone*)—"bla bla bla—Canon Law—bla bla bla—self-centred, sanctimonious hypocrites—bla bla bla—bloody impertinence—bla bla bla—" Ah, here we are. "In consideration of

268

the fact that when this letter is ultimately made public I shall
be in my grave, I feel it to be only fair that the world of Art, to
which I owe so much, should receive from me one final and
unequivocal statement, which is that, with the exception of a
water-colour of a dog executed at Broadstairs when I was
eleven years old, I have never painted a picture of any sort or
kind in the whole course of my life."

ISOBEL *gives a slight cry, puts her hand to her throat and chokes.*

CURTAIN

ACT II: Scene I

A few hours have elapsed since Act I.

The curtain rises on a scene of general dejection.

ISOBEL *is lying on the sofa with her eyes closed.* COLIN *is sitting upstage with a plate of food.* PAMELA *is sitting downstage gloomily turning the pages of an art magazine.* JANE *is sitting in an armchair.* JACOB *is sitting down right.*

JANE: Won't you have some of this pâté, Jacob? It's awfully good.

JACOB: It would choke me.

JANE: You really should try to eat something. Shall I go into the kitchen and ask what's-her-name to scramble some eggs?

COLIN: If the man doesn't want to eat, why badger him?

JANE: He must keep up his strength. Violent shocks to the nervous system are terribly devitalising, besides which he has talked himself into a state of exhaustion.

PAMELA: And a fat lot of good it has done. It would have been much better if we had all gone home hours ago when I suggested it. We shall feel much more able to cope with everything after a good sleep.

JACOB (*raising his head*): A good sleep! Are you mad?

PAMELA: Certainly not. I'm beginning to think that Colin and I are the only sane ones among the lot of you. We always thought Sorodin's pictures were fakes anyway, and said so. Didn't we, Colin?

COLIN (*with his mouth full*): Yes, we did.

JACOB (*with controlled fury*): Without wishing to be rude, Colin, I must frankly say that, where works of art are concerned, I could never consider you or your wife's opinion to be in the least valid, or even interesting.

COLIN: Here, steady on!

JACOB: Please do not think that this is in any way intended as a

reproach. We all aim to be specialists in our own milieux. I
have no doubt whatever that you are an expert on military
strategy and that your wife is an accomplished horsewoman. I
am equally convinced that neither of you could distinguish a
Picasso from a hole in the ground.

COLIN: At least we'd know the hole in the ground *was* a hole in
the ground. (JANE *laughs*.)

JACOB (*savagely*): Well—I wish you'd both find one and fall down
it.

COLIN (*rising*): Ha, ha! Bloody funny! (*Returns glass and plate to
sofa table.*)

ISOBEL (*opening her eyes*): Colin, you know I don't like you to use
that word.

JANE: Do stop baiting Jacob. He's very upset.

PAMELA: I don't see why he should insult Colin and me,
however upset he is.

ISOBEL: I wish you'd all stop bickering. My head's splitting.

JACOB: It can't be true. It must be a trick, some low, blackmailing
trick. I refuse to believe that it is true.

JANE: Nothing can be proved until you actually see the letter and
you can't possibly do that until to-morrow morning because
the bank's shut.

JACOB: Do *you* believe it?

JANE: Yes. I'm afraid I do.

JACOB (*rising*): Do you realise what it would mean if that letter
got into the Press? Do you realise the full implication of this
ghastly situation?

JANE: The letter might be a forgery. We can't tell until the
handwriting is identified.

JACOB: Even if it is a forgery my reputation would be ruined for
ever if the papers got hold of it.

JANE: We must see to it that they don't.

JACOB: This is a nightmare.

JANE: If it is true that father didn't paint the pictures it stands to
reason that someone else did. The first thing to do is to find
out who.

COLIN: Try ringing up the nearest asylum.

JANE: Do be quiet, Colin.

COLIN (*going to* JACOB): It's a very sensible suggestion. Whoever painted "Portrait of Marjorie" must be as mad as a hatter.

PAMELA (*giggling*): Oh, Colin, you do make me laugh sometimes, really you do!

JACOB: I think it would be more helpful if you continued to amuse your wife in the library.

COLIN: I'm quite comfortable here, thanks.

JANE: Do you think Sébastien knows who painted them? I know he swore he didn't, but he might have been lying.

COLIN (*laughing*): Perhaps he did them himself.

JACOB: Whoever painted those pictures was a genius. That is my considered opinion. Not only is it my opinion, it is the verdict of all the finest art critics in the civilised world.

JANE: Do art critics really know?

JACOB: Of course they do. They are most of them men of the highest integrity.

ISOBEL: I have often heard you refer to them as sycophantic sheep.

JACOB: Only on the rare occasions when their opinions have run contrary to my own.

JANE: You are quite convinced, Jacob, that all father's pictures were painted by one person?

COLIN: Or a chimpanzee with a brush in its mouth.

PAMELA (*going into gales of laughter*): Oh, Colin!

ISOBEL (*gently*): I think, dear, that, considering we only laid your father to rest this afternoon, it is not in very good taste to call him a chimpanzee.

COLIN: I didn't. He didn't paint the pictures, anyhow.

JACOB: That has yet to be proved.

JANE: Assuming the worst, that father's letter was true, so far nobody outside this room knows it.

COLIN: Except Sébastien.

JANE: Sébastien can be dealt with.

JACOB: He can sell it to the highest bidder.

JANE: Exactly. We must bid higher.

COLIN: We'll be laying ourselves open to a charge of defrauding the public.

JANE: That can't be helped. The public has been defrauded for years and it might just as well go on being for a little longer.

ISOBEL: I cannot agree to that, Jane. I am sorry, but it is against all my principles.

JANE: Oh, mother, really . . .

JACOB (*rising*): Is it in accordance with your principles to bring ruin and disgrace on a man who has always tried to be your friend?

ISOBEL: What nonsense, Jacob, dear. We all know it isn't your fault.

JACOB: It doesn't matter whose fault it is. My whole reputation is in jeopardy!

ISOBEL: Well, you must admit that it was a little silly of you to let Paul pull the wool over your eyes in the first place, wasn't it? I know we're all liable to make mistakes sometimes but surely it's better, once we know we've been wrong, to come bravely out into the open and say so, don't you think?

JACOB (*with restraint*): No, Isobel, I do not. Nor have I any intention of coming bravely out into the open and saying that I was wrong when I know with every fibre of my being that I was right. I still maintain that whoever painted those pictures had genius.

ISOBEL: Well, I am afraid that I can't agree with you. When you showed me that first picture of Paul's years ago, it was as much as I could do not to laugh outright, really it was. That awful looking woman with a pot on her head!

JACOB (*patiently*): "Market Woman in Algiers" has been acknowledged to be a masterpiece.

ISOBEL: You still can't convince me that women go to market stark naked, even in Algiers. (COLIN *and* PAMELA *laugh.*)

JANE: This is all rather beside the point, mother. Don't you see that we must stand by Jacob.

ISOBEL: I am very sorry, but my conscience would not permit me to uphold, even for a brief period, what I know to be a lie.

PAMELA: I agree with mother. Let's be honest and above board. It pays in the long run.

JANE: That is exactly what it won't do. If this becomes public, not only will poor Jacob be done for but the whole of father's estate will amount to nothing. We must be practical. What possible good could be achieved by bursting this scandal wide open? Surely it is our first duty to find whoever it was father bribed to ghost-paint for him and then it will be up to Jacob to see that justice is done.

ISOBEL: Justice?

JANE: Of course. Jacob must guarantee that whoever painted the pictures will ultimately get the recognition he deserves. I am right—aren't I, Jacob?

JACOB: Yes, my dear.

ISOBEL: I wish Father Flanagan were here.

JANE: I don't see what he could do if he were.

ISOBEL: I know that you don't like Father Flanagan, Jane, but you can take my word for it, he is a very wonderful man; almost a mystic.

JANE: What we need at the moment is a clairvoyant.

COLIN: For once I agree with Jane.

ISOBEL (*reproachfully*): Oh, Colin!

COLIN: Even dear old Mr. Flint would be a damned sight more useful than Father Flanagan. He may not be a clairvoyant but he is a trained lawyer.

ISOBEL: Dear old Mr. Flint wanted to come with us but he couldn't leave his wife.

JANE: Unlike father.

ISOBEL: For shame, Jane.

PAMELA: Why don't we telephone to dear old Mr. Flint and put all our cards on the table?

JACOB (*with dreadful calm*): I can explain to you why we cannot telephone to dear old Mr. Flint, or to Father Flanagan, or to the Pope. It is because we have all agreed not to divulge what has happened to a living soul.

COLIN: Mother hasn't.

JACOB: You must agree, Isobel. I implore you to agree. If Mr. Flint knew, his partners would know, and if his partners knew, his partners' wives would know, and before we knew where we were, the secret would be out and in the papers.

ISOBEL: You have a curious idea of the probity of English lawyers.

JACOB: I have a very definite idea of the incapacity of the human race to keep its mouth shut.

COLIN: This isn't getting us anywhere. Why don't we all go back to the hotel?

    SEBASTIEN *enters by service door.*

SEBASTIEN (*to* JACOB): Did you ring, sir?

JACOB: No, I did not.

SEBASTIEN: How strange. I could have sworn I heard a bell. Perhaps it was a bicycle. Is there anything I can do for you?

JANE: Yes, Sébastien, a great deal.

SEBASTIEN: At your service always, miss.

COLIN: Oh Lord! We're off again!

JANE: You said some while ago that father's letter was witnessed by Marie-Celéste and a head waiter.

SEBASTIEN: Jules Messonier, 80 bis rue de Perpignan.

JANE: Can he speak English?

SEBASTIEN: Oh, no. I believe he picked up a little American during the liberation, but only a few idiomatic words such as okay and demi-tasse.

JANE: He didn't read the letter? They neither of them read it?

SEBASTIEN: No, they only signed it as witnesses.

JANE: Good. To your certain knowledge no one outside this room knows its contents.

SEBASTIEN: To my certain knowledge. I deposited it in the bank myself in a sealed package.

JANE: Had you any suspicion, when you first entered my father's employ, that he wasn't a painter at all?

SEBASTIEN: None, Miss Jane. He explained to me that complete solitude was essential to him when he was working. That was the reason he gave for never painting in this studio. He said it was merely a façade to impress the dealers. Later, of course, when he knew me better, he took me into his confidence.

JANE: Where did he work, then, or pretend to work?

SEBASTIEN: St. Cloud. He rented a studio there under a false name. He used to leave here in the morning gay as a lark and return in the evening exhausted.

JANE: Every morning?

SEBASTIEN: Oh, no! Only when, as he said, he felt the urge.

JACOB: St. Cloud? Where in St. Cloud?

SEBASTIEN: 16 impasse de Louis Philippe.

JACOB: Why didn't you tell us this before?

SEBASTIEN: You never asked me.

JACOB: Have you the keys?

SEBASTIEN: Yes, monsieur.

JACOB: Where are they?

SEBASTIEN: With the letter in the Royal Bank of Canada.

JACOB: Is the studio empty? Is there anything in it?

SEBASTIEN: Only his remaining canvas.

JACOB (*almost screaming*): What!!!

SEBASTIEN: His last great masterpiece, "Nude with Violin".

> *The front door bell rings.*

Excuse me. (*He bows and goes out.*)

JACOB (*wildly and rising*): Remaining canvas! "Nude with Violin"!

JANE: Keep calm, Jacob, for heaven's sake, keep calm.

JACOB: The cunning blackmailing scoundrel! I'll have him arrested, I'll have him flung into gaol!

> *There is the sound of raised voices outside.*

JANE: Jacob! Pull yourself together. You *must* pull yourself together.

> CLINTON PREMINGER, *junior, bursts into the room. He is followed by* SEBASTIEN, *who stands quietly by the door.*

CLINTON: Forgive me for intruding, but I've just had a cable from my editor.

JACOB: I don't care if you've had a cable from President Eisenhower. Please go away.

CLINTON: It's urgent. It's about Sorodin. Where is it?

JANE: Where is what?

CLINTON: Sorodin's posthumous masterpiece, the greatest picture he ever painted. (*He produces a cable from his pocket.*) The cable says it's called "Rude with Violin".

SEBASTIEN (*to above coffee table*): The prescience of the Western Union is almost uncanny.

CLINTON: The news broke in New York yesterday. All the dealers are crazy with excitement. Elmore P. Riskin, the director of the Manhattan Museum of Modern Art, has hopped a plane and is arriving to-morrow. You must let me see it, Mr. Friedland. *Life* Magazine is prepared to carry it on the cover page in colour.

JACOB (*brokenly*): Go away, Mr. Clinton Preminger, junior, just go away.

CLINTON: Oh, please—please—I implore you to let me see it! It may make the whole difference to my approach.

COLIN: Approach to what?

CLINTON: Everything!

JANE: Mr. Friedland is very upset, Mr. Preminger. Please do as he asks and go away. It is quite out of the question for you to see the picture.

CLINTON: But why—why?

SEBASTIEN: It is being varnished.

JANE: Thank you, Sébastien.

CLINTON: This is terribly important to me.

SEBASTIEN: It is terribly important to all of us monsieur.

The front door bell rings.

Excuse me. (*He goes out.*)

CLINTON (*to* ISOBEL): Mrs. Sorodin, I appeal to you. . . .

JANE: Mr. Preminger—you really must stop appealing to my mother, it flusters her.

COLIN: Now see here, Preminger . . .

JANE: Just a moment, Colin. (*To* CLINTON.) I will try to arrange for you to see the picture in the morning.

CLINTON: Do you think it will be dry?

JANE: I can't promise anything but if you will go away quietly now I assure you that I will do all I can.

CLINTON: Okay. I'm sorry—I'll go. Good-bye.

He goes out quickly.

ISOBEL: Americans are curious, aren't they? So abrupt!

JACOB: What are we to do now? If New York had the news yesterday, London will have had it to-day. I shall have all the English dealers pestering the life out of me—Alaric Craigie, Beddington, probably the Tooths.

ISOBEL: What on earth have teeth got to do with it?

SEBASTIEN *re-enters.*

SEBASTIEN: A Princess Pavlikov has called, Mr. Friedland. She seems agitated.

JACOB: A Princess who?

SEBASTIEN: Pavlikov. As the name implies, she is a Russian.

JACOB: What does she want?

SEBASTIEN: To see you, Mr. Friedland. She says it is urgent.

JACOB: Send her away. I can't possibly see anyone now.

SEBASTIEN (*meaningly*): I think, in the circumstances, that it would be wise to grant her a brief interview.

JACOB: What do you mean?

SEBASTIEN: She says she is a very old friend of Mr. Sorodin's. She apparently knew him many many years ago, at the beginning of his career.

ISOBEL (*rising*): I really don't feel up to meeting any more strangers at the moment—Colin—Pamela—— (PAMELA *rises*.)

JANE (*firmly*): Show her in, Sébastien.

SEBASTIEN: Volontiers, mademoiselle. (*He goes out.*)

ISOBEL: Really, Jane, you are being very high-handed. I don't know what has come over you. You've been ordering us about and shouting at us all day long like—like a sergeant-major.

JANE: Please sit down again, darling. This woman may be able to help us—don't you see?

> SEBASTIEN *re-enters.*

SEBASTIEN (*announcing*): Princess Pavlikov.

> *He stands aside and* ANYA PAVLIKOV *comes in. She is a woman of about fifty. Her face is a trifle ravaged but her make-up is excellent. She is discreetly dressed but her jewellery, if it were real, would be worth a fortune.*

ANYA (*to* JACOB): Mr. Friedland?

JACOB: I am Jacob Friedland.

ANYA: Ah, yes. I see now that you could not be anyone else.

JACOB (*stiffly*): I fear I don't understand.

ANYA (*with a charming smile*): It is no matter. (*She looks at* ISOBEL.) This lady—you will please make presentation?

JACOB: Mrs. Paul Sorodin.

ISOBEL (*nodding*): How do you do.

ANYA: Of course, I see also that you could not be anyone else. (*She sees* COLIN.) My God!

COLIN: I beg your pardon?

ANYA (*to* COLIN): Eyes! Not mouth. Mouth is different, but eyes!

JANE (*rising*): I am Jane Sorodin. This is my brother Colin, and this is his wife.

ANYA (*looking raptly at* PAMELA): Beautiful! Quite, quite beautiful! The true English mould. Magnificent!

PAMELA (*embarrassed*): Thank you.

ANYA (*dreamily*): Florence Nightingale, Gainsborough. Clive of India, what a country! I really must sit down. (*Sits.*)

JANE: Please do.

ANYA: Is there brandy in house?

SEBASTIEN: Perhaps Madame la Princesse would prefer vodka?

ANYA (*violently*): No, no, no! I cannot bear vodka. It makes me gay and noisy for a small while, then suddenly tears come and regret and despair fill heart. It is most beastly. Brandy is better, especially after journey.

SEBASTIEN: Very good, madame.

> *He goes out by service door, staring at* ANYA *as he goes.*

ANYA: That man has coloured blood. You can tell by his cheekbones. (*Looking at* ISOBEL.) You are devoted to him?

JANE: We hardly know him. He was my father's servant.

ANYA: Ah! Do not trust him.

COLIN: Thanks. We don't.

JACOB: I understand that you wished to see me urgently.

ANYA: I do. Most urgently. But it is delicate matter, perhaps there is tiny bathroom where we talk privately?

JACOB: Does it concern the late Paul Sorodin?

ANYA: Oh, yes.

JACOB: In that case it also concerns everyone in this room. You may speak freely.

ANYA: Ah! You wish me to say what I say before witnesses. Is idea that?

JANE (*tactfully*): Not exactly. (ANYA *lights a cigarette.*) You see, we are all most anxious to discover as much as possible about my father's earlier years. As you may know, he left my mother in 1925 and we have had no actual contact with him since.

ISOBEL: I cannot feel, Jane, that our private family affairs can be of any interest to Princess Pav—Pav——

ANYA (*laughing gaily*): No Pav-Pav, Pavlikov. It is what you call maiden name. I took it back when my husband showed true colours and went to Düsseldorf with my cousin Masha. He was heartless pig called Flanagan.

JANE: Oh dear!

ANYA: Irish.

PAMELA (*helpfully*): In Ireland Flanagan is a very common name.

ANYA: He was very common man.

SEBASTIEN *re-enters with a balloon glass of brandy on a salver.*

SEBASTIEN: Kniagynia, vashe cognac. (Your brandy, Madame la Princesse.)

ANYA (*taking it*): Spasibo. Pochemou vi ne skazali chto vsia cemia zdez? (*Soft* c.) (Thank you. Why didn't you say the whole family was here?)

SEBASTIEN: Ia doumal chto loutshe vam samoy oubeditsia. (I thought you'd better see for yourself.)

ANYA: Vi mugli predoupredit (*Soft.*) menia. (You could have warned me.)

SEBASTIEN: Mne kazaloc chto eto ne mayo delo. (I did not consider it any of my business.)

JACOB: That will be all, Sébastien.

SEBASTIEN (*crossing to service door*): Very good, monsieur. (*With meaning.*) I shall be just outside the door if you should need me.

He bows and goes out.

ANYA: He speak good Russian but bad accent. Ukraine—harsh on ear. Has he ever been in prison?

COLIN: Frequently, I should think.

ANYA: It always gives people a certain "air". Of course many of my family were in prison from time to time but only for political reason. My uncle Sergei used to tell us wonderful prison tales when we were children in Kief. He once trained mouse to do little dance. La la la—so, he would say—La la la—so! and it would get up on tiny legs and go round and round—how we laughed!

JACOB: Yes! I am sure it must have been most entertaining.

Princess Pavlikov, but we are very eager to hear whatever you have to tell us about Paul Sorodin. It is getting late, and we are all rather tired.

ANYA (*putting her cigarette out*): Very well! Business. (*She looks at* ISOBEL.) You will not mind if I speak truth, Mrs. Sorodin? It is all long ago but I would not wish to wound your heart.

ISOBEL: Please go on. I am fully prepared for whatever revelations you care to make.

ANYA (*enthusiastically*): Fabulous! Wonderful! What a country! What a race! Sir Walter Raleigh, William Pitt, Christina Rossetti. . . .

JACOB (*irritably*): Please say what you have to say, Princess. You knew Sorodin?

ANYA: Yes. (*She sighs wistfully.*) Oh yes, I knew him.

JACOB: Well?

ANYA: How well can one really know anyone? We are all strangers really, lonely strangers groping about in dark. We know face, we know body, we know hands, but soul! That is a thing most different, no?

JACOB: Yes, most different. Therefore we needn't discuss it at the moment, need we? When did you know him?

ANYA: He was my lover from 1925 until 1929.

JACOB: Where did you first meet?

ANYA: Here, in Paris. I was a student at École des Beaux Arts, he trod on my foot in Métro and I bit him.

PAMELA: Bit him?

ANYA: Oh yes! I always bite people when I am suddenly astonished.

JACOB: What were you studying at the Beaux Arts?

ANYA: Sculpture. Feeling of clay intoxicates me. I go quite mad sometimes and dance and shout very loud. (*Laughs.*)

JACOB: When did you start painting?

ANYA (*startled*): Painting! So you know? You have known all the time. You have been most slyboots.

JACOB: I don't *know* anything, but I want to. I want to know all that you can tell me. It may be of vital importance.

ANYA: It was Sorodin who made me give up the sculpting. Clay drove him crazy, all over house nothing but clay. Then one

day we have great great drama and he throw it all in sea, so I
leave him in Algiers and go over mountains to Bou-Sada in
desert.

JANE: Algiers!

ANYA (*to* JACOB): Have you ever been Bou-Sada?

JACOB: No, I have not.

ANYA: Well, don't go. It's ruined now.

JACOB (*persevering*): When did you start painting?

ANYA: When Sorodin came to find me and we were lovers again
and live in house in La Napoule!

JACOB (*striking his forehead*): La Napoule!

ANYA: You remember now?

JANE (*eagerly*): Remember what?

ANYA: Mr. Friedland first meet Sorodin in La Napoule. His car
break at bottom of hill one day when I had gone Nice in bus.
He comes to house and asks for water, and there was Sorodin
in yellow shirt, and together they drink cognac and when I
come back in evening all those silly, silly paintings Sorodin
make me do are no more there.

JACOB: Oh, my God!

ANYA: Mr. Friedland buy all paintings except two, one of lemons
hanging from chandelier, and other triangular fish head on
cushion. They not quite finished, but both he bought later. I
did fish painting with nail scissors because I had broken brush.

JACOB (*sepulchrally*): It is now in the Chicago Museum of Modern
Art.

ANYA: I don't know what happened to picture of stupid old
lemons.

JACOB: It is the treasured possession of one of the greatest
connoisseurs in Beunos Aires.

ANYA (*laughing*): It is great joke, no?

JACOB: No.

ANYA: Sorodin would laugh if he alive now.

COLIN: I'll bet he would!

JANE: How many paintings did you do for my father altogether?

ANYA: I cannot remember, my darling. (*Kisses her on both cheeks.*)
But many, great, great many. He made me go on and on and
on. That was why I leave him really. He thought it was

because I love darling Egmont, but really it was smell of
turpentine. (*To* ISOBEL.) You like turpentine smell?

ISOBEL (*flurried*): Well—no—I suppose I don't actually. I mean—
I don't really know.

ANYA: After long while painting, believe me, it make sick.

JACOB: You left Sorodin and went away with this—this Egmont?

ANYA: That is truth.

JACOB: And you never painted again?

ANYA (*gaily*): Oh, my God, no! Egmont hate painting. Egmont
mechanic.

JACOB: Good for Egmont.

ANYA: We start garage near Grenoble, fine business, many
tourists, Route Napoléon.

JACOB: Did Sorodin try to prevent you leaving him?

ANYA: Oh yes. For three weeks we have the scenes. Sorodin
wish kill Egmont, Egmont wish kill Sorodin. I cry, everyone
cry, then Sorodin give in and make me sign letter.

JACOB: Letter?

ANYA: Yes. I have copy here in bag. Real letter in Swiss Bank
Brussels. Egmont witness letter. Then everyone shake hands,
drink cognac, and we go.

JACOB: Is Egmont alive?

ANYA: I think no. He went Congo 1934 to have better garage, but
Congo bad business for garage.

JACOB: Was the letter a form of contract? Did Sorodin pay you
money?

ANYA: Oh yes. Every year until war. Then no more.

JACOB: Please show me the letter.

ANYA: Certainly. (*Hands it to him.*)

JACOB (*reading it*): This is appalling!

ANYA: True letter in Sorodin's handwriting. Typed copy more
easy to understand.

COLIN: What's in the letter? Is it in English?

JACOB (*still reading it*): Yes . . . yes, it's in English.

JANE: Tell us the worst, Jacob.

JACOB: The gist of it is that Madame Pavlikov agrees to renounce
all claims on her paintings. She also swears solemnly in the
presence of witnesses never to speak or write of the

transaction to a living person. In return for this Sorodin guarantees to pay her an annuity of three hundred thousand francs, to be paid into her account in the National Bank of Switzerland in Brussels.

COLIN: Why Brussels?

ANYA: My stepmother had little business there.

JANE: What sort of business?

ANYA: It is difficult to explain, but it was good until war, then *pouf*! everything break in small pieces—my stepmother die—girls all run away.

COLIN (*to* ANYA): Girls?

ANYA: My step-sisters.

JANE: And you, where did you go?

ANYA: Dublin. Ireland neutral country. That's where I meet Flanagan. But I come back after war to Brussels—then Flanagan leave me. I try to find Sorodin—no Sorodin. I work most hard to live and eat well, then at last I come here again and find Sorodin.

JACOB: When?

ANYA: Five years ago. He shout at me. I bite him. He give me million francs. I take, and now he dies.

COLIN: A million francs! That's a thousand pounds, isn't it?

ANYA: Exchange most bloody.

JACOB: How much do you want, Madame Pavlikov?

ANYA: Money vulgar. I prefer not discuss.

JACOB: You realise of course that this letter is not in any way legal?

ANYA: Not legal maybe but most fine joke for Press.

JACOB: How much do you want?

ANYA (*rising*): I will ask lawyer.

JACOB (*angrily*): You will do no such thing!

JANE: Hush, Jacob, I am sure we will be able to come to some reasonable arrangement with Princess Pavlikov.

JACOB: This is sheer blackmail!

ANYA (*to* JACOB): It is business, Mr. Friedland.

JACOB: If you will deliver the original of this letter to me at my office, number 506 Boulevard Haussmann, within three days, I will draw up a contract guaranteeing you five hundred thousand francs a year for the rest of your life.

ISOBEL: Jacob!

COLIN (*horrified*): The man's barmy!

JACOB: Be quiet and leave this to me. (*To* ANYA.) Well?

ANYA: Belgian francs?

JACOB: Certainly not, French francs.

ANYA: Then no agree. French francs most shifty. Up one day, down next, Government change—wallop!

    SEBASTIEN *enters from service door.*

SEBASTIEN: You rang, monsieur?

JACOB: No, I did not.

SEBASTIEN: How extraordinary! I made sure I heard a bell. It must have been Notre Dame. (*To* ANYA.) Madame would like me to escort her to her car?

COLIN: Car?

SEBASTIEN: Yes, monsieur. I have been having a little chat with madame's chauffeur. A most interesting man.

ANYA (*sharply*): What have you said—you and chauffeur?

SEBASTIEN: We found we had a great deal in common.

ANYA (*to* JACOB): The offer you make just now. It is definite?

JACOB: Yes.

ANYA: Then I accept.

SEBASTIEN: Excuse me, Mr. Friedland, Madame Sorodin, but I venture to suggest that it is a little late in the evening to make final decisions. In the morning, when the brain is clearer and the sun is shining, matters, even business matters, assume quite a different aspect.

ANYA: He make offer before witnesses. I accept before witnesses. No more fiddle-faddle—it is settled!

SEBASTIEN: Oh no, it's not!

ANYA (*visibly agitated, rising*): You and chauffeur—what was said between you?

SEBASTIEN: Ia vass predoupredill ne otkrivat (*Soft* t.) rta. (I warned you not to open your mouth too wide.)

ANYA: Chto vi skazali? (What have you said?)

SEBASTIEN: Eto mayo delo. (That's my business.)

ANYA: Vi ljiote, e vi niskaia svinia! (You are low, lying pig!)

SEBASTIEN: Molchat (*Soft* t.) ouhodite. Eslie vi meite sebia
   derjat (*Soft* t.) dlia vas eto boudette gorazdo polesnie. (Shut up
   and get out. You'll be fairly treated if you behave yourself.)

COLIN: What the hell's going on?

JACOB: What is all this, Sébastien? Kindly explain—in English.

ANYA: You not listen! He stinking half-breed liar!

ISOBEL: Oh dear, I do hope there isn't going to be any
   unpleasantness!

ANYA: I told you not trust him. Look cheek-bones!

JACOB: What were you saying just now? Tell me the truth,
   please.

SEBASTIEN: With pleasure, monsieur. I was merely explaining to
   Madame la Princesse that it was foolish to open her mouth
   too wide and that she would be fairly treated if she behaved
   herself and got the hell out of here.

JACOB: Have you ever met her before?

SEBASTIEN: No, monsieur.

JANE: You weren't here when she called on my father some
   years back?

SEBASTIEN: Alas no, miss. I happened to be staying with friends
   in Barbizon for the week-end. On my return, however, I
   gathered that a fairly stormy interview had taken place.

JACOB: How did you gather that?

SEBASTIEN: Marie-Céleste was hysterical, Mr. Sorodin's left arm
   was severely lacerated, and the sofa had been sent away to be
   re-covered.

ANYA (*almost frantic*): You and chauffeur—what you talk about?

JACOB: The past—what do you mean?

SEBASTIEN: I have a bottle of Armagnac in my room—it was a
   birthday present from Mr. Sorodin. I cannot bear to drink
   alone, and Marie-Céleste has gone to bed, so I invited
   madame's chauffeur to share it with me.

ANYA: What you say? Tell me swiftly!

SEBASTIEN: Armagnac induces a mood of delightful nostalgia,
   very mellowing, inhibitions are released and lost years can be
   recaptured without regret.

JACOB: Come to the point, please. You knew this man before?

SEBASTIEN: Oh yes. Egmont and I are old friends.

JANE: Egmont?

SEBASTIEN: Yes, Egmont Vasquier. He was a garage mechanic, a bluff, cheerful fellow but inclined to become violent when crossed in any way. He was also a trifle unscrupulous in regard to money. That's really what they jugged him for.

COLIN: Jugged him?

SEBASTIEN: Oh yes. That is how we first met, in the late 'thirties. By the strangest coincidence we happened to occupy the same prison cell—in the Congo.

ANYA: You are a dirty filthy blackguardly peasant. Your accent stinks like the fish market in Odessa, and if my great Uncle Vladimir Pavlickovitch were here he would send you bouncing, bouncing in a mule cart to the salt mines of Serbia. Pig, pig, pig!

THE LIGHTS FADE

Scene II

The time is about five o'clock on the following afternoon.
   When the curtain rises, the telephone is ringing. SEBASTIEN *comes in and goes to it.*

SEBASTIEN (*at telephone*): Allô ... ici Invalides 26–46—Ah, Mr. Friedland—Yes, it is all arranged, the camion will be at St. Cloud the first thing in the morning. I will be there myself to supervise everything and return here in it with the canvas.—Certainly, sir, you may rely on me.—Yes, sir, a short while ago. Mr. Elmore P. Riskin is at the Lancaster and Sir Alaric Craigie at the Crillon, I told them both that you would communicate with them personally. Oh yes, sir, the interview went off most satisfactorily—Madame la Princesse became rather violent at one moment and attempted to bite my thigh, but Egmont and I managed to calm her down. Egmont is a very sensible man, and is perfectly prepared to settle for

French francs, unlike myself, who prefers a more stable currency such as dollars. Pray keep calm, Mr. Friedland. Yes, they both went back to Brussels on the afternoon plane and will return to Paris to-morrow with the document. Yes, sir— not at all, sir—In about half an hour? Very good, sir.

With a smile he hangs up the receiver. There is a ring at the front door bell. He rises from the desk, glances round the room to see that everything is in order. JANE *enters.*

JANE: Good afternoon, Sébastien.

SEBASTIEN: Good afternoon, Miss Jane.

JANE: I came on before the others because I wanted to have a little talk with you.

SEBASTIEN: I am both flattered and charmed, Miss Jane. Can I offer you any refreshment?

JANE: No, thank you.

SEBASTIEN: A cigarette, perhaps?

JANE: I have my own, thank you.

SEBASTIEN: A light at least? (*He lights her cigarette.*)

JANE: Perhaps you would like to sit down?

SEBASTIEN: Mademoiselle is most democratic. But if Marie-Céleste should come in and find me lolling about in the presence of my late employer's daughter, it might undermine her morale.

JANE: I suspect that in this particular establishment Marie-Céleste's morale has survived worse shocks than that.

SEBASTIEN: Mademoiselle is so right.

JANE: In any case I didn't ask you to loll about, I asked you to sit down.

SEBASTIEN: I am over-ruled. (*He sits.*)

JANE (*offering cigarette to* SEBASTIEN, *who takes it*): Now then——

SEBASTIEN: I am all attention, Miss Jane.

JANE: I don't doubt that for a moment. You strike me as being a very alert character.

SEBASTIEN: Mademoiselle is too kind.

JANE: Also, a fairly unscrupulous one.

SEBASTIEN: That is correct.

JANE: Will you answer one question absolutely honestly?

SEBASTIEN: That rather depends what the question is.

JANE: Were you genuinely fond of my father?

SEBASTIEN (*quietly, after a slight pause*): Yes, Miss Jane. I was. You may really believe that.

JANE (*with a smile*): Thank you, Sébastien. I do. I too was fond of him in my own mind although I can barely remember him. My mother accuses me of taking a romantic view of him. Am I wrong?

SEBASTIEN: Of course not. You would have adored him; and, if I may say so, I know that he would have adored you. He was a man of remarkable character. Full of charm, vitality and irrepressible humour. Also he was devoted to pleasure, which in Christian communities is always suspect.

JANE: Why did he perpetrate this gigantic hoax?

SEBASTIEN: Because he was the victim of an obsession that tormented him all his life.

JANE: What sort of obsession?

SEBASTIEN: A fanatical, burning hatred of dishonesty.

JANE: You can hardly expect me to believe that when his whole career was founded on a deliberate lie.

SEBASTIEN: Nevertheless, it is true. He loathed cant, jargon, intellectual snobbism and the commercialising of creative talent. Successful art-dealers, critics and so-called experts were his *bêtes noires*. His detestation of them was almost pathological.

JANE: But why? Why should he have minded so much?

SEBASTIEN: Creative talent was his god. He worshipped it ardently, passionately, all the more perhaps because he knew he hadn't a vestige of it himself. Far and away above everything else, he loved good painting.

JANE: If he loved good painting so much, how could he possibly have done what he did?

SEBASTIEN: He was a crusader.

JANE: Crusader? Really, Sébastien!

SEBASTIEN: What I am telling you is the truth, Miss Jane.

JANE: It is hard to believe.

SEBASTIEN: Please try. It is most important.

JANE: Why?

SEBASTIEN: Because of all your family you are the only one he
would have wanted to share the joke with him.

JANE: How can you possibly know that?

SEBASTIEN: Because I knew him, probably better than anyone
else, and because since yesterday I have had the privilege of
knowing you.

JANE: Thank you, Sébastien.

SEBASTIEN (*rising*): Have I convinced you? (*To centre.*)

JANE: There is still a great deal that I find difficult to understand.
Why, for instance, should he have gone to all that trouble and
expense of paying that Russian woman to paint his pictures for
him when he could quite easily have done them himself?

SEBASTIEN: If he had painted them himself they would no longer
have been fakes.

JANE: How do you mean?

SEBASTIEN: Mr. Friedland and all the nabobs of the art world
would have been able to uphold their verdict that he was a
genius in spite of any protestations he might make to the
contrary. Indeed they would have probably used his protestations to prove their point.

JANE: How could they?

SEBASTIEN: By saying that he was a genius whether he knew it
or not and, like so many other men of abnormal creative
power, unbalanced!

JANE: That letter you read out to us with such unmistakable
pleasure. Did you persuade him to write it?

SEBASTIEN (*laughing*): Persuade him? It was the culmination of
his life's ambition. It was his final gesture, a last decisive blow
aimed at the parasites who, in his opinion, had betrayed the
only thing he really respected in human nature, the creative
instinct.

JANE: Thank you so much for clarifying the situation for me—at
least a little.

SEBASTIEN: You are still not convinced?

JANE: I still believe you know a good deal more than you
pretend to know.

SEBASTIEN: How right you are, Miss Jane. But we are friends,
aren't we?

JANE (*rising and holding out hand with a smile*): Yes, Sébastien. (*They shake hands.*) We are friends. But there is still one question that is puzzling me.

SEBASTIEN: What is it?

JANE: Princess Pavlikov left my father in 1929. Who painted the rest of his pictures?

SEBASTIEN: In the idiom of our American cousins, Miss Jane— "search me"!

JANE: Oh dear. Poor Jacob. I really am very sorry for him.

SEBASTIEN (*smiling*): Mr. Friedland is certainly in a most unenviable position. We must all do everything we can to help him, mustn't we?

JANE: You don't like Mr. Friedland, do you, Sébastien?

SEBASTIEN: I share your father's opinion of him. He said he was a pompous, plausible, double-crossing old weasel.

JANE: You don't think he knows anything about painting?

SEBASTIEN: I don't think that anyone knows about painting any more. Art, like human nature, has got out of hand.

There is the sound of voices in the hall.

JANE: Here they are.

SEBASTIEN: I didn't hear the bell.

CHERRY-MAY WATERTON *enters, followed by* FABRICE. CHERRY-MAY *is a blowzy, cheerful middle-aged blonde.* FABRICE *is excessively handsome and looks like an advertisement in a health magazine.*

CHERRY-MAY (*to* SEBASTIEN): Is Mr. Jacob Friedland here?

SEBASTIEN: No, madame.

CHERRY-MAY: They said at his office that he would be.

SEBASTIEN: Have you an appointment with him?

CHERRY-MAY: No, but I must see him. It's terribly important. I'm Cherry-May Waterton. Who are you?

SEBASTIEN: My name is Sébastien. I was the late Mr. Sorodin's valet.

CHERRY-MAY: This is Fabrice. (*He bows.*) He doesn't say much but he's sweet when you get to know him, and he doesn't miss a trick.

SEBASTIEN: I'm so glad.

CHERRY-MAY (*looking round*): Fancy dear old Paul having a valet

and a posh place like this. He did come up in the world, didn't
he?

JANE: You knew my father?

CHERRY-MAY: My God—(*Crossing to* JANE.)—are you Paul's
daughter? I'm a bloody fool not to have recognised you at
once—(*They shake hands.*)—there's a strong likeness. (*To* FAB-
RICE, *in execrable French.*) C'est la fille de dear old Paul. (FABRICE
bows.) I hope we're not intruding, but it really is important that
I see Mr. Friedland. I've got a paper here that will interest him.

JANE: A paper? Oh dear!

SEBASTIEN: Perhaps madame would like to sit down. We are
expecting Monsieur Friedland at any moment.

CHERRY-MAY: Thanks. That's very civil of you. Fabrice, il faut
que nous nous asseyons pour attendre jusqu'au Monsieur
Friedland vien d'arriver. We've been jogging along in that god-
awful bus since lunchtime yesterday.

JANE: Where have you come from?

CHERRY-MAY: Orville-les-Champs, just the other side of Bor-
deaux. Fabrice's mother runs a little café-restaurant there.
Between you and I she's a bad-tempered old bitch—pardon
my French—but she certainly can cook. J'ai dit, Fabrice, que ta
mère est une cuisinière miraculeuse. He's the apple of her eye,
but she gets him down a bit sometimes. That's why we're
here really, I mean I think Mr. Friedland might be willing to
help.

SEBASTIEN: In what way?

CHERRY-MAY: Well, Fabrice wants a chicken-farm—imagine! (*She laughs.*) He got a sort of "thing" about chickens while
he was doing his military service on account of being a cook's
assistant or something. I said a garage would be more lively, or
even a café-restaurant like his mother's, but no, it's got to be
chickens. He's obstinate as a mule once he's set his heart on
anything.

JANE: Have you known him long?

CHERRY-MAY: Four years. Ever since he got out of the army. We
first met on the beach as a matter of fact. He's a gorgeous
swimmer. The moment I clapped eyes on him I said, "Oh
dear!" and then when I saw him do that long slow crawl, I

said, "Cherry-May, you've had it!" J'ai dit, "Fabrice, que vous nagez comme un poisson." (FABRICE *shrugs his shoulders.*)

SEBASTIEN: This paper, you have it with you?

CHERRY-MAY: Oh yes—it's in my bag. Only a copy of course, the original is in Barclays Bank, St. Jean de Luz.

JANE: You knew my father well?

CHERRY-MAY: You bet I did. I was potty about him for nearly seven years. That's why I left the Jackson Girls.

JANE: Jackson Girls?

CHERRY-MAY: Yes, we were working here at the Casino de Paris, as a matter of fact they're still at it, not the same ones natch, all my lot must have fallen apart years ago.

JANE: When did you first meet him, my father?

CHERRY-MAY: Let's see now. (*She pauses.*) It was March or February 1930, yes, it must have been March because I was sharing that flat in the rue Washington with Elsie Williams, she was a hot number if ever I saw one, men, nothing but men morning, noon and night. I used to call the joint the Travellers' Club.

JANE: My father was in love with you?

CHERRY-MAY: Oh yes, I think so, for a little while at least. Anyway, I let him persuade me to go racketing off to Shanghai with him. More fool me—I didn't know what I was in for.

SEBASTIEN: How do you mean?

CHERRY-MAY: Oh, I'd rather not go on about all that just now. I mean seeing that this young lady is his, daughter, well, it wouldn't be quite the thing, would it?

JANE: You needn't worry about sparing my feelings, Miss Waterton. I haven't seen my father since I was three years old. You say you went to Shanghai with him?

CHERRY-MAY: Oh yes, we had a high old time—that is at first.

JANE: And afterwards?

CHERRY-MAY: Now look here, you and me are friends, aren't we?

JANE (*with a smile*): I hope so.

CHERRY-MAY: And I wouldn't want to say anything or do anything to upset you. Your father was a very funny man with very funny ideas. We had a good time together taken by and large, and it was my fault we parted, not his. I just couldn't stand the wear and tear.

JANE: You mean he made you paint pictures?

CHERRY-MAY: Oh, my God! So you know?

JANE: I guessed. That's what the paper's about, isn't it?

CHERRY-MAY: The paper doesn't concern you, dear, that's Mr. Friedland's look-out.

JANE: Had you ever painted before?

CHERRY-MAY: Of course not, and I could only paint then when I had had a few drinks. Paul used to say that alcohol released my dormant genius, that was the phrase he used, I'll never forget it. Finally he made me drink so much that I got jaundice. Ever had jaundice?

JANE: No.

CHERRY-MAY: It's awful! Everything happens in technicolour.

JANE: When did you part?

CHERRY-MAY: August 1939, just before the war.

SEBASTIEN: Where?

CHERRY-MAY: Cairo. We had one of those scenes. Oh dear! He certainly could create all right when he got going. You've never heard such a noise, screaming and roaring and throwing things about! I'm not blaming him, mind you. He treated me very fair. That is, when he calmed down.

SEBASTIEN: You signed the paper in Cairo?

CHERRY-MAY: No, Port Said. It was witnessed by an Arab conjurer and a gentleman from the Lebanon.

SEBASTIEN: Did they read it?

CHERRY-MAY: Oh, no, they couldn't read English. The conjurer had a bit of fun with it, though. He turned it into an egg and then into a rabbit—I must say I couldn't help laughing, but poor old Paul was fit to be tied.

SEBASTIEN: I rather see his point.

CHERRY-MAY: Je vais expliquer cette histoire du papier secret et le lapin, tu le souviens?

> FABRICE *gives a sudden loud guffaw, and relapses into silence.*

That story always makes him laugh, he's got a wonderful sense of humour underneath, but he's a bit moody to-day. I expect it's the bus ride.

SEBASTIEN: Did Mr. Sorodin pay you a lump sum down or give you an annuity?

CHERRY-MAY: Just you ask no questions, sonny-boy, and you'll hear no lies. That's Mr. Friedland's business. I've said too much already.

JANE: Anyhow, you parted good friends?

CHERRY-MAY: Oh yes. He packed me on to a P. and O. and that was that. We said good-bye on the promenade deck, we could hardly hear ourselves speak on account of those bloody bugles, but I could see he was upset. I was too. I cried all through lunch.

> *There is the sound of voices in the hall.* MARIE-CELESTE *opens the doors and* ISOBEL *and* PAMELA *enter.* COLIN *and* JACOB *follow after leaving hats, etc. on the hallstand.* CHERRY-MAY, JANE *and* FABRICE *rise.*

ISOBEL: There you are, Jane! I couldn't think what had happened to you. (*She sees* CHERRY-MAY.) Oh!

JANE (*crossing to* ISOBEL): This is Miss Cherry-May Waterton, mother—(ISOBEL *takes a step forward.*)—she was a great friend of father's. (ISOBEL *takes a step back.*)

ISOBEL (*guardedly*): How do you do?

JANE: And this is her—her protégé—Monsieur—— (*She turns to* CHERRY-MAY *questioningly.*)

CHERRY-MAY: Just call him Fabrice, dear, he hates formality. (*To* FABRICE.) Voici Madame Sorodin, la veuve de tu sais que. Dis bonjour gentiment.

> FABRICE *advances, kisses* ISOBEL'S *hand, then* PAMELA'S *hand. Shakes* JACOB'S *hand, then* COLIN'S, *and goes to the window.*

SEBASTIEN: Miss Waterton wishes to see you on urgent business, Mr. Friedland. It concerns, I suspect, Mr. Sorodin's "Circular" period.

JACOB (*sharply*): What?

SEBASTIEN: She has with her a document.

JACOB: What sort of document?

SEBASTIEN: The usual sort.

CHERRY-MAY (*to* SEBASTIEN): Now listen, sonny-boy, you just leave this to me. It's a private matter.

COLIN (*in a business-like tone*): If it concerns my late father, it concerns all of us.

CHERRY-MAY: That is for Mr. Friedland to decide after he's read it.

JACOB (*crossing to* CHERRY-MAY): Give it to me, please.

CHERRY-MAY (*rising*): Not here, if it's all the same to you. As I said before, it's a private matter—and it's going to be discussed privately or not at all.

COLIN (*pompously*): We wish to see that paper here and now, so please hand it over without further argument.

CHERRY-MAY: Well, well—look who's talking! A chip off the old block and no mistake—must have his own way when he wants it and where he wants it double-quick pronto! I've got news for you, young man. I didn't come all this way to be brow-beaten, and you can put that where the monkey put the nuts.

JANE: Just a moment, Colin.

COLIN: We know it's blackmail and we have no time to waste.

CHERRY-MAY: Oh! Using nasty words now, are we? We'll be throwing the furniture about in a minute if I know the form. Come on, Fabrice—we don't want to get ourselves into a free-for-all. (*She makes a movement to go, but* COLIN *bars her way.*)

COLIN: You are not leaving this house until we have seen that document.

ISOBEL: Colin, dear, there is no necessity to raise your voice. If this Miss—Miss—er Cherry wishes to discuss the matter privately with Jacob, I think she should be allowed to do so.

PAMELA: I think Colin's perfectly right. The paper concerns us all.

CHERRY-MAY (*to* PAMELA): Oh—and who do you think you are when you're at home?

JANE: This is my brother's wife, Miss Waterton.

CHERRY-MAY: I see. Well, I've got a hot flash for her too. (*To* PAMELA.) You stay out of this, dear, unless you want trouble, bad trouble.

PAMELA (*grandly*): Really, Miss Whatever-your-name-is, I am not accustomed to being spoken to in that tone.

CHERRY-MAY: The name is Waterton, Cherry-May Waterton, and now you know, so you can shut up, can't you?

PAMELA (*rising*): How dare you!

CHERRY-MAY: I don't care who you are or what you're accustomed to. I'm just warning you, see? And I'd like to call your high and mighty attention to my young friend over by the window. Just take a good look at those shoulders, dear, and if you don't want to see that pompous, fat-headed husband of yours laid out flat as a pancake you'll keep a civil tongue in your head. Viens, Fabrice—je m'enmerde de tous ces gens. On part.

COLIN: I'm not afraid of your damned gigolo!

ISOBEL: Colin—for heaven's sake . . .

JANE: Be quiet, Colin. You're behaving like an idiot!

CHERRY-MAY (*poking* COLIN *with her parasol*): Stand away from that door, you silly great lout.

COLIN (*to her*): I've already told you that you are not going to leave this room before we have seen that document.

CHERRY-MAY: Oh—we'll see about that! (*She goes up to* COLIN *and slaps his face.*) Fabrice! Continuez le bon travail!

JANE: Oh dear, this is most unfortunate . . .

> With a loud snarl of rage FABRICE hurls himself across the room, and fells COLIN to the ground.
> ISOBEL screams. There is general pandemonium. In the middle of it MARIE-CELESTE enters.

MARIE-CELESTE (*announcing*): Monsieur Obadiah Lewellyn.

> A respectably dressed but very black negro enters. He is holding a document in his hand.

SEBASTIEN: My God! The Jamaican Period!

CURTAIN

ACT III: Scene I

The time is a few hours later.

   When the curtain rises there is, as there was in Act II, Scene I, an atmosphere of general dejection. ISOBEL *is lying on the sofa with her feet up and her eyes closed.* COLIN, *whose forehead is adorned with a large cross of sticking plaster, is seated up stage with a plate of food.* PAMELA *is seated downstage idly turning the pages of an art magazine.* JANE *is sitting at the coffee table, on which there are the remains of a meal.* JACOB *is sitting in armchair holding* CHERRY-MAY'S *hat.*

JANE: I really think you ought to try to eat something, mother—you've had nothing since lunch and you only just picked at that egg thing.

ISOBEL (*hopelessly, with her eyes closed*): It had garlic in it.

JANE: Shall I ask Marie-Céleste to make you a nice plain omelette?

ISOBEL: No, thank you, dear, I couldn't touch it.

JANE: If you don't eat you'll start one of your headaches.

ISOBEL: I've started one already.

COLIN: Why do you keep on badgering people to eat when they don't want to?

JANE: Well, you didn't need any badgering anyway, you've been stuffing yourself for the last hour.

PAMELA: Why can't we all go back to the hotel?

JANE: Because we can't leave until we know what's happening in there.

PAMELA (*glancing towards the library*): They've been at it for ages.

JANE: Oh, I wish I knew what was going on. (*She goes over to the library door and listens.*) Sébastien's still talking.

COLIN: In any particular language or just plain English?

PAMELA (*giggling*): Oh, Colin, you do make me laugh, really you do.

JANE: Well, he doesn't make me laugh. If it hadn't been for his oafish, monumental lack of consideration for other people's feelings, he wouldn't have got into that humiliating brawl with the Frenchman and been knocked out.

COLIN: I was not knocked out. I hit my head against the leg of the chair.

JANE: Nonsense. You went down like a ninepin.

COLIN: He took me by surprise.

JANE: The only surprise to me was that he didn't sock you before. You were overbearing and rude and quite insufferable to that poor woman.

PAMELA: I thought she was a horror.

JANE: And she thought you were a pretentious ass, so you were quits, weren't you?

PAMELA (*angrily*): Jane!

COLIN: Poor woman, indeed. She was nothing but a common tart, and the man was quite obviously a pimp.

ISOBEL: Once and for all, Colin, I will not have you using those expressions in my presence. This isn't a barrack-room.

COLIN: I wish to God it was.

ISOBEL: I don't like blasphemy either. I am afraid the army has coarsened you dreadfully, you used to be so well-mannered and gentle when you were a little boy.

JANE: That's what *you* think, mother.

ISOBEL: And now you seem to be growing more and more like your Uncle Edward every day.

PAMELA (*hotly*): It's not fair of you to say that! Colin isn't in the least like Uncle Edward, and, anyway, Uncle Edward would never have been cashiered if it hadn't been for that Mrs. Falkener.

JANE: I don't really feel that we need argue about Uncle Edward and Mrs. Falkener at the moment, Pamela. We have rather more important matters to discuss.

ISOBEL: I never knew what he saw in her.

JANE: The fact remains that if Colin had not started throwing his weight about and insulting Cherry-May Waterton we shouldn't have had that appalling scene and she and her young man wouldn't have rushed out of the house leaving us with no possible means of tracing them.

PAMELA: I for one don't see any necessity for tracing them, let them both go and a good job.

JACOB: I should have thought, Pamela, that by now even you would have dimly understood that it is vitally important for us to get that document from her and destroy it.

COLIN: And give her an income for life, I suppose. There won't be any estate left at this rate.

JANE: She only wanted a chicken farm.

PAMELA: A chicken farm? What on earth would a woman of that type do with a chicken farm?

JANE: Presumably what people usually do with chicken farms, raise chickens. It's for her young man anyhow, she wants to set him up in life. She was perfectly frank and honest about it, and rather touching really until Colin started bullying her and calling her a blackmailer.

PAMELA: Frank and honest indeed! I know just how frank and honest that type of woman can be!

JANE: It's silly to keep on calling her "that type of woman" when you don't know anything about her. I'm quite certain that there's nothing in the least mean or grasping in her character, on the contrary I should say that she was over-generous if anything, thoroughly sentimental and a very good sort.

COLIN: Good sort! You're dotty.

JANE: She ran away with father years ago because she loved him. She was one of the Jackson Girls.

ISOBEL: Oh no, she wasn't, dear. I knew all three of them when they were young. Veronica, the eldest, came out at the same time as your Aunt Freda. I don't think the other two ever came out at all on account of the war.

SEBASTIEN *enters from library.*

JANE (*going to him*): Oh, Sébastien—what's happened?

SEBASTIEN: Nothing has happened. Nothing at all.

JACOB: You should have let me handle him.

SEBASTIEN: I fear that even your overwhelming persuasiveness would not have achieved any better results, monsieur.

JACOB: Have you got the paper?

SEBASTIEN: Alas no. I have not.

JANE: Have you read it?

SEBASTIEN: Yes. It's more or less the same as the others.

COLIN: How much did you offer him?

SEBASTIEN: He is not interested in money. He is an Eleventh Hour Immersionist.

ISOBEL: Oh dear. That's very unfortunate.

SEBASTIEN: He is a man of strong religious principles and men of strong religious principles are notoriously un-co-operative. Look at Thomas-à-Becket.

ISOBEL: I wouldn't describe Thomas-à-Becket as un-co-operative exactly, he was just——

JACOB: Isobel. Thomas-à-Becket's problems were settled several hundred years ago. Our problems are more immediate. Will you please permit us to concentrate on them?

ISOBEL: There's no need to snap at me. I really don't know what's happening to everybody today.

COLIN: What did he come here with the paper for if he didn't want to get something out of it?

SEBASTIEN: He intends to publish it.

JANE: Publish it! Oh no!

SEBASTIEN: Oh yes. His conscience has been troubling him for a long long time, and when he read in the newspaper of Sorodin's death, the news so shattered him that he ran out naked into a banana plantation and had a vision.

COLIN: Was he reading the newspaper in his bath?

SEBASTIEN: He didn't say.

ISOBEL: What sort of vision?

SEBASTIEN: A vision of your late husband, madame, roasting in hell.

ISOBEL: Good gracious!

SEBASTIEN: His description of it was graphic in the extreme. I will spare you the details but it obviously upset him very much.

ISOBEL: Poor man, it must have.

SEBASTIEN: So much so indeed that he caught the next plane available and came here.

COLIN: But why?

SEBASTIEN: He wishes to save your father's soul, monsieur.

COLIN: He's left it a bit late, hasn't he?

SEBASTIEN: He considers that he was to blame in the first place for having allowed himself to be coerced into painting the pictures.

JACOB: He really did paint them?

SEBASTIEN: Oh yes, every one. He was responsible for the whole of the Jamaican period.

JACOB (*brokenly*): What have I done—what have I ever done to deserve this?

SEBASTIEN: His personal favourite is "Copra Factory at Sunset"—the one that is at present in the Royal Gallery in Copenhagen.

ISOBEL: Is copra that stuff they get from sea-gulls?

SEBASTIEN: No, madame. Copra is produced by the coco-palm.

ISOBEL: I must be thinking of guano.

JACOB: I implore you, Isobel, in this moment of crisis, to turn your thoughts away from guano.

SEBASTIEN: Mr. Lewellyn is firmly convinced that his vision of the late Mr. Sorodin in the—er unenviable situation I have just described, is the direct result of the deception they concocted together. He feels most strongly that Mr. Sorodin's soul, in which I think he takes an exaggerated interest, will never achieve proper celestial recognition until that deception is exposed and the sin expiated.

COLIN: The poor chap's obviously a religious maniac.

SEBASTIEN: Possibly. At any rate he is quite unshakable.

COLIN: What's he doing now?

SEBASTIEN: Praying for guidance. He may start singing at any moment.

COLIN: I hope to God he doesn't.

ISOBEL: Some negroes have lovely voices.

JACOB: He refused absolutely to take money?

SEBASTIEN: Absolutely.

JACOB: The document is a copy, I presume?

SEBASTIEN: As a matter of fact it isn't. He left a copy in the Bank of Nova Scotia, Port Maria, Jamaica.

JACOB: You mean you actually had it in your hands?

SEBASTIEN: No. He was very cunning. He only let me have a quick glance at it to identify the handwriting, then he made me stand at the other side of the room while he read it aloud to me. I did note, however, that he kept it in his wallet, which is something gained at any rate.

JANE: What do you mean, Sébastien?

SEBASTIEN: I mean that it might be possible to extract it if all else fails. I have a friend here in Paris who is an adept at that sort of thing.

JANE: That's quite out of the question, Sébastien.

SEBASTIEN (*with a shrug*): Needs must when the devil drives.

JACOB: You say this friend of yours is here in Paris?

JANE: Jacob!

SEBASTIEN: Yes, monsieur. He was a great chum of Mr. Sorodin's. They used to go to race meetings together.

COLIN: A common pickpocket?

SEBASTIEN: Oh no, sir. He only does it as a hobby. He is actually a pianist by profession. He says it keeps his fingers supple.

COLIN: Was he another of your brother prisoners in the Congo?

SEBASTIEN: No, sir, in Johannesburg.

The front door bell rings.

Excuse me.

He goes out.

COLIN: That man's utterly without shame.

JANE: I envy him.

COLIN: I must say I didn't expect to come to Paris and get caught up with the underworld.

JANE: I always understood that that was the average Englishman's main object in coming to Paris.

CHERRY-MAY and FABRICE enter, followed by SEBASTIEN, who stands by the door. JACOB rises.

CHERRY-MAY (*to* JACOB): I had to come back because I couldn't bear to let the sun go down on my wrath. Besides I left my bloody hat behind. (*Taking hat.*) Ta, dear! I lost my temper and it's no use pretending I didn't. (*To* COLIN.) I hope you will accept my apology in the spirit in which it is offered?

COLIN (*acutely embarrassed*): Oh—er—that's perfectly all right.

CHERRY-MAY (*noticing the sticking-plaster and going to him*): Oh, your poor head! Fabrice, regarde ce que tu as fait! Le pauvre garçon est gravement blessé, tu ne sais pas la force de toi-même! Will you accept Fabrice's apology too?

COLIN: Please don't say any more about it.

CHERRY-MAY: Would you mind if he shook hands with you? He won't be happy till he does. He's been in a terrible state all through dinner, wouldn't touch a morsel. He's very nervy, you know, in spite of being so athletic, and you can take my word for it he won't sleep a wink tonight unless he knows that all's forgiven and forgotten.

COLIN: I still think he might have given me a little warning before hurling himself at me like a thunderbolt.

CHERRY-MAY: Oh, come on, be a sport! It was all my fault really, for flaring up and giving you that slap. I've always been quick off the handle ever since I was a kiddie.

JANE: Be gracious, Colin, it was all a misunderstanding.

COLIN: All right—all right—let's forget it. (*He holds out his hand.*)

CHERRY-MAY: Viens serrer la main avec chaleur, Fabrice.

> FABRICE *rushes at* COLIN *and shakes his hand with enthusiasm.*

There. (*Sitting in armchair.*) Now we're all friends again, aren't we?

SEBASTIEN: I am sure that this most heartwarming "amende honorable" calls for some refreshment. Can I offer you a drink, Miss Waterton?

CHERRY-MAY: Thanks. I don't mind if I do.

SEBASTIEN: Champagne?

CHERRY-MAY: Oh no, champagne gives me the come-ups. A whisky splash if it's not too much trouble, and some ginger-ale for Fabrice on account of he's in training.

> SEBASTIEN *looks inquiringly at everyone else. There is a general shaking of heads to indicate dissent and he goes over to the table.*

CHERRY-MAY (*to* FABRICE): Tout va s'arranger, chéri, c'est inutile d'avoir l'air d'un canard mourant dans un orage de tonnerre.

> FABRICE *grunts morosely.*

You mustn't think he's sulky, it's just that he shuts up like a clam when he's upset. I hope you're enjoying your stay in Paris, Mrs. Sorodin?

ISOBEL (*taken by surprise*): Well, I—er—I'm afraid that in the present circumstances . . .

CHERRY-MAY (*realising her blunder*): Oh dear—there I go again— putting my foot into it up to the neck. I ought to have my head examined.

JACOB (*with studied irony*): Without wishing to disrupt this rather convulsive flow of social amenities, Miss Waterton, I think it would be a good idea to return to the business in hand.

CHERRY-MAY: You mean the paper?

JACOB: Yes. Have you got it?

CHERRY-MAY: Yes, here in my bag—but . . .

JACOB: I fully understand your reluctance to discuss so private a matter in the presence of Paul Sorodin's family . . .

CHERRY-MAY: I don't wish to seem carping, dear, but if only you'd said that before we'd all have been saved a lot of fuss and fume.

SEBASTIEN: Your whisky splash, Miss Waterton.

CHERRY-MAY (*taking it*): Ta.

SEBASTIEN *hands* FABRICE *a ginger-ale and goes to windows.*

JACOB: I understand from Miss Jane Sorodin that you wish to invest in a small chicken farm.

CHERRY-MAY: I didn't say anything about it being small.

JACOB: Well, assuming that everything else is satisfactorily arranged, I really feel that the exact acreage can be discussed later.

CHERRY-MAY: It isn't for me, anyway. Personally I can't bear the bloody things—pardon my French, Mrs. Sorodin.

ISOBEL (*determined to be amiable*): I fear my own French is sadly inadequate. I always regretted that my parents didn't send me to a convent when I was a child. My sister Freda on the other hand speaks it like a native. When she was seventeen she was sent to Geneva to be finished.

CHERRY-MAY: I should think Geneva'd be enough to finish anybody.

JACOB (*with commendable restraint*): Although at any other time I

should be the first to welcome an intelligent discussion of the
League of Nations. . . .

COLIN (*cheerfully*): We've almost formed one ourselves now,
anyhow, haven't we?

PAMELA (*giggling*): Oh, Colin—how can you?

JACOB: God give me strength!

ISOBEL: Jacob, please . . .

JACOB: That was not intended as blasphemy, Isobel. It was a last
despairing cry from a tormented man who is being driven step
by step into a nervous collapse.

JANE: Keep calm, Jacob. You really mustn't work yourself into
another state. You'll have a stroke!

JACOB (*wildly*): I should welcome it!

ISOBEL: You shouldn't say things like that, Jacob, even in fun.

JACOB: I did not say it in fun, Isobel. (FABRICE *leans over* JACOB,
watching him.) The dreadful happenings of the last few days
have banished for ever the word "fun" from my personal
vocabulary. (JACOB *turns and sees* FABRICE.) Go away, you're far
too big. I have tried to keep my head in this appalling
situation. I have struggled, against overwhelming odds, to deal
sanely and practically with the problems that beset us, for your
sake, Isobel, as well as for my own, and have I received the
slightest co-operation? The answer is no! A thousand times
NO! Your lack of concentration both individually and as a
family verges on the pathological. Your unlimited capacity for
irrelevant reminiscence has beaten me to the dust. During
these pregnant hours which so vitally affect the lives of all of
us I have been regaled by descriptions of your sister Freda and
her linguistic abilities; the mystic attributes of your Father
Confessor; the misdemeanours of your brother Edward with a
Mrs.—Mrs.——

PAMELA: Falkener.

JACOB: And when Sébastien emerged from the library a little
while ago, you, Isobel, were engrossed in the social frustra-
tions of the Jackson Girls.

CHERRY-MAY: What's the matter with the Jackson Girls?

COLIN: One of them came out and the other two didn't.

CHERRY-MAY: I'll bet that was Elsie Williams. She was always a pusher. Out of what?

JACOB: I give up. I am defeated. I can do no more and say no more. I am a broken man.

JANE: Give Mr. Friedland a whisky and soda, Sébastien.

SEBASTIEN: Certainly, Miss Jane. (*He goes to the table and mixes a drink.*)

ISOBEL: I'm sure I don't know what *I've* done that Jacob should attack me in that hysterical manner.

JANE: Never mind, darling, he's having a very trying time.

COLIN: So are we.

SEBASTIEN *hands* JACOB *his drink.*

PAMELA: If you ask me, I think he was very rude indeed. Why shouldn't mother talk about Aunt Freda and the Jackson Girls as much as she wants to?

CHERRY-MAY: Here, what *is* all this about the Jackson Girls? Who's been saying what? I can tell you one thing, their routines were just as good as the Tillers' any day of the week!

JANE: It's a slight misunderstanding, Miss Waterton.

CHERRY-MAY (*still a trifle suspicious*): Oh.

SEBASTIEN: With regard to that chicken farm, Miss Waterton. . . .

CHERRY-MAY: What about it?

SEBASTIEN: If Mr. Friedland made you a satisfactory offer, would you be willing to hand over the paper that Mr. Sorodin made you sign?

CHERRY-MAY: I might be willing to consider it.

SEBASTIEN: And would you also agree to sign another paper with Mr. Friedland and his lawyer guaranteeing to keep the whole matter entirely secret?

CHERRY-MAY (*after a slight pause*): Yes—that is—if, as you say, the offer Mr. Friedland makes me is satisfactory.

SEBASTIEN: Good.

CHERRY-MAY: But the paper's in St. Jean de Luz, you know, the real one.

SEBASTIEN: In that case, after your conversation with Mr. Friedland in his office tomorrow morning, would you and

307

Monsieur Fabrice be willing to go to Biarritz, collect the document, and fly back here with it within twenty-four hours?

CHERRY-MAY: Well, I don't know about that—flying gives me the willies.

SEBASTIEN: Perhaps, if your expenses were—er—handsomely defrayed, you might be able to bring yourself to endure the willies?

CHERRY-MAY: All right. Anything would be better than that smelly bus.

SEBASTIEN: You know where Mr. Friedland's office is?

CHERRY-MAY: Yes, we went there this morning.

SEBASTIEN: Would ten o'clock tomorrow be convenient to you, Mr. Friedland?

JACOB: If I am not in a strait-jacket, yes.

> *There is the sound of a deep negro voice in the library singing "Let us Break Bread Together on Our Knees".*

CHERRY-MAY: My God, what's that?

ISOBEL (*rising to the occasion*): A friend of ours from the West Indies.

CHERRY-MAY: It's a good strong voice, isn't it? Is he a pro?

COLIN: Pro what?

SEBASTIEN: He is practising for a religious concert he is giving in Jamaica. (*With meaning.*) In the very near future.

CHERRY-MAY: Écoute, chéri—c'est une jolie voix, n'est-ce pas? (*To the room in general.*) He's potty about music. (*She rises.*) Il faut que nous partions maintenant, nous ne voulons pas dépasser notre bienvenue.

JANE (*holding out her hand and rising*): Good-bye, Miss Waterton. I do hope we shall meet again some day.

> JACOB *rises.* SEBASTIEN *opens the double doors.*

CHERRY-MAY: So do I, dear. You must come to see us at our chicken farm, we'll give you a nice new-laid egg. (*The song changes to "My Lord, What a Morning". To* ISOBEL.) Good-bye, Mrs. Sorodin, it's been a pleasure, I'm sure ... Fabrice, viens dire bonsoir à Madame Sorodin.

> FABRICE *rushes at* ISOBEL, *who shrinks slightly. He kisses her hand and then goes to shake hands with* JACOB *when* OBEDIAH, *still*

> *singing, enters from the library.* FABRICE *shakes his hand.* OBEDIAH
> *shrugs his shoulders and, still singing, goes back into the library.*

JANE (*helplessly*): Oh dear!

CHERRY-MAY: He'll have the plaster off the ceiling if he's not
careful. Well—see you tomorrow, Mr. Friedland. (*She listens.*) I
once knew a man in Belfast with a voice just like that, his
name was Flanagan. Bye-bye, all.

> CHERRY-MAY *and* FABRICE *go out.*

JACOB: There must be just one person in Ireland called O'Reilly.

> *Song changes to "Every Time I Feel a Spirit".*

ISOBEL (*rising*): I really can't stand this any longer—this noise is
going through my head like a knife.

COLIN: All right, mother, Pam and I will take you to the hotel.

> ISOBEL *and* PAMELA *go into hall for coats, etc.* COLIN *goes to the*
> *door.*

JANE: What are we to do about Mr. Lewellyn, Jacob? What are
we to do?

SEBASTIEN: Leave it all to me, Miss Jane. You can rest assured
that I will handle Mr. Lewellyn with the greatest tact.

JANE: Oh dear ... I don't like it.... (ISOBEL *re-enters.*) I really
don't.

COLIN: Come on, Jane. (*The singing stops.*) Mother's exhausted.

JACOB: Go with your mother, dear. I'll deal with this.

JANE: But Jacob ...

ISOBEL (*at the door, stiffly*): Good-night, Jacob. (JANE *goes.*) I hope
that you will feel better in the morning.

> ISOBEL *sweeps out, followed by* COLIN.

SEBASTIEN: You'd better go too, sir. You need a good night's
rest.

JACOB: What are you going to do?

SEBASTIEN: I haven't the faintest idea. I always allow circumstances to dictate my course of action in a crisis. Improvisation is
my strong suit. I will telephone you first thing in the morning,
monsieur.

JACOB: But Sébastien, I really think that ...

SEBASTIEN: I insist on you going home to bed, Monsieur
Friedland. You are in a highly excitable state. I suggest a glass

of hot milk and two tablets of seconal. If my efforts to coerce Mr. Lewellyn should fail, we must seek other alternatives in the morning. But please go now.

JACOB (*rising*): All right. Thank you, Sébastien. I am most grateful.

SEBASTIEN: De rien, Monsieur Friedland. Good-night. Allow me.

JACOB (*as he goes out*): Good-night. (SEBASTIEN *closes the doors.*)

The voice in the library continues humming "Swing Low, Sweet Chariot". SEBASTIEN comes quickly back, goes to the telephone.

SEBASTIEN (*at telephone*): Clichy 56–57?—Allô—Ici Sébastien. Oui, très bien—Joe est là? Bon—J'attends. (*A slight pause.*) Joe? Joe?—Pop round here there's a good boy, there's a bit of trouble on and I need your help—no, no knives or firearms necessary, it's just a question of finesse—you might slip a cosh into your pocket in case of unforeseen developments. Okay. (*He hangs up.*)

The voice is now singing "Swing Low". SEBASTIEN switches off the lights, takes off his jacket and goes towards library rolling up his sleeves.

THE CURTAIN FALLS

Scene II

The time is about eleven a.m. on the following morning.

In the window on an easel, facing the audience, is a vast canvas. Standing before this, with an ecstatic expression on his face, is CLINTON PREMINGER, *junior. Down right is* GEORGE, *a Press photographer with a camera and flash bulbs.*

SEBASTIEN is sitting negligently on the arm of the sofa, smoking a cigarette.

CLINTON: This is the greatest moment of my life.

SEBASTIEN: I'm so glad.

CLINTON: Get one from this angle, George—sort of oblique.

GEORGE: Okay. (*He takes a flash picture.*)

SEBASTIEN (*glancing at his watch*): Time's up. They'll be here in a minute.

CLINTON: One more, please, one more.

SEBASTIEN: Very well, but hurry up.

CLINTON: I want you in this one, just gazing with a rapt expression.

SEBASTIEN: Certainly not.

CLINTON: Come on, be a pal. *Life* Magazine will just eat it.

SEBASTIEN: If I could be sure of that I might oblige.

CLINTON: "Great man's faithful valet, blinded by tears, looks his last at posthumous masterpiece".

SEBASTIEN: Great man's faithful valet, blinded by flashlight, looks a bloody fool.

CLINTON: Please, just one, the personal touch means so much.

SEBASTIEN: Who to?

CLINTON: The whole of the United States.

SEBASTIEN: In that case I dare not refuse. (*He crushes out his cigarette.*) Where do you want me to stand?

CLINTON (*indicating*): About here. Is that okay for you, George?

GEORGE (*laconically*): I'm beyond caring.

SEBASTIEN: Aren't you interested in photographing modern paintings?

GEORGE: No sir. Not when they look like that.

CLINTON: If you saw that picture for the first time; what would you say?

GEORGE: I'd say, "Boy, is that dame in trouble!"

CLINTON: It's a great masterpiece.

GEORGE: Okay, okay, it's a great masterpiece. I'm not arguing, let's shoot.

SEBASTIEN: The latest offer for it, from one of your own countrymen, was eighty thousand dollars.

GEORGE: Don't think I'm boasting, mister, but we got suckers in America the same as anywhere else. Turn your head a bit to the left—ready— (*He flashes.*) Okay.

SEBASTIEN: My mouth was open.

GEORGE: So was mine. (*To* CLINTON.) Finito?

CLINTON: Yes. That's all—rush them through.

GEORGE: I can't wait.

He goes out.

SEBASTIEN: A rugged character.

CLINTON (*depressed*): I can't bear it—I just can't bear it.

SEBASTIEN: What?

CLINTON: This God-damned philistinism, this dumb, ignorant hostility to anything that's progressive in Art—it gets me down sometimes. When you think of what Sorodin has done for the world, and then a jerk like that comes along and sneers, it's heartbreaking.

SEBASTIEN: Cheer up. The avant-garde is always in a vulnerable position. You must steel yourself against the slings and arrows of the multitude.

CLINTON: He photographed that picture, he looked at it from every angle, but never for one moment did he really see it. He never even noticed the brushwork.

SEBASTIEN: You cannot go through life expecting people to notice brushwork.

CLINTON: I know, I know—I guess I mind too much. After all it's been the same all through the history of Art, hasn't it? Do you ever think of Wagner?

SEBASTIEN: Constantly.

At this moment ISOBEL, JANE, PAMELA *and* COLIN *enter.*

ISOBEL: Good morning, Sébastien.

SEBASTIEN: Good morning, madame. (*They shake hands.*)

ISOBEL: Where is Mr. Friedland? He told us to meet him here.

SEBASTIEN: I am expecting him at any moment, madame.

ISOBEL: I hope he won't be late—we're catching the one o'clock plane.

CLINTON (*crossing to her and shaking her hand*): Good morning, Mrs. Sorodin. I guess I owe you an apology.

ISOBEL (*politely*): Oh, indeed—what for?

CLINTON: For getting in your hair so much.

ISOBEL (*startled*): Getting in my hair?

CLINTON: I mean always busting in and out and intruding on your sorrow.

ISOBEL: Oh! My sorrow! (*She laughs.*)

CLINTON: But I've seen it now—and photographed it and

everything's fine—so I won't trouble you any more. Good-bye, and thanks a lot.

> CLINTON *goes out quickly.*

ISOBEL: You know, I cannot understand a single word that young man says. Oh dear. (*She catches sight of the picture.*)

COLIN (*staring at it*): Good Lord! Look at this, Pam.

PAMELA: Oh! (*She goes into gales of laughter.*)

JANE (*she looks at the picture*): Oh! It can't be true—it really can't. (*She also breaks down and laughs helplessly.*)

COLIN: Is that the one they're coming to see? The one that they're making all the fuss about?

SEBASTIEN: It is, sir.

JANE: Look, mother, you really must look! (*She is in paroxysms of laughter.*)

ISOBEL: No dear—really—I'd rather not——

JANE: I insist.

> *Choking with laughter she forces* ISOBEL *to look at the picture.*

ISOBEL: No, no—I really—Oh! (*She collapses with laughter and chokes.*)

JANE (*hysterically*): Water, Sébastien—quickly.

> SEBASTIEN *runs to the table, pours out a glass of water and brings it to* ISOBEL. *She attempts to sip it and chokes again. Everyone but* SEBASTIEN *is now out of control.* JACOB *comes in. His face looks harassed and drawn. He stands at the door for a moment looking at the scene in astonishment.*

JACOB: What on earth is happening?

ISOBEL: Jacob—I'm sorry—I can't help it——

> *She chokes again and* JANE *thumps her tenderly on the back.*

JANE (*gasping*): It's the picture, Jacob—we've just seen it.

ISOBEL (*with an effort*): Do stop doing that, Jane, you'll knock my hat off.

JACOB: Control yourself, Isobel, for heaven's sake! Have you all gone mad?

SEBASTIEN (*to* JACOB): Hysteria has set in, I'm afraid, monsieur.

JANE (*wiping her eyes*): We'll be all right in a minute, Jacob, just give us a little time.

PAMELA: It's those feet! They're such a funny shape—— (*She goes off again.*)

JANE: Do stop. We *must* pull ourselves together.

JACOB: I should like a small brandy and soda please, Sébastien. I am not feeling very well this morning.

SEBASTIEN (*going to the table*): Certainly, monsieur.

JANE (*contritely*): Oh, I am sorry, Jacob.

ISOBEL: The dreadful thing is that it *has* got a distinct look of poor Mrs. Etheridge—Oh—Oh—Oh——! (*She presses her handkerchief to her eyes.*)

JANE: Mother!

ISOBEL: I don't know what I shall do the next time I run into her in Sloane Street——

SEBASTIEN (*to* JACOB): Your brandy and soda, monsieur.

JACOB: Thank you. (*Drinks.*)

JANE: Tell us what's the matter, Jacob. I think we're over the worst now.

JACOB: I haven't closed my eyes all night—my whole world is crashing round me and I find you all in hysterics.

JANE: We couldn't help it, really we couldn't.

SEBASTIEN: Cheer up, monsieur. I have good news for you. Mr. Obadiah Lewellyn is at this moment on his way back to Jamaica.

JACOB (*jumping*): What?

SEBASTIEN: I tried to telephone you first thing this morning but your line was out of order.

JACOB: The paper. What about the paper? What happened last night?

SEBASTIEN: He tore it up, monsieur.

JACOB: *He* tore it up? What do you mean?

SEBASTIEN: It took rather a long while to get him into the right mood but we succeeded ultimately.

JANE: We?

SEBASTIEN: Before attempting to reason with Mr. Lewellyn I took the precaution of telephoning to a few of my friends. I felt it wise to be prepared for any eventuality.

JANE: You didn't do anything to him, did you, Sébastien?

SEBASTIEN: Oh no, Miss Jane. As a matter of fact the boot was on the other foot.

COLIN: What are you talking about?

SEBASTIEN: Actually it was he who did something to us.

JACOB: What do you mean? What could he do to you?

SEBASTIEN: He saved us, monsieur.

JACOB: Saved you?

SEBASTIEN: Yes. That is, we encouraged him to believe that he had.

COLIN: What the hell are you talking about?

SEBASTIEN: When I went into the library last night after Mr. Friedland had left I was prepared, if gentle persuasion proved unavailing, to extract the document by force.

JANE: Oh Sébastien, how horrid of you.

SEBASTIEN: I had no intention of hurting him, Miss Jane, I merely intended, with the assistance of my friends, to overpower him, remove the paper from his wallet, and see to it that he was firmly escorted to Orly airfield and sent back to Jamaica.

JANE: The poor man, how could you!

SEBASTIEN: Fortunately however, such a drastic course of action turned out to be unnecessary.

JACOB: Go on, what happened?

SEBASTIEN: As you remember, Mr. Lewellyn had been singing for some time before you left——

COLIN: Singing! He was bellowing his lungs out.

SEBASTIEN (*to* COLIN): It is a well known psychological fact that, in certain highly religious emotional types, continued singing can induce a state of extreme exaltation.

COLIN: It doesn't in me.

SEBASTIEN: With all due respect, sir, I would hardly describe you as a highly religious emotional type.

JANE: Don't interrupt, Colin. (*To* SEBASTIEN.) Go on.

SEBASTIEN: When I entered the library, Mr. Lewellyn was not only singing himself into an ecstatic trance, but he was also undressing.

ISOBEL (*startled*): Undressing? Whatever for?

SEBASTIEN: A not uncommon Freudian impulse, madame.

COLIN: A sort of Revivalist strip-tease!

PAMELA (*giggling*): Oh, Colin, you are dreadful.

ISOBEL: I hope you stopped him.

SEBASTIEN: Oh no, madame. That would have been most dangerous. To attempt to frustrate anyone in a state of such spiritual abandon might lead to the most appalling consequences. All I could do in the circumstances was to fold his garments neatly, as he discarded them, and let him rip.

ISOBEL: Did he take *everything* off?

SEBASTIEN: Everything but his glasses, madame.

ISOBEL: How very surprising! He looked such a mild respectable man. There's no accounting for what people will do nowadays. Do you remember that clergyman in Bletchley?

JACOB (*irritably*): Isobel, please——

JANE: Go on, Sébastien. What happened then?

SEBASTIEN: Oh, from then on everything was easy. When my friends arrived he stopped singing and invited us to join him in prayer.

COLIN: That must have shaken them a bit.

SEBASTIEN: Oh no, sir, being men of the underworld they took in the situation at a glance. We moved in here on account of the library being a little cramped and, taken by and large, the service went off very well.

JANE: Service?

SEBASTIEN: Not perhaps according to accepted professional standards but quite satisfactory within its limits. There was slight confusion over the hymn singing, but, taking into consideration the language difficulties, we acquitted ourselves very favourably. Then Mr. Lewellyn exhorted us to see the light, to which we agreed unanimously, and finally, after a little reasonable persuasion from me, he agreed to destroy the paper as an act of Faith.

COLIN: Well, I'll be damned.

SEBASTIEN: I took the liberty on your behalf, Mr. Friedland, of promising him a new stained-glass window for his church. I told him that the money would be cabled to Jamaica immediately.

JACOB: How much?

SEBASTIEN: His rough estimate amounted to thirty-five pounds seventeen shillings and sixpence. I suggested that fifty pounds would be safer in case of unforeseen extras.

JACOB: Thank you, Sébastien. You did very well. I am most grateful.

ISOBEL: I presumed he dressed again before going to the airport?

SEBASTIEN: Oh yes, madame. When his ecstasy subsided he became quite normal. He actually complained of the climate being a bit nippy.

JANE: I can see why my father was so fond of you, Sébastien. You are certainly resourceful.

SEBASTIEN: Mademoiselle is most flattering.

JANE: What do we do now?

COLIN: How do you mean?

JANE: The three great periods of my father's painting have been accounted for and disposed of. What about the fourth?

SEBASTIEN (*suavely*): The fourth, Miss Jane?

JACOB: That is precisely what has been keeping me awake all night.

JANE: That monstrosity. (*She points towards the easel.*) Who painted that?

SEBASTIEN: Your directness of approach does you credit, Miss Jane.

JANE: Did you paint it yourself?

SEBASTIEN: I thought that that was in your mind, Miss Jane.

JACOB: Stop beating about the bush, Sébastien. Did you or didn't you?

SEBASTIEN: No, monsieur, I did not.

JACOB: Well, if you didn't, who in heaven's name did?

SEBASTIEN: Just a moment, monsieur!

> *One of the double doors slowly opens and* LAUDERDALE'S *head appears.*

LAUDERDALE (*coming in and crossing to the picture*): Then it's true!

SEBASTIEN: Lauderdale. Why aren't you at school?

LAUDERDALE: How could you do such a cruel, wicked thing? You've broken your promise.

SEBASTIEN: Control yourself, Lauderdale. (*To* ISOBEL.) Forgive this abrupt intrusion, madame. This is my son.

JANE: Your son!

SEBASTIEN: Dis "Bon Jour" gentiment, Lauderdale.

LAUDERDALE (*stamping his foot*): I won't!

ISOBEL: What a dear little boy. Why is he called Lauderdale?

SEBASTIEN: His mother had ideas above her station. She was a Lithuanian refugee who ultimately settled in Cheltenham.

LAUDERDALE (*beginning to cry*): I'll never forgive you—never, never, never!

ISOBEL: Why are you crying, little boy?

LAUDERDALE: Because my father is a bastard.

SEBASTIEN (*smoothly*): As a matter of fact that is about the only thing we have in common.

ISOBEL: Well, really I—I hardly think—— (*She breaks off.*)

SEBASTIEN: Run away now, Lauderdale, like a good boy. I will explain everything later.

LAUDERDALE: You promised on your word of honour not to show it to anyone until it was finished.

JANE: Oh—I'm beginning to understand.

JACOB: Good God! Do you mean ... (*To* LAUDERDALE.) Was it you who painted that picture?

LAUDERDALE: Of course it was. It's my masterpiece. I had to do quite a lot of it on a ladder. Oh, father, how could you—how could you? (*He sobs loudly.*)

SEBASTIEN: My son has painted ever since he was seven years old. On three different occasions his pictures have been shown at L'Exposition d'Art d'Enfants. One was actually reproduced in *L'Illustration*.

LAUDERDALE (*sobbing*): Vilain—Goujat! Tu m'a trahi—Tu m'a trahi!

SEBASTIEN: Tais-toi. Je vais tout t'expliquer un peu plus tard, mais tais-toi maintenant.

JACOB: You say that one of his pictures was reproduced in *L'Illustration*?

SEBASTIEN: Yes, monsieur, but you need not be alarmed. It was only a little water-colour "Pastorale" of an ox pulling a cart and, anyhow, it was painted under a nom-de-plume.

JACOB: What the devil does it matter what name it was painted under? This is dangerous.

SEBASTIEN: Calm yourself, monsieur. No one could possibly connect this—this Chef d'Œuvre with a wishy-washy little water-colour.

LAUDERDALE (*stopping crying*): What do you mean wishy-washy? It won a prize, didn't it?

SEBASTIEN: Now look here, Lauderdale. This picture is my property, finished or unfinished. You have been well paid for it.

LAUDERDALE (*contemptuously*): Well paid! Two hundred francs and a box of Carlsbad plums.

SEBASTIEN: *And* a matinée at the Opéra Comique.

LAUDERDALE: It was only *The Tales of Hoffmann.*

SEBASTIEN: Be that as it may, if you don't go immediately to your room and wait there until I come to you, I shall pack you off tomorrow to your mother in Cheltenham and you know how you'd hate that.

LAUDERDALE: But, papa——

SEBASTIEN: Do as I say at once. Va t'en.

LAUDERDALE: But the painting isn't finished. Won't you please let me fix it? The right breast's all wrong.

SEBASTIEN: Both breasts are all wrong. Go away.

LAUDERDALE (*starting to cry again*): I'll never paint another picture for you again—never as long as I live.

SEBASTIEN: Don't be too sure of that. Run along now. (*He pushes him towards the door.*)

LAUDERDALE: Don't touch me. I hate you. You have no soul!

He wriggles away from SEBASTIEN'S *grasp and rushes out, slamming the door behind him.*

ISOBEL: Poor little chap.

JANE (*collapsing in laughter*): Oh dear, oh dear—this is really too much!

JACOB: Do you mean to tell me that that child painted that picture unaided?

SEBASTIEN: Yes, monsieur. Under my supervision. His colour sense is not as yet fully developed and his draughtsmanship still leaves a lot to be desired, but he is a diligent boy, and when he grows up and matures, he should go far.

COLIN: No farther than Wormwood Scrubbs.

SEBASTIEN: The other canvases of course are more abstract.

JACOB: Other canvases?

SEBASTIEN: Yes. About thirty, all told. Mr. Sorodin signed them all.

JACOB: This is grotesque!

SEBASTIEN: He described them as his "Neo-Infantilism" period. He dearly loved a good joke. (*He laughs.*)

JACOB: Where are they?

SEBASTIEN: In a warehouse in Passy, monsieur.

COLIN: They must be destroyed immediately.

SEBASTIEN (*crossing to* COLIN): I think not, monsieur. That would be a futile gesture of vandalism. If judiciously placed on the market during the next few years they should fetch anything up to a hundred thousand pounds. I have already insured them for eighty thousand.

JACOB: *You* have insured them?

SEBASTIEN: Yes, monsieur. They are my property. Naturally enough really, considering that my son painted them. Mr. Sorodin saw the justice of that, which is the reason he assigned them to me to dispose of as I saw fit. He suggested that you and I might come to some sort of arrangement.

JACOB: I'll see you damned first! I'll expose the whole abominable swindle!

SEBASTIEN (*suavely*): Wouldn't that be a little inconsistent, seeing that you have already paid off Princess Pavlikov, Miss Waterton and Mr. Lewellyn? I really do advise you to think carefully, Mr. Friedland. If you expose the whole abominable swindle, as you call it, you also expose yourself to the ridicule of the world.

COLIN (*rising*): On behalf of my mother and my family I would like to say that I entirely agree with Mr. Friedland. The scandal must be exposed and we must face the consequences. Don't you agree, mother?

ISOBEL: Yes—I suppose so—but——

COLIN (*sitting again*): But what?

ISOBEL: I was thinking of that dear little boy—after all that work—he'll be dreadfully disappointed.

SEBASTIEN: Not only will *he* be disappointed, the whole world of modern painting will be humiliated and impoverished. The casualties in Hollywood alone will be appalling. The bottom will fall out of the market and thousands of up-and-coming young artists will starve. It will be a cataclysm! Many of the great masters too will be flung into disrepute, their finest pictures will be viewed with suspicion and distrust. If the news leaks out that the great Sorodin's masterpieces were painted by a Russian tart, an ex-Jackson Girl, a Negro Eleventh Hour Immersionist and a boy of fourteen, the rot will spread like wildfire. Modern sculpture, music, drama and poetry will all shrivel in the holocaust. Tens of thousands of industrious people who to-day are earning a comfortable livelihood by writing without grammar, composing without harmony and painting without form, will be flung into abject poverty or forced really to learn their jobs. Reputations will wither overnight. No one will be spared. Not even Grandma Moses.

ISOBEL: I see no reason to drag in the Old Testament.

SEBASTIEN: Pause and consider, Mr. Friedland, before you unleash this chaos. It will not only be ridicule that you have to fear, it will be crucifixion! Your colleagues alone will see to that. (*The front door bell rings.*) Here are two of them now.

JANE: What are you going to do, Jacob?

SEBASTIEN (*to* JACOB): Is our little secret to be kept inviolate, monsieur, or laid wide open?

JACOB: Come to my office this afternoon. We'll discuss it there.

SEBASTIEN: And Sir Alaric and Mr. Riskin?

JACOB (*despairingly*): Show them in.

SEBASTIEN: Very good, monsieur. (*He bows to* ISOBEL, *then to* JACOB, *and opens the double doors.*)

THE CURTAIN FALLS

Methuen World Classics
include

Jean Anouilh (two volumes)
John Arden (two volumes)
Arden & D'Arcy
Brendan Behan
Aphra Behn
Bertolt Brecht (six volumes)
Büchner
Bulgakov
Calderón
Čapek
Anton Chekhov
Noël Coward (seven volumes)
Eduardo De Filippo
Max Frisch
John Galsworthy
Gogol
Gorky
Harley Granville Barker
  (two volumes)
Henrik Ibsen (six volumes)
Lorca (three volumes)

Marivaux
Mustapha Matura
David Mercer (two volumes)
Arthur Miller (five volumes)
Molière
Musset
Peter Nichols (two volumes)
Clifford Odets
Joe Orton
A. W. Pinero
Luigi Pirandello
Terence Rattigan
  (two volumes)
W. Somerset Maugham
  (two volumes)
August Strindberg
  (three volumes)
J. M. Synge
Ramón del Valle-Inclán
Frank Wedekind
Oscar Wilde

Methuen Contemporary Dramatists
include

Peter Barnes (three volumes)
Sebastian Barry
Dermot Bolger
Edward Bond (six volumes)
Howard Brenton
(two volumes)
Richard Cameron
Jim Cartwright
Caryl Churchill (two volumes)
Sarah Daniels (two volumes)
Nick Darke
David Edgar (three volumes)
Ben Elton
Dario Fo (two volumes)
Michael Frayn (two volumes)
Paul Godfrey
John Guare
Peter Handke
Jonathan Harvey
Declan Hughes
Terry Johnson (two volumes)
Bernard-Marie Koltès
David Lan
Bryony Lavery
Doug Lucie
David Mamet (three volumes)

Martin McDonagh
Duncan McLean
Anthony Minghella
(two volumes)
Tom Murphy (four volumes)
Phyllis Nagy
Anthony Nielsen
Philip Osment
Louise Page
Stewart Parker (two volumes)
Joe Penhall
Stephen Poliakoff
(three volumes)
Christina Reid
Philip Ridley
Willy Russell
Ntozake Shange
Sam Shepard (two volumes)
Wole Soyinka (two volumes)
David Storey (three volumes)
Sue Townsend
Michel Vinaver (two volumes)
Michael Wilcox
David Wood (two volumes)
Victoria Wood

If you enjoy the work of 'The Master', why not join
the Noël Coward Society? Members meet on the
anniversary of Coward's birthday at the Theatre Royal,
Drury Lane to see flowers laid on his statue by
a star such as Sir John Mills, Alan Rickman or
Vanessa Redgrave. Groups go to Coward productions,
places of interest and celebrity meals.

Members receive a free copy of our regular colour
magazine, *Home Chat*, as well as discounts on
theatre tickets, books and CDs. All are welcome to join –
serious students, professional and amateur performers,
collectors of memorabilia or simply fans.

Visit our regularly updated website: www.noelcoward.net
for a membership form
or write to the Membership Secretary:

Noël Coward Society
29 Waldemar Avenue
Hellesdon
Norwich NR6 6TB
UK

Methuen Modern Plays
include work by

Jean Anouilh
John Arden
Margaretta D'Arcy
Peter Barnes
Sebastian Barry
Brendan Behan
Dermot Bolger
Edward Bond
Bertolt Brecht
Howard Brenton
Anthony Burgess
Simon Burke
Jim Cartwright
Caryl Churchill
Noël Coward
Lucinda Coxon
Sarah Daniels
Nick Darke
Nick Dear
Shelagh Delaney
David Edgar
David Eldridge
Dario Fo
Michael Frayn
John Godber
Paul Godfrey
David Greig
John Guare
Peter Handke
David Harrower
Jonathan Harvey
Iain Heggie
Declan Hughes
Terry Johnson
Sarah Kane
Charlotte Keatley
Barrie Keeffe
Howard Korder

Robert Lepage
Stephen Lowe
Doug Lucie
Martin McDonagh
John McGrath
Terrence McNally
David Mamet
Patrick Marber
Arthur Miller
Mtwa, Ngema & Simon
Tom Murphy
Phyllis Nagy
Peter Nichols
Joseph O'Connor
Joe Orton
Louise Page
Joe Penhall
Luigi Pirandello
Stephen Poliakoff
Franca Rame
Mark Ravenhill
Philip Ridley
Reginald Rose
David Rudkin
Willy Russell
Jean-Paul Sartre
Sam Shepard
Wole Soyinka
Shelagh Stephenson
C. P. Taylor
Theatre de Complicite
Theatre Workshop
Sue Townsend
Judy Upton
Timberlake Wertenbaker
Roy Williams
Victoria Wood

For a Complete Catalogue of Methuen Drama titles
write to:

Methuen Drama
215 Vauxhall Bridge Road
London SW1V 1EJ

or you can visit our website at:

www.methuen.co.uk